INDIA

HIMALAYAN
ODYSSEY

Frontispiece Approaching the top of the Khangkyong plateau (10 November 1949)

HIMALAYAN ODYSSEY

Trevor Braham

London   George Allen & Unwin Ltd
Ruskin House   Museum Street

First published in 1974

ISBN 0 04 910054 8

Printed in Great Britain
in 12pt 'Monotype' Barbou type
by W & J Mackay Limited, Chatham

PREFACE

Although this book is partly biographical it does not pretend to be a biography. While it is not, in the technical sense, a mountaineering book it is mainly about mountains; or rather, about my personal involvement with mountains. The setting is exclusively Himalayan, a term used in its widest geographical sense to include the numerous ranges, extending from Afghanistan in the west to Assam in the east, which divide the Indian subcontinent from the great Central Asian landmass to the north. The book records the events of various travels in some of these regions; but unlike a number of books with a Himalayan flavour, it lays no claim to respectability by the criterion of some singular achievement or success.

For over thirty years, through a combination of chance and a clear affirmation of choice, I have dwelt within proximity and sometimes within sight of the great ranges of the Himalaya. Such exceptional good fortune has provided opportunities for acquiring some intimacy with these mountains, enriching yet unacquisitive, which has made them a personal and an essential part of my life.

It would be disingenuous to say that I have never hoped one day to try to convey to others something of this experience. But despite occasional encouragement from friends, doubts have always held me back from setting down thoughts into words: the description would never match the experience; and without the justification of some vital or supreme adventure would the effort be worthwhile?

The day seems to have passed when the amateur or the idealist practised his pastime in his own individual way. Mountain climbing, like most other activities is becoming increasingly professional, demanding whether we like it or not many of the symbols of professionalism. I have approached the mountains with the amateur's undemanding indulgence. There was never any question why: I simply had to. The need to find reasons and justification and to define these in words came much later. When I began first to visit the mountains, their beauty and their isolation appeared to be the initial compelling factor; but I could sense vaguely even then that the appeal was not purely physical. In spite of the need to pursue a professional career unrelated to mountains,

I have found it possible to continue my indulgence because one always finds the means to do the things one really wants. Sometimes it was preferable to have half a bite at the cherry, such as a brief mountain journey with a limited objective, than to have nothing at all.

There are no tales of daring or heroism in this book. Those uninvolved with mountains often suspect that climbers are strongly motivated by the dramatic element which is inherent in their environment. But this accounts for a small portion of the overall appeal. There is an intense personal feeling, almost a magical quality, which provides the main driving force for most mountaineers. If some of them differ about the object that drives it is because different temperaments naturally emphasise different aspects of the opportunities which mountaineering offers. Thus there are bound to be some who disagree with this book's underlying ethic, unable to discover the mainsprings of much of the action described. There are many for whom any involvement with the mountains without the spur of physical challenge or victory such as mine is incomprehensible.

This record of my Himalayan travels is concerned mainly in describing my impressions of places and people rather than in presenting a saga of remarkable occurrences. I have been involved one way and another with Himalayan regions for the major part of my life. A series of wanderings, across a wide variety of country spreading through to the extreme ends of the ranges from east to west, has provided me with the thrills and the excitement, the wonder and the serenity that await all those who travel amongst high mountains. Writing about my journeys has helped me to see them through other eyes: an error of inexperience, an opportunity lost, an exaggerated self-assurance; failings which make me the more grateful for the proliferation of riches which it has been given to me to gather. Sometimes, especially during the early years, when I found myself in the presence of big mountains the impact was so great that words seemed an irrelevance. Impressions too numerous to assimilate crowded the mind and I gradually entered a new world, becoming aware of unsuspected sensibilities and responses.

The people whom I have encountered of different races, faiths, tribes, and sects have seemed to me to possess a characteristic similarity in their qualities. Their lives are governed by the fundamental needs of a primitive society; toughness, austerity and resourcefulness are their common attributes, enabling them to deal with the capricious forces of nature. Envy or greed are rare. There is a godfearing and unquestioning acceptance of the inexorable hand of fate. They possess an inborn gentility which is reflected in the openness of their hospitality; and how much more appealing is their simple courtesy and charm than the laboured graces of our social conventions. For many years I have accepted and responded to the intimate loyalty and affection of many of these peoples. But I have not attempted here, for this is not a biography, to draw a too personal picture. By making no more than a passing mention of my contact with the people I have thought to retain a greater objectivity.

Mostly, I have allowed my diaries to take over the narrative of the journeys. I have retained their original blend of wonder and infatuation in an attempt to recreate the atmosphere of the period. Thus the observations and impressions written down in some cases three decades ago may seem to read strangely. The tide of enthusiasm, so strong during the early years, has risen rather than ebbed. Because experience has widened its channels a humbler acceptance of the rewards gradually emerges in my later diaries indicating a deeper relationship with the mountains which, being more sensitive requires less embellishment.

Many of the regions which I have described are filled with picturesque associations from the past. Their events are well known and are amply recorded. But I have added, at the beginning of almost every chapter or region, fragments of history with the object of providing some background. When I have followed in the footsteps of the pioneers, advancing confidently where often they had to move cautiously forward, I have sometimes become aware of a singular sensation: has it not been an acknowledgement of their exploits that has made my own welcome more cordial? I have included a limited bibliography together with a Notes section, which enlarges on such brief references to the past as I have made; but, intentionally, I have separated this from the main text so that some readers, if they prefer, may omit it altogether. Limited use of vernacular and mountaineering terms has been unavoidable, and these are explained in a glossary. I have expressed heights throughout in feet, both in the text and on the sketch maps. I have done so in order to retain uniformity with the Survey maps which I used on my journeys. The only exception occurs in Chapter IX where I have adopted metres in conformity with modern sketch-maps now available.

The willingness with which my wife has rescued my original handwritten pages filled with corrections producing a neatly typed script is a monument to her patience and to her loyalty to a cause in which at least she believed.

I have benefitted much from advice given to me by numerous friends, who have read through sections of the book. They have shared some of my mountain adventures and I hope that it is not because of this alone that they have been generous in offering encouragement. For their assistance, I would like to thank in particular Professor Kenneth Mason, John Kempe, Sally and Michael Westmacott, John Tyson, Peter Holmes. Whilst to Fred Dangar, for his valuable work in compiling the index, I owe special thanks.

For the area-maps of Nepal and Garhwal I am indebted to Professor Mason's lucid sketches in *Abode of Snow*; to John Tyson for his original maps of the Kanjiroba region of West Nepal; to Henry Day for his sketch of the Siri Dara basin; to J. Wala of Krakow for his admirable maps of the Hindu Kush. I am grateful to them for permitting me to use their work as base material for my sketch-maps. All the illustrations are from photographs taken by me with the exception of illustrations numbers 14, 26, 28 which are from photographs taken by Dennis Kemp, Gene White and Wolfgang Stefan respectively. I am grateful to them for allowing me to reproduce these.

London
February 1974   T.H.B

CONTENTS

ILLUSTRATIONS

MAPS

I

Historical Background

*Romance almost became a reality. The gods were very near
at hand. We touched as it were the skirts of their garments. Yet even
at the culminating moments of these strenuous dream-days there still
lingered the sense of incompleteness, of something lacking. The secret
was almost disclosed, but never quite, the veil never entirely withdrawn.*

Sir Martin Conway
Karakoram 1891

During my earliest years I had regarded mountains and those who
climbed them with a special awe. The outer Himalaya were then only
sketchily known, and serious interest was beginning to be taken in the
highest peaks during the 1920s. The pioneers who had made an immense
contribution to early exploration of the Himalayan range were followed
by a new generation; and the stage had been set for the opening of an
era that was probably the most important in the history of Himalayan
climbing. Activity began to grow and flourish and, except for a break
caused by the Second World War, culminated in the Himalayan
'Golden Age' which flourished about thirty years later.

As a small boy living in India during the late 1920s, the impressions
created by Himalayan expeditions of that time were very real and in my
fancy they seemed to take on a dream-like quality. My parents took no
more than a mild interest in the British-dominated activities of those
days, and I am thankful for the understanding which they showed when
my own interest was stirred during summer visits to Darjeeling, which
was then the starting-point for several of the major expeditions, and the
main recruiting centre for Sherpa porters. In later years this understanding withstood greater tests; for, although I do not think that they

ever wholly approved of my mountaineering, they gave me, in their kindness, nothing but encouragement and support whenever I was in need of both.

Darjeeling in those days was a fashionable hill station, the summer seat of the Bengal Governor, garrisoned by British and Indian regiments. It possessed the uncrowded atmosphere of an English country town, with summer homes built in Tudor, Georgian or Victorian style in a setting of neatly trimmed lawns and flower beds. If the atmosphere of Simla could be described as a mixture of Surrey and Tibet this could have been said equally of Darjeeling. Here, during the summer and autumn seasons, a calendar of social and sporting events was enjoyed by the ruling clique of civilian and military officials, merchants from Calcutta, and their wives.

There were cloudless days in late autumn and early spring when the southern wall of Kangchenjunga stood out white against a sky of deep blue supported on a plinth of purple foot-hills; or monsoon days when the town was enveloped for weeks in cloud, with pine trees and cottages only vaguely seen through the floating mists. On a clear morning it was a moving experience to visit Observatory Hill. Several pathways from the Mall led up to the crest, which was marked by a Buddhist shrine. My recollections are of a neat circle of prayer flags fluttering in the breeze; the sound of bells and gongs and the smell of incense. There were lamas from Tibet, Bhutan and Nepal, some in silent meditation, others spinning prayer-wheels with a begging-bowl by their side. The view from there, no matter how often I saw it, never failed to arouse a mixture of excitement and desire: from Nepal in the west across Tibet to the north and Bhutan in the east, 200 miles of snow-covered ranges, filled the horizon, with Kangchenjunga as the centre-piece. There were visits to Birch Hill, a forest park and a favourite family picnic spot, now the site of the Himalayan Mountaineering Institute. There were also visits to Tiger Hill, six miles to the south-east; from its crest, at nearly 9,000 feet, there was a panorama of the ranges to the north, which included a distant view of Makalu, Everest and Lhotse, and the infinite stretch of the Bengal plains to the south. We used to visit this hill-top on a clear morning to see the sunrise, and I can remember starts by lantern-light from Senchal Rest House, 850 feet below, or departures from Darjeeling on horseback in the early hours.

There existed in those days in Darjeeling a large floating population of Sherpas, Bhutias and Tibetans. Many were immigrants in search of work, and with their sturdy physique they took on occupations as rickshaw-pullers and coolies. The women with their colourful home-spun aprons and their ready smiles carried conical baskets on their backs, supported by a head-band; the men sat in groups around their rickshaw stands noisily enjoying their favourite dice-game. They were fond of a gamble, and not a small proportion of them were fond of spirits. I remember moving nervously away from the path of one festive trio reeling down a hill in the broad light of day. Many of these groups had settled permanently in Darjeeling, and as the demand for expedition porters grew they were sure of steady employment during the summer. They were slow to integrate with the local population, and they used to live exclusively in their own ethnic groups on the outskirts of the town, in villages like Bhutia Busti and Toong Soong Busti. Many of the older men trained by Kellas, Bruce and Ruttledge had established their reputation as high-altitude porters, a tradition which was being handed down to a younger generation.

It was during my childhood years in the early thirties, spent between Calcutta and Darjeeling, that my deepest impressions were formed. At that time it was accepted without any sense of dishonour that attempts upon the major Himalayan peaks by one strong team after another should be repulsed. It is fashionable nowadays to underrate the achievements of the early Himalayan climbers. The routes they attempted were the easiest that could be devised. Their failure to reach the summits is sometimes regarded as being due to lack of skill or resolve. But account is seldom taken of the mental reservations that accompanied early Himalayan climbing. 'It is not remarkable that Everest did not yield to the first few attempts; indeed it would have been very surprising and not a little sad if it had, for that is not the way of great mountains.' Eric Shipton expressed those feelings in 1943.

It was inevitable that an aura of mystery should have surrounded the efforts of the pioneers. The atmosphere was comparable with that which had prevailed in the Swiss Alps a hundred years earlier, except that the bigger scale and higher altitude of the Himalaya provided greater justification. We know that familiarity with the high peaks came slowly to the peasant dwellers of the upper Swiss valleys; the Sherpas and other mountain dwellers of the Himalaya and Karakoram were no different from their European counterparts. But other factors often tend to be overlooked. The radical change in climbing techniques evolved in recent years, which has brought about a different evaluation of climbing problems, was itself brought about by a compulsive search for 'firsts'. The older generation had achieved their 'firsts'; the younger had to have theirs. By modern standards the early explorers were ill-clothed, improperly equipped, poorly fed and meagrely supported by their porter teams. The photograph of Mallory and Norton, taken on Everest at about 26,800 feet on 21 May 1922, wearing light alpine boots and puttees, tweed jackets and felt hats seems to symbolise perfectly the heroic efforts of those days. Physiological and scientific knowledge was scanty, and there were limited reserves of experience upon which the climber could draw in order to base his judgements. It is not often appreciated that many of the pioneers were extended to the limit of their resources. It was from their efforts that knowledge grew.

When the original Himalayan surveys were carried out in the middle of the nineteenth century, instructions were given that time should not be wasted over uninhabited regions above 18,000 feet. But there were many surveyors who possessed outstanding ability and enterprise. In 1856 Montgomerie established a survey station at 16,000 feet on a spur of Haramukh mountain in Kashmir. The distinction for the discovery of one of the world's greatest glaciers went to Godwin-Austen in 1860–1, who explored the Baltoro which is thirty-six miles long. Other surveyors sketched the Hispar and Biafo systems, which have a combined length of seventy-six miles. The extension of mountain surveys during the period 1865 to 1885 was largely due to the *'pundit'* explorers, native mountain dwellers, intelligent and exceptionally loyal, who were meticulously trained by J. T. Walker and T. G. Montgomerie of the Great Trigonometrical Survey to carry out work across the frontiers where British surveyors were forbidden to travel. Chilas, Gilgit and Chitral were then unexplored, and the sources and drainage of the Tsang Po river in Tibet were unknown. These men, the most famous of whom was 'AK' (all of them were known by code numbers or initials), through patient work and accurate observation, and generally travelling in disguise, brought back extensive information. They included a 1,200-mile journey in Tibet, following the course of the Tsang Po for 600 miles; the first circuit of Mount Everest; the exploration of the Indus gorge to Bunji; the first map of Swat, which was then an independent tribal state.

Limited knowledge of the geography of the Himalaya and the great distance of the mountains from the populated areas of India, called for careful forethought and meticulous preparation before any lengthy mountain journeys could be contemplated. In 1883 W. W. Graham was probably the first to come to the Himalaya, accompanied by an Alpine guide, purely to climb mountains. In 1887 Sir Francis Younghusband reached the 18,000-foot Muztagh pass, crossing the main Karakoram range. Sir Martin Conway* in 1891 led the first climbing expedition to the Karakoram's largest glaciers, traversing the entire length of the Hispar and Biafo and reaching the head of Baltoro. In 1895 A. F. Mummery, generations ahead of his time, pioneered a route to 21,000 feet on the south-west face of Nanga Parbat, on which he lost his life. In 1899 D. W. Freshfield first drew attention to the possibility of climbing Kangchenjunga. By this time, with the consolidation of British administration in India and the extension of roads and railways, access to the mountains was becoming gradually easier. But during the period of the Himalayan forerunners the ascent of high peaks was practically unknown, and travel in glaciated country was exceedingly rare.

In 1907 Dr T. G. Longstaff ascended 6,000 feet in one day to the 23,360-foot summit of Trisul, the highest yet climbed. In 1909 the Duke of Abruzzi explored the glaciers surrounding K2. C. G. Bruce spent over two decades during the early years of the century exploring and climbing in little-known areas of the Himalaya often accompanied only by Gurkha orderlies from his regiment, whom he trained in the use of rope and ice-axe. Dr A. M. Kellas, between the years 1910 and 1912 climbed four peaks above 22,000 feet in northern Sikkim and explored large areas north and south of Kangchenjunga, ascending several smaller mountains. He was the first to provide elementary mountaineering training to Nepalese and Bhutia porters. Sir Aurel Stein's extensive geographical surveys, which took place between the years 1900 to 1916, though not strictly relating to the Himalaya, covered large areas north of the main range; and probably no single traveller has added more to knowledge of Central Asia and Turkestan.

There were many others, famous as well as unnamed—such as the lone Englishman who at the turn of the century and with a handful of local men crossed a 15,000-foot ice-pass from Nagar into Ishkuman, which had never been crossed before, and has not been crossed since; or the Survey of India *khalasi* who in 1860 carried his signal pole to the summit of a mountain above 20,000 feet on the borders of Spiti and Ladakh. There was a jest once current in India that if Everest had to be climbed an order should merely be issued to the Survey of India that a trigonometrical station was required on the top!

During the decade that followed the 1914–18 war, the pioneers were no longer active. Himalayan climbing in the early twenties was dominated by three successive Everest expeditions. While George

* Later, Lord Conway of Allington.

Mallory became a legend, the tragedy and mystery that surrounded Mallory and Irvine's disappearance on the north face of Everest in 1924 seemed for a while to damp enthusiasm for major ventures. But exploration on a small scale continued, financed largely by private resources. The Survey of India meanwhile was busy extending the limits of its knowledge. Kashmir and the northern borders of India were re-surveyed, generally in the charge of single highly skilled officers going out for several months with very limited resources in men and material. Two such ventures come to mind, both in 1926: Mason's search for the source of the Shaksgam river, and Angwin's triangulation of the Kaghan valley.

Small groups of friends had begun to travel and climb in the Himalaya, the forerunners of expedition groups that were to follow during the next four decades. One of these, in 1927, comprised T. G. Longstaff and H. Ruttledge, who visited the southern rim of the Nanda Devi basin. C. J. Morris and H. F. Montagnier in the same year visited Shimshal. In 1928 Admiral Lynes' party, including Hugh Whistler, spent four months in Kashmir, carrying out extensive ornithological and botanical studies. There were other private expeditions devoted almost exclusively to survey. Between the years 1899 to 1912 the Americans, Dr and Mrs Bullock-Workman, visited the Karakoram six times. Much of their work was exploratory and devoted to survey, but some of the information they brought back was disproved by later explorers; and their mapping was not always accurate. The Dutch explorer Dr Visser and his wife carried out four expeditions to the Karakoram between the years 1922 to 1935, covering areas in the east such as Nubra, Saser and Shyok; also the Khujerab and Shimshal in the west, spending the winter of 1930 in Yarkand. In 1929 the Duke of Spoleto carried out a photogrammetric survey of the Baltoro glacier, preparing the first map on a scale of 1:25,000 of the south and south-east sides of K2. His party of twelve included the geologist Ardito Desio, who in 1954 led the expedition which made the first ascent of K2.

The Himalayan Club was founded in February 1928.[1] Douglas Freshfield had suggested in the *Alpine Journal* in 1884 'the formation at Calcutta or Simla of a Himalayan Club prepared to publish narratives of science or adventure'. Though the idea must have recurred to many who were in India in the intervening years, much time was to elapse before it took shape. It is largely due to the initiative and energy of Sir Geoffrey Corbett of the Indian Civil Service and of Kenneth Mason of the Survey of India that the club 'was born on the path behind Jakko',

a hill above Simla, on 6 October 1927. The inaugural meeting of the
club was held on 17 February 1928 at Army Headquarters, Delhi, with
F.M. Lord Birdwood, C-in-C India, as President and Corbett as Honorary Secretary. Among its founder members were the Viceroy of
India, Lord Irwin, the Governor of the Punjab, Sir Malcolm Hailey,
the Surveyor-General of India, Sir Edward Tandy, the Director of
Geological Survey of India, Sir Edwin Pascoe; also Sir Francis
Younghusband, Sir Martin Conway, Freshfield, Collie, Bruce, Longstaff, Norton, and many others noted for their pioneer work. Before the
founding, invitations to join the club were issued to notable mountaineers
in many countries of the world and the 127 founder members were 'a
solid core of men who have done things'. Corbett, in his introduction to
the first volume of the Club's journal, said 'and so the Himalayan Club
is founded and we hope great things of it . . . my own hope is that it
may help to rear a breed of men in India, hard and self-reliant, who will
know how to enjoy life on high hills'. The Mountain Club of India was
formed independently in Calcutta on 27 September 1927; its moving
spirit was W. Allsup and its original members numbered sixty-four.
General C. G. Bruce was its president. On 14 December 1928 the
Mountain Club amalgamated with the Himalayan Club 'for the benefit
of the common aims of the two clubs'.

In its early days the Himalayan Club flourished largely through the
activities of men from the civil and defence services in India who had
the inclination and leisure not only to travel in the Himalaya but also to
devote their spare time to honorary duties as the Club's office-bearers.
It should be remembered that mountain climbing was then not the
exclusive nor even the predominant attraction for men visiting the
Himalaya; there was *shikar*, fishing, skiing, and various branches of
science for which the Himalaya provided a vast, almost untouched
field. The Club performed a useful role, appointing not only local
secretaries covering practically all the regions, but also a wide range of
technical and scientific correspondents, all experts in their field; for
example, Sir Aurel Stein in archaeology, Dr DeGraaff Hunter in geo-
physics, Lt.-Col. C. H. Stockley in zoology, Hugh Whistler in ornithology,
and so on. The Himalayan Club became a clearing house for information, and a source of assistance to all who were planning Himalayan
journeys. Expeditions from abroad were helped with local arrangements
and transport, and in the early years it was usual for a member of the
Himalayan Club to accompany the larger expeditions from Europe in
order to provide practical assistance in the field, especially with porters.

The local secretary of the club in Darjeeling began to collect the names of Sherpa porters with expedition experience. Gradually a porter register was compiled. No Darjeeling porter felt that he had acquired status until he possessed a numbered H.C. book, containing his photograph and a complete record of his experience, mainly written up by expedition leaders. A Sherpa's most coveted prize was the 'Tiger' badge awarded by the club for exceptional devotion to duty at high altitudes. Not least of the club's activities was the publication of its journal. The first volume of the *Himalayan Journal* appeared in 1929; it appeared annually thereafter until 1940, increasing in importance as a record of Himalayan activity, and becoming an authoritative source of reference. The club was fortunate to have had for twelve years continuously an editor of the calibre of Kenneth Mason, ideally suited by his qualifications and experience. Although he left India early in 1932 on his appointment as Professor of Geography at Oxford, he continued to edit the journal from England until 1940, after the outbreak of World War II.[2]

These were lasting achievements. A tradition was being built, the benefits of which were to be felt by succeeding generations of Himalayan travellers and climbers. The founding of the Himalayan Club seemed to mark the beginning of a new era. Himalayan travel and exploration, excluding official survey work, had hitherto taken the form either of a large expedition sponsored by some wealthy individual or scientific society, or as an indulgence of the solitary explorer limited to his own meagre resources. The 1930s ushered in for the first time two distinct categories of Himalayan expedition: the large publicly-backed enterprise aiming at the ascent of a major peak, and the small privately organised group of friends seeking unvisited glaciers and unclimbed peaks. The first was typified by repeated British and German attempts to climb Everest and Nanga Parbat, and the second by the achievements of individuals like E. E. Shipton, F. S. Smythe and H. W. Tilman. This was the decade to which my earliest recollections belong and which stimulated my interest in the Himalaya. First impressions are often the strongest; and I can still recapture the boyish excitement it gave me to hear about those exploits while they were being enacted—the Germans on Kangchenjunga, the climbing of Kamet, the struggles on Nanga Parbat and Everest.

In 1929 a young Bavarian, Paul Bauer, came out to the Himalaya with a party of eight climbers who wanted 'to test themselves against something difficult . . . some mountain that will call out everything of courage, perseverance and endurance'. The enterprise was devoid of publicity; yet their objectives were similar in scale to those of the groups who came out forty years later looking for 'ultimate' problems on the faces of Annapurna, Nanga Parbat and Everest. Bauer and his friends pioneered a route up a long and difficult ice spur on the north-east side of Kangchenjunga. There were many dangerous sections and their perseverance was fully stretched when almost every advance was followed by a retreat due to storms; ice-caves had to be dug for protection where tents could not be placed. A four-day storm dictated final retreat, which was carried out under extremely severe conditions. Bauer made another attempt on Kangchenjunga by the north-east spur two years later, with a party of nine which included three of his original team. Familiarity with the route did nothing to diminish its technical problems, and after forty days of continuous effort, with the climbers ferrying their own loads, the party reached the top of the north-east spur at about 25,500 feet. They were faced with an ice slope leading to the north ridge, with the summit of Kangchenjunga still over 2,500 feet above them. They judged the condition of the ice slope to be dangerous and called off the climb. Bauer's two efforts in 1929 and 1931 had introduced new standards to Himalayan climbing.[3]

Another attempt to climb Kangchenjunga was made in 1930 by an International Expedition led by Professor G. O. Dyhrenfurth; the party included Marcel Kurz, Erwin Schneider and Frank Smythe. Many errors were made in the organisation and conduct of the expedition, not uncommon in those early days of large expeditions; for many lessons had to be learnt the hard way. The major error was the choice of an impracticable route from the north via the Kangchenjunga glacier. The party was only convinced about the dangers of this side when a massive avalanche killed a Sherpa porter and very nearly wiped out several other climbers. Other climbs were made in the region, notably Jongsong Peak (24,416 ft), the first confirmed ascent of a Himalayan peak above 24,000 feet.[4] A cine-film of the expedition was produced, the first of its kind, which received well-deserved praise. I remember the unbelievable thrills it gave me at a showing in Darjeeling.

In the Karakoram in 1929 the Duke of Spoleto's party spent over two months surveying the main Baltoro glacier, also attempting to make a journey round K2. Whilst one group crossed the 19,030-foot Muztagh pass over to the north, they failed to find an exit to the east into the valleys draining from the Shaksgam.[5] In 1930 Professor G. Danielli, travelling under his own resources, carried out two months' geological and botanical survey of the Siachen glacier, through its 45-mile length from snout to head.[6]

The distinction of being the first to climb a peak above 25,000 feet, went to F. S. Smythe's privately organised party, seven of whom, including a Sherpa and a Dhotial, reached the summit of Kamet (25,447 ft) in June 1931. The climb was followed by exploration of glaciers to the south and south-west including the climbing of several peaks.[7]

The Germans began their long series of attempts to climb Nanga Parbat in 1932, when Willy Merkl brought out his first expedition. It was a modestly organised venture. A route was pioneered on the northern flank via the Rakhiot valley, and this was followed by every subsequent expedition including the successful one of 1953. Its sheer length, five miles from the base to the last camp and three and a half miles from that camp to the summit, made it vulnerable in the event of bad weather. Its merit was that it was technically easier than any other route on the mountain. The 1932 team climbed the West Chongra peak (20,480 ft) and Rakhiot peak (23,170 ft), and were determined to come back in order to complete a route by which they felt certain the summit could be reached.[8] Merkl returned in 1934 with nine climbers and three scientists, including Professor R. Finsterwalder who prepared a large-scale map of the Nanga Parbat region. On 6 July five Germans and eleven Sherpas were in the top camp at 24,650 feet when a storm struck. This continued almost unabated for nine days, and in their attempt to retreat the party got hopelessly strung out in twos and threes under the most appalling conditions, devoid of food, shelter and communication. Four Sherpas struggled to safety four days later, and one miraculously stumbled into camp alone after eight days. Three Germans and six Sherpas died, including Merkl, whose Sherpa Gaylay perished by his side neglecting his own safety.[9]

A strong German party of nine came out again in 1937; the leader was Karl Wien, and several of the team had already climbed either on Nanga Parbat or on Kangchenjunga. They were dogged by bad weather; and it was mid-June by the time they had set up a camp below Rakhiot peak, from which they intended to launch their assault; the site was near to that used by the two preceding expeditions, and also by the successful expedition of 1953. On the night of 14–15 June, when seven Germans and nine Sherpas were sleeping there, the entire camp was wiped out by an avalanche. This disaster seemed even greater than the one in 1934.[10] But with characteristic determination the Germans returned in 1938 with eight climbers, headed by Paul Bauer. An innovation was the use of an airplane which dropped a total of seventy loads at the glacier camps. After two and a half months of effort, hindered by bad weather, the attempt was called off at the Silver Saddle, a prominent feature leading to the summit structure of Nanga Parbat; here the bodies of Merkl, Gaylay and others who had died in 1934 were discovered.[11] The Germans, beginning to recognise the vulnerability of this lengthy northern route, sent out in 1939 a reconnaissance team comprising Peter Aufschnaiter and Heinrich Harrer to examine Mummery's route on the Diamir side. But many years were to elapse before this team returned home, for they were interned in India after the outbreak of World War II and later escaped to Tibet. Many more years were to pass before the Diamir face was eventually climbed in 1962.

Nine years after the 1924 tragedy on Mount Everest another British expedition was sent out. Nepal was closed. Permission from Tibet had always been difficult to obtain, and the issue was decided usually on a personal level by virtue of the mutual trust that had existed between Sir Charles Bell,* a former Political Agent in Sikkim, and the Dalai Lama. The 1933 party, led by Hugh Ruttledge, comprised fourteen British and seventy-two Sherpas. Since the monsoon reached the Everest region by early June, an early start had to be made, and the semi-wintry conditions encountered during the long march across the Tibetan plateau was a harsh introduction. Gaining from the experience of three previous expeditions, and better equipped, the party were able to build a line of camps up a tried route, every climber contributing to the effort as a whole. The top camp was about 600 feet higher than that of 1924. The Sherpas were given loads of no more than fifteen to twenty pounds for their carries to the two highest camps, and most of the eight who achieved this feat were awarded 'Tiger' badges by the Himalayan Club. One of these was Angtharkay; one porter, on dumping his load at 27,400 feet, with a grunt of relief immediately demanded a *chit*. Oxygen was taken, but it was not used for climbing; indeed, there were still some ethical objections to its use. There were two summit attempts. P. Wyn-Harris† and L. R. Wager examined the north ridge in order to establish whether this route, favoured by Mallory, was to be preferred to the traverse of the north-east face. Suffering from the effects of anoxia, they thought that two prominent steps on the rock ridge looked too difficult. Below the first rock step they discovered an ice-axe, around which much speculation has arisen over the fate of Mallory and

* See Chapter II, Note 2.   † Later, Sir Percy Wyn-Harris, KCMG.

Irvine. Smythe and Shipton made a second attempt, following Norton's 1924 route across the face. Snow lying on the outward sloping rock rendered the climbing tricky and unsafe, and the highest point reached, 28,100 feet, was about the same as that reached by Norton in 1924.[12]

Only in retrospect is it possible to appreciate the physical and psychological barriers which these climbers must have faced. Twenty years later, when the Swiss guide Lambert and Tenzing reached a height little greater than this from the south, assisted by oxygen, it was hailed as an achievement. The southern route by which Everest was climbed in 1953 had one great advantage over the northern in that its main technical difficulties were lower down. On the pre-war route, the serious climbing began above the 21,000 foot camp situated at the foot of the north col slopes, involving an ascent of over 8,000 feet within a distance of nearly four miles; the last 1,000 feet posed the greatest problems, and the highest camp was situated 1,600 feet below the summit. In 1953 the camp below the Lhotse face at 22,000 feet left about two and a half miles of climbing, with the top camp placed 1,000 feet below the summit, and with the main technical difficulties over-come. Above all, in 1933 oxygen on Everest was not accepted as it is nowadays, a piece of equipment as fundamental as crampons or an ice-axe.

In 1935 a reconnaissance team led by Eric Shipton was sent out to Everest with the object of extending the survey of the region, selecting a team for a full-scale attempt the next year and judging the suitability of the post-monsoon period. The party of six carried out extensive exploration in the course of which twenty-six peaks over 20,000 feet, were climbed. A post-monsoon attempt was ruled out, though many continued to argue in its favour.[13] The 1936 expedition was organised on a similar scale to that of 1933, and the leader was again Hugh Ruttledge; but after only three nights spent on the North Col the climb was abandoned, heavy monsoon snowfalls having begun by mid-May.[14]

There was another attempt in 1938, led by Tilman and run at a cost of £2,000, about a fifth of the costs incurred by each of the two pre-ceding expeditions; each member contributed what he could afford and there was no newspaper backing. Despite an earlier start, monsoon conditions were established by the time the top camp could be set up near the site used in 1933. Oxygen was used, but the apparatus was in-efficient. None of the assault teams were really fit enough, under the trying conditions, to tackle the serious difficulties involved in the final stages of the climb.[15] This attempt was followed by protracted discussions about the respective merits of big and small expeditions. Shipton and Tilman argued strongly in favour of the latter, based upon their own considerable achievements during that decade. But the majority opinion supported the belief that the scale and the importance of the objective should determine the size of the expedition. Fourteen years later it was this principle which guided the planners of the successful British expedition. Few persons had a closer acquaintance with Mount Everest than Eric Shipton, and it was fitting that exploration of the eventual ascent route was carried out by a small reconnaissance party under his leadership in 1951 when at last Nepal opened its doors to mountaineering expeditions.

Two serious attempts were made by American teams to climb K2: but there were differences in the organisation and conduct of the two expeditions of 1938 and 1939. The first, led by Charles Houston, was a model of careful planning and was preceded by a reconnaissance of three sides of the mountain before the south ridge, on which the Duke of Abruzzi had camped in 1909, was selected. This has been the route followed by all subsequent expeditions, including the successful one in 1954. In twelve days four Americans and three Sherpas set up a high camp on the ridge and reached a prominent shoulder above it, continuing to about 26,000 feet. They turned back with the knowledge that a way had been found to the summit. The 1939 attempt led by Fritz Wiessner seemed on the other hand to disregard basic principles of planning and teamwork. The camps, strung out along the ridge, became depleted and isolated whilst Weissner with Sherpa Pasang Dawa carried out two ill-prepared summit attempts above the shoulder. During a period of storm one American and three Sherpas were lost in a rescue attempt.[16]

In 1934 Professor G. O. Dyhrenfurth's International Expedition carried out a reconnaissance of Gasherbrum I (26,470 ft). They climbed the west summit of Sia Kangri (c. 23,500 ft), then referred to as Queen Mary peak, and also the east summit of Baltoro Kangri, (23,786 ft) known as the Golden Throne. A French party led by de Ségogne attempted in 1936 to climb Gasherbrum I. They set out from Srinagar in Kashmir with 500 coolies for the 300-mile march to Askole, which took one month; from there 670 coolies were engaged for the journey up the Baltoro glacier. Four weeks after setting up a base they placed a camp at about 23,000 feet, from which they had to retreat during a ten-day storm.

In 1935 John Hunt and James Waller reconnoitred Saltoro Kangri

(25,400 ft), opening up a route to about 24,800 feet, by which the mountain was climbed in 1962 by a Japanese party. Masherbrum (25,660 ft), was first attempted in 1938, when J. B. Harrison and R. A. Hodgkin climbed to over 25,000 feet on their summit attempt. In the same year a reconnaissance of Rakaposhi (25,550 ft) was carried out by M. Vyvyan and C. Secord, who climbed a peak of 19,700 feet situated on its north-west ridge; they also reconnoitred the Kunyang glacier below Disteghil Sar (25,868 ft), climbed by Austrians in 1960, and Kunyang Chish (25,760 ft), climbed by Poles in 1971. In 1937 Shipton's survey north of the main Karakoram filled large blanks in the Shaksgam and Shimshal areas, sorting out the existing confusion in subsidiary glaciers flowing from the Hispar and Biafo and those north of K2. Their fieldwork lasted six months and they produced a map covering 2,000 square miles of mountains and glaciers, proving what a competent party was capable of achieving in extremely difficult country.[17]

It was in Garhwal in 1934 that Shipton and Tilman demonstrated the possibilities open to small parties, given the required toughness and ability. For five months they explored the difficult country surrounding Nanda Devi and the Badrinath and Kedarnath groups. There could have been no better proof of the confidence their three Sherpas had in them than their unquestioning willingness to follow them, at the height of the monsoon, into completely unknown country subsisting for a while on jungle roots. Shipton's description of this expedition resulted in one of his most attractive books.[18] In 1936 Tilman and Odell reached the 25,645 foot summit of Nanda Devi;[19] and in 1939 a Polish party reached the 24,391-foot east summit of the mountain.[20] The Japanese entered the Himalayan scene in 1936 with their ascent of Nanda Kot (22,530 ft), completing Longstaff's 1907 route.[21] Marco Pallis' venture to the Gangotri glacier in 1933 was typical of many subsequent expeditions organised by groups of friends and limited in cost to what each member could contribute personally; they climbed two peaks of 22,000 feet, quite a respectable achievement for newcomers. The Gangotri glacier was the scene of a German expedition in 1938, led by Professor Schwarzgruber, when three peaks above 22,000 feet were climbed. By this time the Survey of India had carried out extensive work in Garhwal in the charge of G. H. Osmaston and R. A. Gardiner,* resulting in the publication of new maps. The heights of all the main summits were accurately fixed and the position of main and subsidiary glaciers clearly shown.[22] F. S. Smythe spent the summer of 1937 botanising in the

* Later, Brigadier G. H. Osmaston, MC, and Brigadier R. A. Gardiner, MBE.

Bhyundar valley; and with Peter Oliver* he climbed several mountains between 20,000 and 22,000 feet, including Mana peak (23,860 ft). A Swiss expedition in 1939, led by André Roch, climbed Dunagiri 23,184 ft.

Bhutan had always been closed to Europeans. Kingdon Ward and others made three botanical expeditions into this primitive country in the early 1930s. A notable expedition was that of G. Sheriff and Ludlow, who during nine months' travel in 1936 collected, among others, sixty-five varieties of primula and sixty-nine varieties of rhododendron. Whilst Kingdon Ward's journeys had covered most of west, central and east Bhutan, theirs penetrated north, towards the Tibet border. In 1938 they did an eight months' botanical journey through south-east Tibet, obtaining glimpses of two high peaks situated on the Assam–Tibet border, Namcha Barwa (25,445 ft), and Gyala Peri (23,460 ft). F. Spencer Chapman, after spending six months in Lhasa as private secretary to the Political Officer in Sikkim, Basil Gould,† succeeded in obtaining permission for an attempt on Chomolhari (23,999 ft), situated on the Bhutan–Tibet border. He climbed the mountain on 26 May 1937 with the Sherpa Pasang Dawa.

The scene of many small expeditions was Sikkim, containing scores of unclimbed mountains over 20,000 feet, and being easily accessible for those with limited time available. In 1935 C. R. Cooke, then stationed in Calcutta, climbed Kabru (24,075 ft), a southern outlier of Kangchenjunga.[23] In 1937 he was joined by John Hunt,‡ also stationed near Calcutta at the time, and they spent the months of October and November climbing in the Zemu area. Cooke was searching for a new route on Kangchenjunga as an alternative to the difficult north-east spur. Accompanied by two Sherpas, he climbed to within 600 feet of the North Col. As a route, this did not seem suitable, because between the North Col and the summit lies the north ridge, over two miles long and of unknown difficulty. Hunt ascended Nepal Peak, south-west summit, 23,500 feet. Erwin Schneider in 1930 had climbed a neighbouring summit (23,470 ft) from the Nepal side.[24] In 1936 Paul Bauer, with Karl Wien, G. Hepp and A. Göttner, visited the Zemu glacier, looking for some new climbs in preparation for their visit to Nanga Parbat the following year. Wien who led that expedition was the only climber to escape the avalanche; Hepp and Gottner were engulfed with five others. The beautiful peak of Siniolchu (22,597 ft) was climbed by its

* Lt.-Col. P. R. Oliver, killed in action in Burma in 1942.
† Sir Basil Gould, CMG, CIE.
‡ The Lord Hunt of Llanvair-Waterdine, CBE, DSO, DCL, LLD.

difficult west ridge; also the highest summit of Simvu (22,346 ft). Both climbs were made during the monsoon. The party explored out of the Zemu valley north into Lhonak, and south over the Simvu saddle, descending the difficult Talung gorge.[25]

Those were some of the highlights of the 1930s; a decade which, during my most impressionable years, filled me with the inspiration and provided me with the impetus to venture into the Himalaya.

1. The northern flank of Kangchenjau; the west ridge is on the right (19 November 1949)

2. Unexplored peaks of the Khangpup group (16 October 1962)

3. South-west face of Kangchenjunga from Base Camp. The great ice shelf runs diagonally across the upper centre of the picture with the main Kangchenjunga icefall in the centre (2 May 1954)

II
Sikkim

*If I ever write an autobiography it will be as other men have done
—with the most earnest desire to make myself out to be the better
man in every little business that has been to my discredit; and I
shall fail, like the others, to make my readers believe anything
except the truth.*

Mark Twain

Sikkim covers an area of approximately 3,000 square miles. Tibet lies
on its northern and eastern borders, with Bhutan in the south-east
corner and Nepal in the west. The country's original inhabitants were
Lepchas, an ancient tribe who emigrated from southern Tibet. There
is scant trace left now of pure Lepcha stock and the present population,
descendants of immigrants from Nepal and Tibet, far outnumber the
original Lepchas. The ruling family of hereditary maharajas is of
Tibetan ancestry, the area having been once a part of the wider
principality of Tibet. Although the Lepchas were animists, there are
now thirty-seven monasteries in Sikkim, varying in size and importance,
the oldest dating from 1697 is at Choling, Buddhism having been
introduced during the seventeenth century.

From this period, when the tangible history of the country really
begins, it was known to be closely associated with Tibet, and its
customs and institutions have always been guided by those of Lhasa.
It was during the period following the Gurkha expansion, when
British forces helped to contain the eastward advance of the Nepalese,
that Britain signed a treaty in 1817 by which she was granted certain
protective rights over Sikkim. In 1835 the tract that now comprises
Darjeeling was ceded to the British by the Maharaja of Sikkim. An act
of indiscretion on the part of the Prime Minister of Sikkim in 1849 led
to friction between the Government of India and the State. Dr A.
Campbell, Superintendent of Darjeeling, and Dr Joseph Hooker, the

noted botanist and explorer[1] were seized and imprisoned while encamped on the road to the Cho La north-west of Gangtok. Following
this incident, a portion of the country south of the Rangit river, now
covered mostly by valuable tea gardens, was occupied by the British.
A fresh treaty, signed in 1861, re-established good relations between the
British and the Sikkimese, which continued for many years. Tibetan
influence, however, continued to gain strength and when Tibetan
militia, often present on the eastern borders, advanced across the
frontier to construct a fort, the British despatched a punitive expedition
in 1888 to drive them out. As a result, a convention was established in
1890 declaring Sikkim a semi-independent state with clearly defined
borders, administered by a Maharaja and his council under the guidance
of a political officer appointed by the Government of India. This status
quo was more or less maintained after Britain handed over power in
1947. Geographically and ethnologically, the extreme northern area of
Sikkim is a part of the Tibetan zone, with broad windswept uplands
supporting a scanty population of yakherds. Until the opening years of
the twentieth century, the Lhonak area* was claimed by Tibet; and
there are still to be seen the remains of walled fortifications well inside
the approaches to the high passes leading to Tibet.[2]

It is interesting here to digress briefly on the historical sequence to
the treaty of 1890, the signatories to which were Lord Lansdowne, as
Viceroy of India, and the Chinese Resident in Tibet, representing the
Emperor of China under whose suzerainty Tibet lay. Tibet, acting
independently of China who was then engaged in a war with Japan,
failed to observe the terms of the treaty, and in distrust of British
intentions sought to obtain protection from the north by means of
independent overtures to the Russian government. It was then that
Lord Curzon, Viceroy of India, decided to act, and the Tibet Mission
was despatched in 1903 under Col. F. E. (later Sir Francis) Younghusband's leadership, with permission from London to proceed to
Khamba Dzong in order to negotiate with the Tibetan government.
Following five months of persistent refusal on the part of the Tibetans
to negotiate, the Mission turned into a Military Expedition, eventually
in 1904 fighting its way through Gyantse to Lhasa. Although the Dalai
Lama had gone into exile in Mongolia, a convention was negotiated
between Britain and Tibet with provision for closer ties including the
exchange of trade.[3] The British thereupon withdrew. But the Chinese
were not slow to seize the occasion of this withdrawal for a strengthen-

* *Lho* = south; *Nak* = black.

ing of their political influence, confirming this later with movements of their armies from the east. By December 1909 when the Dalai Lama eventually returned to Lhasa after over five years abroad, the Chinese were in almost complete control, and by February 1910 their troops were in occupation of Lhasa. Ten days later the Dalai Lama, with six of his ministers, reached India. They lived there for over two years, mostly in Darjeeling and Kalimpong, as guests of the Government of India. It was during this period of exile that Tibetan suspicions of British intentions were at last dispelled. When revolution broke out in China in November–December 1911, Chinese control over Tibet soon disintegrated, and by January 1912 the Dalai Lama was back in Lhasa as spiritual and constitutional head of his people. Four decades later his successor, the 14th Dalai Lama (born in 1935) departed from Lhasa in circumstances closely resembling those of 1910. Within one month of his formal installation in November 1950, Chinese forces invaded Tibet and he moved to Yatung where he set up a temporary government. He undertook a series of travels later, visiting Peking for six months in 1954–55 and India in 1956 to attend the twenty-fifth centenary celebrations of the birth of Buddha. In April 1957 he returned to Lhasa, but owing to the presence there of a Chinese army of occupation, the move was symbolic rather than significant. The population of pre-1950 Tibet has been variously estimated, in the absence of any published census, as between 2 to 4 millions; and that of Lhasa as about 20,000. Though the Dalai Lama was situated traditionally at the apex of power, a good deal of authority used to be exercised by a small number of families in the capital city comprising the priesthood and the nobility. When the Chinese occupation began, guerrilla warfare was waged for several years by the inhabitants of practically all the Tibetan provinces, with more than 50,000 men involved during the height of the resistance campaign. In March 1959, serious fighting broke out in Lhasa following the action of the Chinese army to quell an open rebellion. The Dalai Lama, accompanied by a small escort of ministers and priests, finally fled from the city, making his way towards India through the hills north of Assam. He arrived in Tezpur on 18 April, and since then he has lived in exile in India. He describes his life and thoughts in his book *My Land and My People* which was published in London in 1962. The divinity which he represents sprang from reforms introduced by the great religious teacher Tsong Kapa (1357–1417) who established a new sect of Lamas, the order of the Yellow Hats, devoted to spiritual learning and observing a strict moral code. Looking realistically to the future, in the face of greater upheaval than any of his previous incarnations have known, the present Dalai Lama, while preaching a doctrine of universal friendship and goodwill, does not profess any hatred for the Chinese people; and he is undoubtedly aware that he might well be the last in a 600-year-old line of divine incarnations.

In order to visit Sikkim in the 1940s, a start had to be made from Calcutta by the overnight train to Siliguri, which is situated at the northern end of the Bengal plains. The train left Sealdah station every night at nine. The tumult of an Indian railway-station at departure time has to be experienced to be believed, with frantic crowds of travellers pursued by overladen coolies, voices pitched at the highest level, fighting for a foothold in overcrowded carriages. I can recall the interior of the carriages in which we travelled: dimly lit, upholstered in dark green leatherette and containing four or five sleeping berths; the windows were fitted with venetian, wire-mesh, and glass shutters, none of which worked. Once the steam engine got under way, whistling through the hot night, coal dust and smoke would enter and smother the carriage. From Jalpaiguri, before dawn, if the weather was clear, there was a startling view of Himalayan peaks, over a hundred miles away. The train reached Siliguri at seven; ahead stood the massive barrier of the Himalayan foothills rising 5,000 feet above the plain. In between lay the Terai. In this forest belt travellers on foot or horseback before the turn of the century often had encounters with tiger and wild elephant.

We usually breakfasted in the railway dining-hall at Siliguri before commencing the 52-mile journey to Darjeeling. Outside, the taxi-stand was filled with a variety of aged vehicles which resourceful hill drivers contrived to keep roadworthy. A more adventurous method of travel was by the narrow-gauge railway drawn by diminutive steam engines manufactured in England in the early years of the century. The track of the Darjeeling Himalayan Railway is a remarkable piece of engineering, often providing excitement with its loops and sidings. Because of its more leisurely ascent into the hills, it provides a marvellous introduction to the country. On steeper sections the overworked engine is assisted by a fireman who sits on its fender scattering sand on the rails. The train, with its black and white passenger coaches, would puff into Darjeeling about six hours after leaving Siliguri, and nobody minded too much if it arrived an hour or two late. The complete change of atmosphere during the ascent from the plains is not confined to the air alone, fresh and cool as it feels after the sultry heat. The population of lean and sallow Bengalis has given way to the rosy-skinned and stocky people of the hills, going about their business in a cheerful and carefree manner.

Apart from Darjeeling the other town of importance in British-administered territory was then Kalimpong. It was the terminal point on the trade-route from Tibet, mule caravans bringing in wool for exchange with Indian merchandise.⁴ Here in 1900 Rev. John Anderson Graham of the Missionary Youngmen's Guild founded St Andrew's Colonial Homes; later the orphanage was expanded, and around it grew a boarding school, a hospital and a handicrafts centre which today are still growing and flourishing. From Ghoom, the village of eternal mist, the road to Kalimpong descends steeply through the tropical forest, alive with the humming of cicadas, to the bridge over the Tista river at 2,000 feet. From there, Kalimpong is six miles away and more than 3,000 feet above.

The roads through these hills are frequently washed away during the monsoon, keeping gangs of roadworkers busy for most of the year. On several occasions I have had to walk across a landslip to fresh transport on the other side, hiring coolies to ferry baggage there. Sikkim and the Darjeeling district possess an abundance of tourist rest-houses maintained by the Public Works or Forestry departments. I have visited twenty-three of the fifty-seven bungalows that are scattered over the country at altitudes between 550 feet to 13,000 feet. Much care was obviously taken when selecting the sites for these buildings which command the finest possible viewpoint, and are separated by distances convenient for a day's walking. They are mostly sturdy stone constructions distinguished from afar by their red-painted roofs, and many of them have beautifully kept gardens. One of the most popular tours from Darjeeling used to be the walk to Singalila situated at 12,000 feet on a high ridge stretching north towards the mountain groups below Kangchenjunga. This ridge forms the boundary between Sikkim and Nepal and it provides spectacular views which extend westwards to Everest and Makalu; and eastwards to Chomolhari in Tibet.⁵

In April 1942 I found myself on holiday in Darjeeling. I spent my days combining strenuous morning sessions of tennis with four-mile walks around Birch Hill in the afternoon. On the northern side of Birch Hill I paid a visit to St Joseph's College; four years there under the stern discipline of Belgian Jesuits had taught me self-discipline and the value of a sense of humour. The school dormitory was situated on the top floor of the neo-gothic building; from my bed I could see the clear outline of Kangchenjunga on a moonlit night, and I often wondered what it would be like to sleep out there under the snows. Once, on a still autumn day I watched, through the school telescope, clouds of wind-driven snow sweeping across the south-west face of the mountain.

It was almost at the end of my holiday that April when I met a group planning a tour to the Singalila range, who needed a fourth to make up their party. I was twenty and bursting with fitness. I jumped at their invitation to join them. We travelled in the style hallowed by British traditions of the past three decades; a pony and a *syce** for each of us, plus an orderly carrying our personal baggage; a 'tiffin' coolie to trot alongside, laden with food for the journey; a cook trained in English ways; and a *sirdar* to preside over the whole assembly. Our cook was Dawa Thundu, famous later on Everest, and Ajeeba was one of our porters. I found them an immensely cheerful crowd; they brought old items of expedition kit, including ice-axe and goggles, which created a suitable impression, although umbrellas would have been more appropriate. Each evening, after a leisurely outing lasting about five hours, including a halt for lunch, we would reach a rest-house which our men had long since made comfortable, with the tea-table set beside a fire, with our beds made up and hot water ready for washing. On arrival, the ponies were relieved of their saddlery and, after rolling on their backs in the grass, whinnying with delight, they were tethered and fed; grazing was not allowed because of the aconite which grows wild on the slopes above 10,000 feet, especially in spring, and which is poisonous to horses, cattle and sheep.

We spent the first night at Tonglu (10,069 ft) and the next at Sandakphu (11,929 ft). We were pursued by bad weather practically all the way. Recollections of this brief trip are few. One is a glimpse of the Everest group from Sandakphu; there was only a partial view between clouds in the evening light, but it was wonderfully real compared with the fragment seen from Tiger Hill. One afternoon on the ridge beyond Tonglu, clouds stretching northwards for over forty miles right across the foothills emphasised the distance separating us from the peaks, the upper tips of which were just visible beyond the billowy sea. On our last evening I walked outside at dusk; mists were gathering and the isolation and silence filled me with a curious loneliness mixed with awe. On our return, the village of Manebhanjan could be seen 1,000 feet below. I left the pony route and raced with a porter along narrow tracks plunging steeply down the face, marvelling at his speed and sureness of foot despite the load of thirty-five pounds that he carried.

* *Syce* = groom

One lasting impression was the feeling that came to me at the end; I had tasted something I had never known before. When returning to Darjeeling I looked back with a strange desire at the now distant ridge that we had traversed and I knew that I had discovered something permanent and that I would have to return.

In the early 1940s Himalayan climbing had come very nearly to a stand-still, there being other preoccupations more urgent at the time. But it was always possible to snatch two weeks' leave, or a bit more, for a visit to the nearest mountains. The Darjeeling Sherpa population which only a few years before had seemed insufficient to meet a growing demand from expeditions, now had great difficulty in finding employ-ment. A handful had obtained full-time jobs as personal servants or orderlies; but most of them were out of work, and many returned to their homes in Sola Khumbu. The few that were left obtained sporadic employment with parties of servicemen from India, Burma and Malaya who would come to Sikkim to see the incredible display of orchids and rhododendrons in the spring, or to reach the high passes overlooking Tibet in the clear autumn weather; a few even came to climb peaks. The former local secretary of the Himalayan Club in Darjeeling was no longer available to assist these parties of trekkers or climbers over recruitment of porters; and it was very largely through the agency of Karma Paul that porters were engaged. A Tibetan, he had acted as porter *sirdar* for the successive Everest expeditions since 1924, and had now grown prosperous, running a taxi service in Darjeeling and own-ing a number of racing ponies. Daily rates for porters were often fixed arbitrarily; and it was not until about five years later, when the Himalayan Club were able to find a new local secretary, that a standard tariff was fixed and enforced. However, a few of the leading Sherpas could be contacted independently, and they could be relied upon to handle all the necessary arrangements; pre-eminent amongst these were Angtharkay, Wangdi Norbu, Pasang Dawa, and later, for he was then away from Darjeeling, Tenzing. If your ambitions extended to travelling above the snowline, the porters could always conjure up remnants of old expedition equipment which had passed into their hands, and which they were glad to hire out for a reasonable charge.

By 1945, when the Burma war was at its height, leave was less easy to obtain. By then the Aircrew Mountain Centre had been set up in Kashmir by Wing Commander A. J. M. Smyth; its activities have been

Northern Sikkim and Kangchenjunga

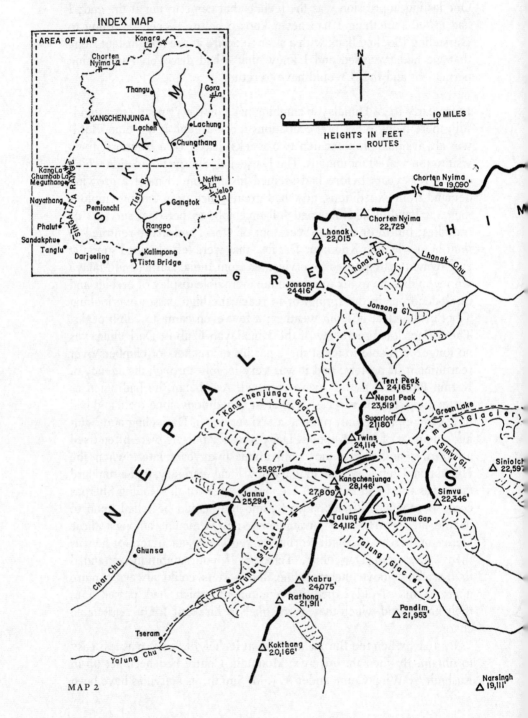

INDEX MAP

AREA OF MAP

Kongra La

Chorten Nyima La

Thangu

Gora La

KANGCHENJUNGA

Lachen

Lachung

Chungthang

S I K K I M

Tista R.

Kang La
Chumbab La
Meguthang

Nayathang

Pemionchi

Nathu La
Jelep La

Gangtok

Phalut

Rangpo

Sandakphu
Tanglu

Darjeeling

Kalimpong
Tista Bridge

SINGALILA RANGE

N

0 _____ 5 _____ 10 MILES

HEIGHTS IN FEET
------ ROUTES

Chorten Nyima La 19,090'

Chorten Nyima 22,729'

G R E A T

Lhonak 22,015'

Lhonak Gl.

Lhonak Chu

Jonsong 24,416'

Jonsong Gl.

H I M

Tent Peak 24,165'

Nepal Peak 23,519'

Sugarloaf 21,180'

Green Lake

Zemu Glacier

Twins 24,114'

Simvu Gl.

Kangchenjunga Glacier

25,927'

27,809'

Kangchenjunga 28,146'

Jannu 25,294'

Talung 24,112'

Zemu Gap

Simvu 22,346'

S

Siniolch 22,597'

N E P A L

Ghunsa

Yalung Glacier

Char Chu

Talung Glacier

Kabru 24,075'

Rathong 21,911'

Pandim 21,953'

Tseram

Kokthang 20,166'

Yalung Chu

Narsingh 19,111'

MAP 2

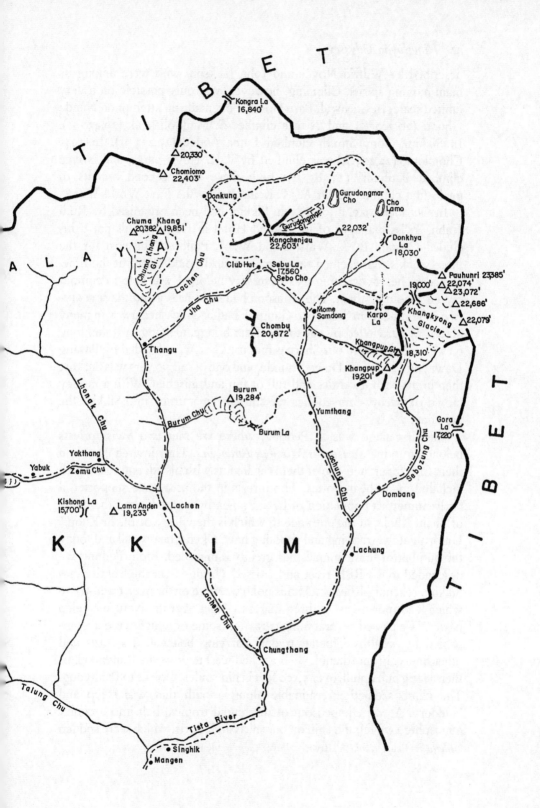

described by Wilfrid Noyce and John Jackson, who were among its main moving spirits. Climbing, however, was only possible on a very limited scale. In Garhwal, Basil Goodfellow made an attempt on Nanda Ghunti (20,700 ft) and Noyce climbed S. Maiktoli peak (19,430 ft). In Sikkim, Tony Smyth climbed Lama Anden (19,233 ft). In 1945 Chomiomo (22,403 ft) was climbed by T. H. Tilly's party, and Noyce climbed Pauhunri (23,385 ft); both these were second ascents of peaks first climbed by Dr A. M. Kellas before the First World War.[6]

In October 1945, a journey in Sikkim had been organised by Rudi Hahn, Swiss manager of the Grand Hotel in Calcutta; his party included Captain R. A. Watson and W. M. Phillips. The cost for the three week's tour seemed rather more than I could afford at the time, and some heart-searching was necessary before I was able to commit myself to joining them. The monsoon had been heavy and the seventy-two-mile road from Siliguri to Gangtok had been washed away in many places. We travelled by car to the Tista bridge, arriving in Kalimpong on 2 October, where our Sherpas met us. They were headed by Pasang Dawa; our cook was Dawa Thundu, and one of our porters was Sarkay, then in his early twenties and full of fun and mischief. With a motley crowd of twenty-four coolies we started our journey into Sikkim the next day.

Our first stage was to Pedong, where we met two Swiss priests belonging to the *Société des Missions Etrangères*. They invited us to join them for supper, and one of them regaled us with his adventures, which included many bear stories. The forests in the area once supported a fairly numerous population of bears; a nearby gorge having the name of Bhalu Khola, at the entrance to which is the village of Bhalu Khop.* Unfortunately, trapping and shooting have taken a heavy toll and today the number of these animals has greatly diminished. From Pedong we descended to the Rishi river and crossed a bridge over the frontier into Sikkim, reaching Rhenok. At this point we were on the main trade-route which leads north-east in three stages to Tibet over the Natu and Jelep passes. We passed several mule caravans, some of which were accompanied by wealthy Tibetan traders carrying bejewelled swords and other finery. From Rhenok we branched west to cross the Rangpo Chu; then a long pull uphill, over 5,500 feet in nine miles, took us to Pakhyong. The climb seemed interminable along a path that was steep and bouldery. As we climbed out of the humid tropical belt into a cooler atmosphere we felt the chill on our shirts and shorts, which were sodden

* *Bhalu* = Bear; *Khola* = River-valley; *Khop* = plentiful

with sweat. I recall an intense thirst, and when we arrived at the rest
house, which had been tantalisingly visible for over an hour and a half,
I drank the entire contents of a four-pint jug of cold water.

Gangtok looked a delightful spot when we arrived there the next
day. Its large bazaar was surprisingly clean, and the row of three
modern rest-houses on the hill above were more luxurious than any we
had seen. One of them was occupied by a wireless officer whose job it
was to maintain contact with Lhasa. We met two parties of travellers,
one of which had returned from a journey to Phari Dzong in Tibet.
The other party, bound for northern Sikkim, had Tenzing as their
sirdar, quietly competent with his attractive smile. That was the first
time I met him, two years were to pass before I saw him again.

Through the evening mist I observed a figure with an ice-axe climbing up the hill towards the bungalow. He wore a battered felt hat and
had a climbing boot on one foot and a canvas shoe on the other. When
I visited him later, he introduced himself as Capt. C. W. F. Noyce.[7]
His room was scattered with climbing gear and food, and an expedition
odour filled the air, a smell compounded of human bodies, wood-smoke
and leather. Hesitantly, in a self-effacing manner, he told me about his
ascent of Pauhunri (23,385 ft) with Angtharkay. The weather was
poor; he had not acclimatised fully, and Angtharkay had a suppurating
sore. But two clear days gave them the chance which they needed.
Angtharkay leading, uncertain that they could complete the lengthy
snow ridge to the summit; Noyce panting behind, persuading him to
take a look just beyond the next bit. I was attracted by Wilfrid Noyce's
diffidence and reserve, which seemed to underline an essential integrity
of character, and he made a deep impression upon me. Our friendship
ripened in later years; and often, when seeking to round the sharp edges
of my character, I have wondered to what extent his qualities have
influenced me. It was delightful to meet Angtharkay, whose exploits
were well known to me from Eric Shipton's books. He was quietly
spoken and completely sincere, and he gave me a copy of the printed
leaflet which he had prepared for guided tours. During those years
there were few opportunities for mountain journeys, and none for long
expeditions.

From Gangtok our daily marches continued in easy stages between
rest houses. The first three days, at altitudes between 2,000 and 5,000
feet, provided an introduction to Sikkim's tropical forests. I saw for the
first time foliage so dense that sunlight could not penetrate. Amidst this
lush vegetation are creepers and ferns of every variety. A striking

feature of these monsoon-fed forests is the profusion of torrents and waterfalls of infinite variety, from boiling foam gushing between boulders to wind-blown spray, rainbow-hued, falling from cliffs 1,000 feet above. With its dank odour and oppressive character, this zone is very different from the upper forest belt of pine, fir, holly and oak trees, with a profusion of orchids, rhododendrons and magnolia.

The road northwards from Gangtok climbs to the Penlong La, then descends about 4,000 feet in nine miles to Dikchu. Not far beyond Penlong village a track crossing the river to the right leads to Tumlong, which preceded Gangtok as the state capital and the seat of the Maharaja in the days when the ruler who was also the spiritual head, followed the life of a recluse. The monastery at Tumlong, founded in 1740, is still one of the most important in Sikkim and it used to house about 125 monks. It was at Tumlong that Dr A. Campbell and Dr Joseph Hooker were held prisoner in 1849–50. Before reaching Dikchu we crossed a bridge over the Dik Chu, which has its source near the Cho La and joins the Tista river at this point. The bungalow is situated in a garden filled with citrus trees, directly above the roar of the Tista. It is an attractive situation, although at 2,000 feet it is probably warm in summer and mosquito-ridden.

After four inches of rain had fallen in the night we encountered several minor landslips on the Singhik track, which was overrun with small streams. At the Rongrong Chu we crossed a suspension bridge, 200 feet long, high above the river. In the early afternoon we reached the village of Mangen from where there is a view of the Talung gorge. This has been traversed by only a handful of Europeans; half-way up, a subsidiary valley leads to the isolated Talung monastery. The country beyond that is very little known and leads to the Kishong La with Lama Anden to the east and the southern Zemu peaks to the west.

Singhik rest-house is built in a clearing deep in the forest and the chowkidar took a great pride in his flower garden. Here Pasang introduced us to *marwa*, the indigenous drink of Sikkim. It is prepared from fermented millet seed, which is placed in a bamboo pot filled with warm water. After a few minutes the contents are sucked through a bamboo straw; the result is a mild cider-like beverage. One pot can last a whole evening; when it is dry more water is added, and you have a fresh brew. The visitors book, thirty years old, which contained familiar names from the early Kangchenjunga and Everest expeditions, made interesting reading. It may have been the *marwa* which put Pasang into a reminiscent mood, for he produced his Himalayan Club book and 'Tiger' badge, and recounted some of his experiences with Weissner on K2 and Spencer Chapman on Chomolhari.

The next morning was clear, enabling us to see the famous view up the Talung gorge; this revealed the steep south-east face of Kangchenjunga and the Simvu massif, with Pandim (22,010 ft) surprisingly close. By eight o'clock, when we set out, only a few summit tips were visible. About seven miles beyond Singhik we crossed the Tista river; then we began to climb through country of which Freshfield had written 'the nearness of the great mountains begins to make itself felt', where sharp breezes refreshed our bodies heated by the climb of 1,200 feet. Chungthang, or the Monk's meadow, is situated at the apex of an angle made by the Lachen and Lachung rivers which unite here to form the Tista. A bridge above the village is of interest because of a rock promontory to its left, from which condemned criminals used to be flung into the river.

From Chungthang we travelled up the Lachen valley. A month earlier a huge landslide had carried down about 1,000 feet of the hillside, damming the river and forming a lake from which the waters escaped through a narrow channel. The villagers lived under the constant threat of the bursting of this dam. The old track up the valley had been destroyed and a new pathway had been devised which climbed steeply upwards through forest and undergrowth above the shattered hillside. We got away at 6.30 am., after a breakfast by candle-light, and spent two and a half hours on the detour. We made our ascent mostly in shadow and were badly stung by nettles. On steeper bits, branches and shrubs provided the safest support. The descent went more easily, but we had to fix a rope at one bad place where a rickety step-ladder was suspended across a cliff. At the end of the detour we found that we had advanced barely two miles up the valley from Chungthang.

At noon the whole party halted for a meal in the cool glade at Menshithang, where the porters, basking in the sunshine, gorged happily on unripe walnuts. At this place Sikkimese and Tibetan warriors were said to have met in a great battle around 1890. Our path beyond this climbed steadily until at about 7,500 feet the appearance of the country gradually became more alpine, containing wide green meadows and sturdy stone-built homesteads. When we arrived in Lachen (8,800 ft) it was cold, the sun having long since left the sheltered valley. The peak of Lama Anden seemed to stand just beyond the ridge above the village; in fact, it was over 10,000 feet above us, sharply etched in the clear evening sky.

We allowed ourselves a rest-day at Lachen, spending the morning sorting and packing loads for our journey up the Zemu glacier. Later we visited the monastery dating from 1860 which had in residence about fifteen permanent monks; but there was present a large group of visiting monks for the seven-day observance of the death of a former head Lama. There are two main buildings, one of which is almost completely filled by a one-ton prayer wheel, the largest in Sikkim. It is brightly painted in green, gold and vermillion, and it requires the entire strength of one man to set it in motion which he does by means of pendant thongs. At every revolution a lever strikes a bell which announces that so many thousand prayers have ascended to heaven. A second building contains the main shrine, hung with brightly coloured *thankas*, which are printed prayer banners of rich brocade; also a library filled with manuscripts bound in wood or leather of rectangular shape built into the walls. We watched a service which was in progress, accompanied by a full orchestra comprising the long Tibetan horn, not unlike the alpine horn, drums, cymbals and pipes. There was a suggestion of rhythm, but without a trace of melody or harmony, and the noise was appalling. A small Finnish mission headed by a Miss Kronquist was closed, but a seamstress showed us round their workshop, where hand-made carpets and rugs were prepared. At Lachen we saw our first yaks, and tasted our first Sikkim apples, sour-sweet, but crisp and juicy.

Departing on 11 October, we left the main path three and a half miles north of Lachen to enter the Zemu valley. The track up the Zemu Chu is narrow and overgrown; it peters out when the last herdsman's hut is reached at Yakthang. Practically the whole of the first stage is across waterlogged forest and undergrowth with fallen tree-trunks rotting in the bog and half-submerged rhododendron thickets blocking the way. I remember finding this very hard work, and thinking that if this was what mountaineering was about I was probably not very interested. It took us almost as many hours to cover nine miles; and when we arrived at Yakthang 11,000 feet, it was cold with wet snow falling. The next day bad weather persisted; following the Zemu Chu close above its left bank we stopped at midday in quite heavy snowfall by a cave called Yabuk; the snout of the glacier was just visible through the mist about half a mile away. There was sleet and snow all afternoon and I think that all of us felt pretty gloomy; the only cheerful note was Sarkay's grinning face as he handed into the tent a huge plate of steaming dinner.

We began to appreciate the scale of the glacier, about ten miles from its snout to the upper ice, and a further six miles from there to the base of Kangchenjunga. We toiled up the moraine in misty weather the next day, getting short of breath; all the mountains around us were hidden. Reaching the broad ablation valley on the north side of the glacier, known as Green Lake Plain, we found it covered by snow. Lower down we passed one of Paul Bauer's camps, with a few rusty remains scattered about. But the porters had pressed on, placing our camp at what they referred to as Marco Pallis' camp; this was situated in a sheltered corner of the plain at about 15,500 feet. In this valley there was an abundance of juniper scrub, and a really large camp fire cheered us that evening. Shortly after sunset the clouds lifted and the startling white peak of Siniolchu (22,597 ft) was revealed, with its needle peak to the right.

We had intended to spend about four days here, making excursions up the glacier, but the weather never showed any real sign of improving and on the third day we decided to return to Lachen. Twice we walked up the valley to the shores of the Green Lake (16,190 ft). Ice-encrusted streams criss-crossed the snow-covered plain, but a few of the hardier primula and gentian were scattered about; and we saw several marmots, also a herd of antelope. Despite persistent cloud there were glimpses of Simvu, the Zemu gap and the lower slopes of Kangchenjunga's north-east spur. The next day, less troubled by the altitude, we walked on the moraine towards the more level central part of the glacier. Although Kangchenjunga refused to reveal itself fully, there were brief views of the Twins, Nepal Peak and Tent Peak thrillingly close.

We were back at Yabuk on the third evening, sharing the camp-site in typical snow and sleet with Captain Langton Smith, who was accompanied by Rinzing and two other Sherpas. He was aiming to climb Sugarloaf Peak (21,180 ft). We talked late into the evening and I gathered that this was his first Himalayan climb. Langton Smith did not return from this expedition. He and one of his Sherpas were last seen in camp at 18,000 feet when a storm struck. The other Sherpas were unable to find any trace of the bodies.

When we returned to Lachen on 16 October, Watson had approached the end of his leave and had to depart. The rest of us set out for the next part of our journey, which led north to Thangu and over the Sebu La (17,560 ft) into the Lachung valley. Bob Watson possessed a tremendous sense of fun and we would miss his amusing anecdotes and comments.

Hahn, at forty, was the oldest in the party; he was heavily built and had developed a nasty cough following an injudicious bathe in Zemu Chu. Walter Philips, a tireless walker in tennis shoes and corduroy shorts, impressed the porters by his phlegmatic acceptance of any situation, no matter how gloomy. At the Lachen bungalow we chatted with the Maharaj Kumar of Sikkim, then a lad of twenty and now ruler of the State, while he packed his kit in preparation for a journey to the Chorten Nyima range in the extreme north-west.

In clearer weather we were able to enjoy the walk to Thangu (12,860 ft), obtaining a glimpse of the twin 19,000-foot peaks of Burum Khang, about seven miles to the east. The walls of the living room at Thangu bungalow were covered with pages cut from *The Tatler*, *The Sketch* and *Punch* of thirty years earlier, probably a labour performed by some weather-bound traveller. The good weather held out for another day and we moved up an attractive alpine valley to the north-east towards the grazing grounds where the Jha Chu hut stands. Between 1936 and 1938 the Himalayan Club made funds available for the construction of two huts at Jha Chu and Mome Samdong, linking the route over the Sebu La. These were built and maintained by the Sikkim State Engineer, conforming in design to an alpine climbing hut, with stone walls and wooden interior, stoves for heating and cooking, and a loft containing sleeping quarters. Both these huts are sited at about 15,000 feet, leaving 2,500 feet of ascent on either side of the pass. From the Jha Chu hut there is an impressive view of the unclimbed peak of Chombu, (20,872 ft).

Bad weather set in on the following day as we crossed a small crevassed glacier below the slopes leading to the Sebu La, and the climb to the crest took four hours, as we were slowed down by two feet of powder snow on the long north-west face. The La, a narrow rock ridge, is marked by a cairn and strings of prayer banners; snow had been falling for some time, and as the pass was covered by thick cloud we did not tarry. On the descent we met a party of four British soldiers ascending with twelve coolies; despite the weather they were obviously enjoying their unusually-chosen holiday. The stream which issues from the Sebu Cho, a lake situated at about 15,950 feet on the east side of Chombu, joins the Lachung river below Mome Samdong. We traversed the moraine above the lake, and a mile further on we passed a hot sulphur spring, its waters bubbling and steaming in the surrounding snow.

Very early the next day, from Mome Samdong, we watched a yak

4. Advanced Base, 18,000 feet, at the head of the Yalung glacier (8 May 1954)

5. Monsoon clouds sweeping into the upper Gangotri glacier (18 July 1947)

6. Kedarnath peak from camp on Chaturangi glacier (24 July 1947)

7. Tenzing, Ang Dawa and Ang Norbu (14 August 1947)

caravan moving across the snowy landscape towards the Donkhya La (18,030 ft), like a line of battleships visible through the white-out. A mule train was setting out in the other direction towards Yumthang ten miles away, and we decided to follow in its furrow. The snow was often knee-deep and at about half-way the muleteers stopped for a rest. Dawa Thundu, always the sturdiest of our group, went into the lead and beat out tracks for the rest of the way. Through the conifer forest there was a conventional Christmas-card atmosphere; but a shout was all that was needed to produce a minor avalanche of snow from nearby branches. During the six-hour plod my mind was dulled into semi-consciousness, reconstructing themes from familiar symphonic works in order to keep my body awake. Inside the Yumthang bungalow, one of the biggest in Sikkim, we got three large fires going and were soon able to dry out all our soaked possessions.

By the time we reached Lachung the weather had improved, and the contrast from snow and sleet to sunlit green fields was delightful. We found this village less Tibetan in character than Lachen; it was larger and its inhabitants looked cleaner and more prosperous. An abundance of streams and waterfalls are diverted into their fields, where barley, corn and potatoes are cultivated, sufficient for their needs. We met Miss Doig of the Scottish Mission, dwelling in a stone cottage reminiscent of the Cairngorms. This dedicated lady, then aged seventy-two, had spent about a quarter of a century in the valley, and was much respected for her medical and educational work. An apple orchard surrounded the rest-house and the fruit which was just ripening was the nicest we had tasted.

The Lachung valley supports a larger and more attractive population than the narrow and steeper Lachen valley. Below Lachung the path led through ripening fields between small groups of well-built houses. In the mild glow of the autumn sunshine, the agreeable colours of the landscape seemed to match the cheerfulness of the inhabitants. At Chungthang we rejoined our outward route, and three days later we were back in Gangtok. A lingering memory of that uncrowded hill town is of the bells of mule caravans setting out on the road over the passes into Tibet, recalling an age that has long since passed.

There seemed to be a wealth of opportunity in Sikkim for beginners, and a year later I went there again. Walter Phillips joined me; also Captain J. H. Fleming, then stationed at Fort William in Calcutta. We reached Gangtok on 8 October and were met by Pasang Dawa with

Sarkay, Sonam and young Karma, who came as a cook, though I think that we must have been his first victims. While these four Sherpas stayed with us throughout, Pasang had brought from Darjeeling fourteen other porters, including five women, who came as far as Thangu, where we made a stores dump. We were rather green in those days, and our overburdened caravan provoked an amused smile from Angtharkay, whom we met a few days later near Thangu. Pasang, at that time, was a ministering priest in Darjeeling, and I had seen him there on one occasion dressed in the traditional lama robes of silk brocade, surrounded by a group of acolytes. I think that he sometimes tended to extend that atmosphere to his journeys into the mountains. Besides, I found him rather grasping, unlike Angtharkay, who as I discovered later, always had an eye for economy.

Before setting out from Gangtok we visited the State office in order to obtain a permit for our journey to an area near the northern border. We also called at the Residency in order to meet the Political Officer, Mr A. Hopkinson. At Singhik we shared the bungalow with Captain Jim Thornley, a Gurkha officer, and I envied his ability to converse with his men in fluent Gurkhali. He was returning from the Zemu glacier, where he had made an unsuccessful attempt to find Captain Langton Smith's body, although he discovered remains of their final camp, including two rolls of exposed film.[8]

The detour on the Chungthang–Lachen road had been improved and there was only one unpleasant section, where a bamboo platform twelve inches wide, was suspended across a cliff. The weather was mostly wet, and when we arrived in Thangu on 13 October the snow-line was at about 14,000 feet. Pasang had not visited the Tasha Phu valley to the north, and on the evening of our arrival at the rest house he was unable to obtain much information about it from a semi-inebriated old chowkidar. The next morning we climbed a hill about 1,500 feet high behind the bungalow, and from there we caught glimpses between clouds of the Chumakhang peaks. The highest, 20,382 feet, had been climbed by H. W. Tilman in 1938. Its neighbour, 19,851 feet, was unclimbed and we decided to approach it up a subsidiary valley three miles east of the Tasha Phu.

Our first camp was on moraine at about 16,000 feet and the next was at 17,500 feet on the glacier leading to the south-east ridge of our mountain. After setting up the tents at midday, we advanced up a snow ridge with Pasang giving a confident lead. When we reached ice with an eight-inch snow cover he proceeded cautiously for two rope-lengths, kicking and clearing steps to about 18,500 feet. There was no difficulty, but the late afternoon weather looked threatening, with *poissons* in the sky, and we turned back. The next morning we were completely snowed up, so we packed and returned to Thangu. There, for the next three days, we were marooned inside the bungalow while snow blanketed the hillsides down to 11,000 feet.

We set out again on 22 October, heading for the Jha Chu hut, but there was so much fresh snow that it took us a day and a half to get there. We attempted a mountain of 17,850 feet, north-east of the hut. Battling through a morass of soft snow we reached a col at about 17,500 feet between our peak and its neighbour of similar height. Beyond this, in the deep snow, swimming motions rather than climbing would have been more appropriate, and we called it off. A little discouraged now by the conditions and the weather we thought it would be wise to move north in order to escape from the influence of what looked like late-monsoon storms. Climbing out of the Jha Chu valley, we reached a plateau at 16,500 feet directly under the steep south face of Kangchenjau 22,603 feet. It was a wonderful situation, and there were views of Chombu, Chumakhang and Chomiomo, with Kangchenjunga and the Twins in the distance. On the way down we picked up a track which we followed to the small settlement of Donkung (15,750 ft); this is situated on the main route to the Kongra La, with Khamba Dzong about twenty-five miles away.

Three stone shelters were occupied by yakherd families, but a fourth was placed at our disposal; it was indescribably squalid, with a roof that stopped leaking only when the temperature at night reached freezing. The heavy mastiffs which always accompany Tibetan herdsmen are terribly fierce animals and quite powerful enough to kill a man; when I was approaching the settlement one of these creatures rushed towards me with teeth bared and I was grateful to Pasang for placing himself in front of me. The Tibetan settlers had killed an aged yak, whose meat would provide food for several days; their method is to make an incision in the heart; not, as in Nepal, by breaking the spine. The yak, like the camel to the desert Arab, faithfully serves its owner as much after its death as during its lifetime, providing meat, wool, rope and leather, as well as milk, butter, cheese, fuel and transport. There is a pungency in the smell of a yak-dung fire that seems to outlast all the other odours of a journey, penetrating sleeping bags, clothing and food; fires are kindled in the age-old manner by striking a flint on tinder. Two days earlier a Tibetan had died and he was cremated ceremoniously by the river above Thangu; he was a man of some standing, otherwise the usual practice is to dismember the body, which is then thrown to the vultures.

We had escaped from the bad weather, though the clouds were still visible massing in the south. In the clear atmosphere we experienced the sharp winds which sweep across the Tibetan plateau and temperatures were appreciably lower. On 26 October, at a camp four miles north-west of Donkung, we recorded 7°F at 16,500 feet. From that camp, one afternoon, we climbed for thee hours up scree and snow to about 18,750 feet on the shoulder of Chomiomo's north peak (20,330 ft). The next morning Walter Phillips and John Fleming made another attempt, reaching the broad summit snowfield at 20,000 feet; but they found it too exhausting, burrowing through waist-deep snow to continue to the highest point which seemed about 400 yards away. They had a magnificent view of the main peak of Chomiomo, and of Kang-chenjau and Pauhunri, with the Tibetan plateau stretching away to their right.

For the return journey to Gangtok we had to engage six local porters. They were a thirsty group and all of them, including Pasang, tended to get rather out of hand pausing to refresh themselves at every spirit shop that we passed. Each village has its 'pub', an establishment displaying the owner's name and the licence issued by the State authorising him to sell the local brew; as the latter differs from place to place, I suppose that our men regaled themselves with quite a wide variety.

I had learnt much from this journey; that there was a special attraction in visiting little-known areas and that the depth of one's experience did not depend upon whether a summit had been reached. Also I felt that, when organising another venture, my main emphasis would be on lightness and mobility. These were not new ideas, but conviction had come to me from personal experience.

Having now really caught the mountain fever, fresh ideas kept entering my mind for more extended journeys. It seemed unthinkable to allow a single season to go by without fulfilling some cherished plan, and the months between were spent poring over maps and books, learning as much as I could and storing up ideas. From now on, planning a Himalayan expedition became my most pleasurable occupation.

In 1949 I had become Honorary Secretary of the Himalayan Club, whose central section had recently been shifted from Delhi to Calcutta. The labour of joining together the broken strands and resuscitating the Club's activities after the hiatus of the war years was taken up by the newly-elected President, C. E. J. Crawford, who had climbed on Chomolhari with F. Spencer Chapman in 1936. For over six years there had been few who could spare the time to keep the Club's affairs going, and it is largely due to Charles Crawford's energy that the Club began to take on a new lease of life. The first task was to bring the list of members up to date, which enabled us to pick out those who were still actively interested, and to seek new local secretaries and correspondents. The equipment store, then housed in a small room provided by the Geological Survey of India in Calcutta, had to be refurbished; and a home had to be found for the valuable library, still stored in the crates in which it had been shifted from Delhi. Soon we were able to organise members' meetings in Calcutta, and the *Himalayan Journal* appeared again after an interval of about seven years, Wilfrid Noyce having agreed to edit the first post-war volume. With the re-emergence of the Club, membership began to increase and I found that we started to receive a flow of correspondence. It seemed as though the pent-up frustration of the war years had burst into a flood of enthusiasm.

Initially the emphasis was on small groups with little or no financial backing. It was not until the French had climbed Annapurna in 1950 that the large nationally-backed expedition re-appeared, several countries vying with each other to achieve 'firsts'. As in other sports a lively spirit of competition emerged; a strong motivating force that is not excluded from mountaineering. The field was now wide open, for the decade had begun that probably deserves to be remembered as the 'golden age' of Himalayan climbing. It was during the fifties that all the highest peaks of the Himalaya, Karakoram and Hindu Kush were climbed. I think that it was then still possible, as it seems no longer possible now, to relate the attitudes of the climbers of the day to those of the Himalayan pioneers whose feelings were aptly expressed by Mallory after his return from Everest in 1921: 'Principles must be respected in the ascent. The party must keep a margin of safety. It is not to be a mad enterprise, rashly pushed on regardless of danger. The ill-considered acceptance of any and every risk has no part in the essence of persevering courage. A mountaineering enterprise may keep sanity and sound judgement and remain an adventure. And of all the principles by which we hold the first is mutual help.'[9]

Some of the pre-war climbers were still active in the fifties. I remember entertaining H. W. Tilman in Calcutta before his first Nepal expedition, and F. S. Smythe before his last visit to Darjeeling in 1949, where he was suddenly taken ill. But it was mainly for younger climbers

from all over the world that the Himalaya had now become a playground. When H. E. Riddiford wrote to me from New Zealand in 1950,
seeking a suitable objective for a party of four, I suggested Mukut
Parbat (23,760 ft) because I knew that Smythe the year before had
hoped to climb that mountain. It was interesting to deal with a wealth
of inquiries that poured in from all over the world. Some were keen
merely to follow a familiar journey, others had ambitious objectives;
all demanded a host of detail for a number of regions. Sometimes the
answers called for greater knowledge than I possessed; but I enjoyed
ferreting out information which was nearly always available from the
Club's library and records. Happily, the Himalayan Club at Calcutta,
together with its sections at Delhi, Bombay and Darjeeling, was able
to continue its traditional role as a source of assistance to parties coming
out from abroad. The Club was especially fortunate when in 1951 Mrs
Jill Henderson, whose husband's tea estate was situated near Darjeeling, agreed to become local secretary. Relations with the Sherpas
were never closer than during her term of office. The Club was able to
award many 'Tiger' badges during that period; indeed a number of
Sherpas were placed in a new category as guides.

In 1949 Sikkim loomed large in my thoughts again. Costs had become
an important consideration. Ten or twelve rupees per person per day
was estimated in the 1930s as the average cost of a journey to the
Himalaya. In 1945 my quarter share of the cost for twenty-six days was
750 rupees, almost a threefold increase. The next year three of us contributed 1,000 rupees each; and in 1949 I budgeted for a similar cost.
My plans were to visit the extreme north-eastern corner of Sikkim,
where there was an area that seemed scarcely known, and had not been
fully explored. I was joined by M. Hruska, a Czech, thirty-five years
of age, living in Calcutta, who had been a keen skier and athlete. I had
written to Angtharkay about porters and I was delighted when he
agreed to come himself, bringing four other Darjeeling men. Having
experienced bad weather during two previous visits in October, I
planned to make a later start.

Hruska and I arrived on 1 November in Gangtok, where we found
Angtharkay awaiting us; Dawa Thundu came again as cook, also
Ajeeba, Sonam and Mingma Sitar. Angtharkay's reputation was founded,
I think, not only on his natural qualities as a mountaineer, but also on
his ability as a manager. The confidence and trust which he inspired
gave one the comforting assurance that if a solution to any problem

existed he would find it. He managed his men by example, invariably carrying a load himself and apportioning the loads of others in order to make sure that there were neither malingerers nor victims. Often, as he kept his men together on the march, did I enjoy their jokes and chatter, as I did his shopping ventures at villages on the way. I think that his finest quality was his integrity.

Engaging four baggage mules at Gangtok, we walked in four stages to Lachung. From there the mules, accompanied by one of our men, proceeded to Mome Samdong where, after making a stores dump, they were released. Hruska and I, with five Sherpas, travelled north-east from Lachung up the Sebozung Chu, halting the first day at Dombang 10,040 feet. Here the cultivation of an indigenous medicinal plant is carried out, and we were accommodated in a small hut constructed by the State in 1936. That evening, by the camp-fire, there was an entertainment put on by the Sherpas in the moonlight, Angtharkay singing and dancing lustily with the rest. The hut-keeper at Dombang was not aware of any Europeans having passed this way; but the amount of detail shown on the Survey of India map-sheet indicated that surveyors must have penetrated far up this valley.[10]

Our first camp was placed eight miles beyond Dombang at 12,300 feet, and the next was at 14,000 feet, near the snout of the Khangkyong glacier; near this camp we spotted a herd of *barhal*. We were able to follow a pathway up to a point near the junction of two streams below the glacier. From there the track continues east to Tibet over the Gora La (17,220 ft); a lesser track leads north-west over the Karpo La (17,660 ft) to Mome Samdong. The first is a frequented route, but the second is not in general use, bisecting a glaciated area and ringed by several peaks between 18,000 and 19,000 feet. Ahead of us stood a wall of high peaks rising from the Khangkyong plateau, which is an ice basin about four miles wide guarded by a heavily-broken icefall. The weather was settled and we had wonderfully clear skies; but, as expected, it was cold with night temperatures averaging about 10°F. The late autumn days were short, and we seldom had more than six hours of sunshine a day, reaching us as late as 8.30 a.m. In the evening it was usually quite dark soon after five o'clock.

Our way lay north towards the head of the Khangkyong glacier; our objective was to find a way on to the plateau, and from there a passage out to the west. Since we estimated that there was over 4,000 feet to go, we spent a day on reconnaissance. Following the moraine on the left bank of the glacier, we gained 1,000 feet and were relieved to discover that the way continued without serious difficulty, by-passing the worst sections of the icefall. But with short daylight hours and fatiguing conditions on the snow-plastered moraine, we required two days and two more camps to reach the plateau. Arriving there on 10 November we placed our fifth camp at 18,000 feet on a prominent island of red rock. It was a wonderful situation. The plateau was almost two miles deep; it was surrounded by a row of five peaks, two over 23,000 feet and the remainder over 22,000 feet, which formed a striking watershed dividing Sikkim from Tibet. Hruska had been unable to acclimatise to the altitude; he had grown progressively weaker as we ascended, suffering from headache and an inability to retain any food. His skis had been laboriously carried thus far and I think that he was sustained solely by the prospect of a high-level run, battling on bravely to the top of a pass which we reached the next day.

On the broad slopes approaching the pass we took it in turns to stamp out a track through knee-deep powder snow. Our pass, the height of which we estimated at almost 19,000 feet, was the main western outlet from the upper Khangkyong basin. Due east a sharp line of ice peaks did not reveal any possible exit towards Tibet. The watershed ridge continuing due north was marked by a line of three high peaks, the farthest of which was Pauhunri. I was too elated at the time to feel any regret that we were unable to climb one of these mountains, in particular a peak on the eastern rim marked 22,079 feet, which looked quite feasible; most of the others seemed difficult of approach. From the pass the slopes fell away gently to the west, assuring us of a straightforward descent and enabling Hruska at last to put on his ski. As he glided smoothly, noiselessly down the long slopes the Sherpas' reaction was first one of amusement then of envy. There were superb views to the south-west of Chombu and Kangchenjunga. At the foot of the snowslope we put on the rope in order to cross a badly crevassed section of the upper Jakthang glacier.

Reaching the moraine, we camped that afternoon by a small lake at 17,000 feet in the Jakthang valley. We were situated at the upper limit of scrubwood, and the peaks on the Karpo La divide formed our southern background. Climbing above our camp in the evening, I called out to Angtharkay to join me; in the clear atmosphere to the north-west there was a striking view of Kangchenjau, which was our next objective. A five-hour descent of the valley the next day brought us out on to the Donkhya La track, one mile above the Mome Samdong hut. As far as I know the Khangkyong plateau has not been visited again; together with the glaciers lying immediately to its north and south, it is one of the very few areas left in Sikkim containing groups of unclimbed mountains filled with exciting opportunities.

Snow lay thickly around the vicinity of the Himalayan Club hut, and we found that the building had been made almost uninhabitable by local herdsmen, with several windows smashed and the stove badly damaged. Hruska, who had not recovered fully, decided to return to Gangtok whilst the rest of us set out for the next part of our journey. After Kellas had climbed Kangchenjau in 1912 from the north via a col of 21,000 feet, he observed that an easier approach to his col would be possible from the east. It seemed interesting to try to follow this up, especially as the mountain had not been climbed since.

Travelling north-east from Mome Samdong, we crossed the Donkhya La on 15 November. Although the pass is over 18,000 feet high there was little snow on its crest, and in the marvellously clear atmosphere there were views of the peaks of Northern Sikkim and of the vast plateau of Tibet, with Khamba Dzong clearly visible about thirty miles away. Near the pass we saw the remains of old Tibetan fortifications. We descended into the broad sweeping uplands that comprise the extreme northern zone of Sikkim; there, in 1934, the geologist J. B. Auden had discovered ammonite fossils in the shales and limestones. In former years it was not uncommon to find herds of *ovis ammon* distributed over this region, though the population is very scanty, if not non-existent, today. Skirting the shores of Cho Lamo we came across two yak caravans. Impressions seemed almost unreal; the lake was a rich blue colour and the intense light on the brown plain contrasted with the dazzling peaks of Gurudongmar and Pauhunri on either side. We camped that afternoon at about 16,000 feet, north of the larger of two Gurudongmar lakes. Later I advanced almost a mile above the snout of the Gurudongmar glacier, which debouches into the smaller of two lakes. I was expecting to be able to see the approach to Kellas' col on Kangchenjau from this eastern side; but, probably failing to advance sufficiently far round to the right, I could not distinguish any obvious signs, and I decided unwisely to move over to the north-east side of the mountain in order to search for Kellas' original ascent route. What followed was the fruit of inexperience.

Entering the wrong valley south of Donkung, we reached a saddle situated at about 18,000 feet on the western flank of Kangchenjau and found ourselves overlooking the Jha Chu valley. Above us rose the west ridge of the mountain, two miles of steep ice and rock leading to the untrodden west summit. We built a cairn and returned to the tents at 17,000 feet, where I felt quite unworthy of the delicious scones which Dawa Thundu had prepared for tea. We spent a rest day in Donkung. A sheep was purchased for eighteen rupees and the Sherpas spent most of the day killing, dissecting and cooking it; we ate very well. I walked up the slopes to the north in order to gain a better perspective of Kangchenjau, picking out Kellas' col and fixing landmarks below it.

I left Donkung on 19 November accompanied by Angtharkay, Dawa Thundu and Ajeeba, and we camped at 19,000 feet below the slopes leading to the 21,000-foot col. There had been a sharp wind all day, and at night I had to emerge in the darkness in order to struggle with the loosened guy-ropes of my tent. In the morning the wind had dropped only slightly and the temperature was minus 4°F. For once the Sherpas were late in stirring, and we got under way at 9.30 a.m., when a sun devoid of warmth reached us. We carried a tent and food for a camp on the col, though I had observed that its lower slopes, which faced north, were in constant shadow while its crest received only a couple of hours of sunshine in the morning. We made good progress at first up a firm wind-crust. After three and a half hours we struck ice at an angle of 45° and we judged that there was still about 650 feet to go. We were cold, and I had long since lost sensation in my toes and fingers. I caught up with Angtharkay who had been in the lead throughout. When I suggested retreat he looked dismayed but put the question to Dawa Thundu and Ajeeba, who were below. It seemed that the unpleasant decision to turn back would have to be mine. I think that with Angtharkay out in front the others would have followed, however reluctantly.

An opportunity lost is seldom regained and a dozen times since have I regretted my decision. I had not learned yet to judge my limits and to draw the dividing line between what was feasible and what was unjustifiable. Each man has his own critical point, and the secret lies in knowing exactly when that point has been reached within the limits of safety to himself and to others. That was the lesson which came home to me from this failure. As far as I know, Kellas' 1912 ascent of the east summit of Kangchenjau has not been repeated.[11]

By 1950 Tibet, about one-sixth of whose population consisted of monks, was in the throes of upheaval. Many years earlier Percival Landon* had

* See Nepal Note 1. Landon first visited India in 1904 as a newspaper correspondent for *The Times* when he accompanied the Younghusband expedition to Lhasa.

written: 'The Potala unconsciously symbolises the vast erection of power and pride which separates the priestly caste from the religion they have prostituted.' China, re-emerging as the greatest power in Asia, had not only taken active steps to re-establish her suzerainty over Tibet, but had demolished the ancient religious autocracy headed by the Dalai Lama in Lhasa, setting up her own military and civil administration to exercise control of the country. The areas bordering India, historically always sensitive, were now even more so; Gangtok was being gradually built up as a forward outpost of the Indian army. For the first time in over half a century travel restrictions were introduced in Sikkim. My last visit to Sikkim in 1952 was my least fruitful.

Landslides had washed away the Siliguri–Gangtok road in several places. When I reached the Indian border town of Rangpo (950 ft), where I had to spend a night, police officials seemed over-eager to examine my pass and to inquire about my intended movements. Arriving in Gangtok on 3 October, I called on the Dewan, who was responsible for political liaison between the Government of India and the State. My efforts to obtain permission for another attempt on Kangchenjau were in vain; I was not permitted to travel north of Thangu. The Indian army seemed to be in evidence everywhere and two of the State rest-houses were occupied by officials. My spirits seemed to match the gloomy weather, when Angtharkay's grinning face appeared through the mists and hopes seemed to revive.

I left Gangtok with Angtharkay and five Sherpas, walking up the Lachen valley to Thangu in almost continuous rain. Leeches pestered us in the forest and I found many changes in the route, a good deal of the original pathway having been destroyed by heavy monsoon rain. In September 1950 a large section of the icefall south of the Sebu La had collapsed into the Sebu Cho, which is one of the main sources of the Lachung river. When the waters, which were blocked for several months, eventually broke out there was widespread flooding, which caused much damage to fields and villages and carried away a suspension bridge six miles below Chungthang.

From Thangu on 9 October we moved up to the Himalayan Club hut in the Jha Chu valley, now barely habitable following damage caused by local herdsmen. After sitting out a day of bad weather we crossed the Sebu La, obtaining fairly clear views of Chombu (20,872 ft). It did not seem surprising that this mountain was still unclimbed; a difficult north-west ridge appeared to be the only way to a shoulder at about 20,000 feet, from where a fairly broken ice ridge leads to the summit.[11] We studied the icefall above the Sebu Cho, now visibly reduced in size; and were struck by the devastation, the old route to Mome Samdong, having been obliterated. We pitched our tents that night near the remains of the Himalayan Club hut. It was now devoid of windows and doors and its roof had been severely damaged.

Two short excursions were made. The first was up the Khangpup glacier. We entered this valley about two miles south-east of Mome Samdong, finding a beautiful camp-site at 16,000 feet, near the upper névé of the glacier. From that camp on 13 October we climbed a peak marked 18,310 feet, putting on the rope to tackle a final 300 feet of steep rock plastered with snow. Angtharkay and Ang Nyima built a cairn on the top, which we reached in thick mist. Had the weather not turned bad on us again, our next climb would have been the highest peak of the group (19,201 ft), along its easy-looking north ridge. Instead, we descended in the snow and rain to Yumthang.

From there we began our second excursion on 16 October, entering the Lako Chu to the north-west, a tributary draining from a lake below Burum La. This area, like the Khangpup, was very little known and none of its peaks had been ascended. We crossed the Burum La (16,000 ft) in wet mist; there is a track westwards down the Burum Chu which enters the Lachen valley about three miles above the Zemu Chu. A small lake below the pass is fed by an icefall from the Burum glacier. We failed in an attempt to overcome this obstacle, which is confined between narrow rock walls; above it a cirque of peaks would have been reached, including the highest of the group (19,284 ft). There seemed to be several tributaries issuing from a glacier basin north of the pass, though we obtained only partial glimpses through the persistent low cloud. After two frustrating days, with camps placed both east and west of the Burum La, we packed up and began the journey back to Gangtok. We were able to see how badly Lachung had suffered from the previous year's flood; half of this attractive village, along with its fertile fields, had been wiped out; boulders and debris reached up to within a few hundred yards of the rest-house, destroying most of the apple orchard.

On the return march Angtharkay provided excellent meals; his hot buttered scones served with tea were a special treat. Amongst his like-able qualities was his incredible modesty and his sense of humour. He was wearing the wrist-watch that Shipton had given him the year before on the Everest reconnaissance expedition, and he spoke with affection of Mrs Jill Henderson, whose kindness and understanding had earned her a sort of head-of-family status among the Darjeeling Sherpas. When he talked philosophically about the long winter months in Darjeeling, during which many Sherpa families possessed no means of livelihood, it was because as a leader in his community he felt a special responsibility. Later, it was good to hear that he was able to find a permanent occupation on contract with the Government for road construction in the State—though, not long after, big expeditions once again claimed his services.

III

Kangchenjunga

*All men dream: but not equally. Those who dream by night in
the dusty recesses of their minds wake in the day to find that it was
vanity: but the dreamers of the day are dangerous men, for they
may act their dream with open eyes, to make it possible.*

T. E. Lawrence

It seemed to me, after such a fruitless journey to the mountains in 1952,
that I ought to pause in order to examine my motives. I think I realised
that my main interest did not consist in trying to test my strength; nor
was it essential for me to achieve some victory. The mountains had
taught me about life. I needed to learn that comfort and security are
not essential prerequisites to a sense of satisfaction; also that, when
shorn of conventional attitudes and symbols, all men are equal, and
that if thrown together in a trying situation, their finest as well as their
ugliest qualities will rise to the surface; I think that what I desired was
respect earned in such a situation. The mountains had already given me
physical fitness and friends, a deeper appreciation of the planet in which
we live, a clearer perception of values, distinguishing the stable and the
essential from the petty and ephemeral.

Those were some of my reasons. But the mountains themselves were
the main reason. They seemed to symbolise power and immutability as
well as solitude and beauty. I was clearer about what I disliked than
about what I really desired. The sight of a crowd of climbers gathered
together at the foot of a route awaiting their turn was a denial of the
detachment to which I attached the highest value. Preoccupation with
a single cliff for a whole day or for several days could never satisfy me.
In my mind the mountains were of primary importance; men's achievements, though obviously important, were secondary. The presence of
mountains aroused feelings of humility, free from all pretence or deceit.
Mountaineering had to be the whole mountain experience—the huts in

the valley, the shepherds in the upper meadows, the flowers by the glacier stream, the upper icefield, the snow ridge, the rocky crest, the lonely summit. It was sufficient that the mountains were aesthetically satisfying. I did not need to seek difficult climbs, although I tried to acquire competence to deal with difficulties that might arise in my quest for perfect accord with the mountain environment.

I felt that I would go on. There was much more that the mountains could give me, and the involvement had already grown too deep. It was not until many years later that I felt I had come near to winning the freedom of the mountains, and I knew that this had developed out of a balance of physical and aesthetic experience. This gave me an assurance of the rewards which I could always obtain; knowing exactly my strength and my limitations, and relating my powers to those with which I had to contend.

In 1948 and again in 1951 I spent two weeks climbing in Switzerland. On both occasions I engaged Arthur Lochmatter as a guide. A scion of the celebrated St Nicklaus family of guides, he was then in his mid-twenties, enthusiastic and keen to establish his reputation. I paid him a daily rate, and when the weather was good we spent long days out on the peaks, both of us seizing the opportunity with equal enjoyment. He was an excellent companion, and I learnt a good deal from him about technique.

Climbing in the Swiss Alps was a new experience for me. By way of training I walked for two weeks through the South Downs of England with a rucksack on my back, sleeping each night at a farm or youth hostel, and I followed this with a week's fell-walking in Wasdale and Langdale. My climbs in Switzerland added a good deal to my enjoy-ment of the mountains. There was the tiny shop in the valley where the climber could procure everything he needed. Then the long climb up to the hut, a test of physical fitness. In the hut a small group of climbers, and for supper huge helpings of soup with bread and sausage. The reluctant early start, half-awakened by a cup of hot coffee; then the reward of seeing the sunrise from half-way up a mountain, moving out of the cold shadow into its warmth. The presence of tracks all the way up the mountain diluted my sense of satisfaction over reaching the summit. Finally, the return to the valley, the luxury of a hot bath, and dinner in the elegance of the Monte Rosa Hotel dining room at Zermatt. In 1948 we did the Sudlenzgrat, Dom, Allalin-Alphubel traverse; then we crossed over by the Col d'Herens to Arolla for a few more climbs.

I am grateful that I visited the Swiss Alps in the days when they were still relatively unspoilt and uncrowded; tourists and cars were at a minimum, and the latter were in any case not allowed into the upper valleys. Arthur Lochmatter was busy during the first week of my two weeks' holiday in 1951, so I went alone to the Bernina area, where I did three climbs. The experience was valuable. With my Himalayan orientation I tended to overestimate distances and heights, the smaller Alpine scale filling me with comforting illusions. I recall the last climb done in stormy conditions, when limbs and senses were sharply alerted in order to avoid hidden dangers. During the following week the bad weather persisted; Lochmatter and I were able to climb only the Rimpfischhorn, Dufourspitze and Castor and Pollux. At 3 a.m. on our final day we left the Monte Rosa Hut (special treatment from Mrs Alexander Graven because I knew her husband) and climbed the Dufourspitz in time for me to catch the train to Brig that afternoon.

I spent one week walking in the Cévennes in south-west France, fulfilling a schoolboy wish to follow the travels of Robert Louis Stevenson. It was naive not to expect the country to have changed, but I found much that was still attractive. My visit to the Trappist monastery near La Bastide, a desolate spot in Stevenson's day, was memorable for the droves of tourists loading their cars with cheese and wine prepared for sale by the monks.

A few years later I visited the Spanish Pyrenees, grateful to find some of the upper valleys still unspoilt. Based mainly at Espot and Areu, I was able to spend long days scrambling and ridge-walking by myself, the smaller scale flattering the tally at each day's end. Areu, at the head of the Val Ferrera, was such an isolated agricultural settlement that it seemed impossible to find someone among the dialect-speaking community who could converse in French let alone English. From the top of Pico d'Estats there was a view of the Spanish and French Pyrenees with Andorra spread out below. The low cost of travel was a pleasant surprise, and one did not mind accepting a ride to the railhead in the milk-van, especially as that happened to be the only transport available. Returning to Barcelona in a train filled with Sunday trippers I was fascinated by the conversation, carried out at the highest pitch by seven volatile and demonstrative Spanish with whom I shared a railway carriage.

In the autumn of 1952 proposals for a joint Anglo-Swiss attempt on Everest were dropped, and the Mount Everest Committee in London moved ahead with its plans for a strong attempt in 1953. The Himalayan Club in Calcutta received a confidential copy of John Hunt's planning memorandum. Jill Henderson[1] in Darjeeling was asked to contact Tenzing. He had been high on Everest twice that year, and after the second Swiss expedition he had spent a few weeks in hospital. He told her at first that he was not quite well and would not go. Some persuasion was required before he changed his mind. I sometimes compare the organisation of that expedition to Everest in 1953 with the international expedition eighteen years later. The latter had two leaders, a heterogeneous group of thirty-one climbers from ten nations, television teams, and commercial pressure brought about by a budget of £100,000. When bad weather and sickness were added, the overall factors against success were overwhelming. The Himalayan Club organised an Everest Dinner in Calcutta at the end of June 1953 to welcome back John Hunt's successful team. At this function we were privileged to hear first-hand accounts of the climb from Hillary* and Hunt. Tenzing had drawn heavily upon his physical reserves; I found his round face and powerful body looking worn, but the familiar smile was there. Hunt, already looking ahead, had turned his thoughts to Kangchenjunga. His interest in the mountain began in 1937 when he and C. R. Cooke had explored its northern side.[2]

I first met John Kempe† in Calcutta in the summer of 1953. He was then headmaster of a school in South India and he had just returned from Sikkim, where with G. C. Lewis he had climbed the North summit of Kabru (23,750 ft). Kempe told me that from Kabru their view of Kangchenjunga had shown a definite line of weakness on the south-west face and that an attempt from that side merited serious consideration. In 1899 D. Freshfield, after journeying round Kangchenjunga, mentioned the south-west side as one of three possible ascent routes, provided an ice-shelf, conspicuously seen from Darjeeling, could be reached. He described it as 'a very direct route . . . but a prodigious climb'. F. S. Smythe later wrote off this face as 'unjustifiable'.[3] In 1905 the infamous A. Crowley made an attempt from this side with a small party that included the Swiss, Dr J. Guillarmod; it was abandoned after W. Pache and three porters were killed in an avalanche.[4] In 1920 H. Raeburn and C. G. Crawford explored the upper Yalung glacier to about 20,000 feet. Otherwise the south-west side of Kangchenjunga was virtually untouched. Kempe got in touch with Hunt, who showed

* Sir Edmund Hillary.

† J. W. R. Kempe, now Headmaster of Gordonstoun School, Elgin, Morayshire.

interest. But neither the Himalayan Committee in London nor the Alpine Club were then in a position to organise an attempt. Kempe was assured of support as well as financial backing from the newly-constituted Mount Everest Foundation[5] and he agreed to organise a reconnaissance of Kangchenjunga in 1954, which, if successful, could lead to a full-scale British attempt the following year.

Lewis was available again; Kempe invited J. W. Tucker, who had been on the reserve list of climbers selected for the Everest expedition in 1953, and S. R. Jackson, an experienced rock climber with a record of good climbs to his credit; both were new to the Himalaya. Kempe invited me to join, and he inquired whether I could suggest a doctor to complete the party. I suggested Donald Matthews, a New Zealander, who had a lucrative practice in Calcutta. Although he had practically no climbing experience he played a useful role in the team, possessing a temperament that combined stoicism and humour in the right proportions.[6] The expedition was organised on a private basis, each of us contributing equally to the overall cost, although a grant from the Mount Everest Foundation went some way towards meeting the expenses of Tucker, Jackson and Lewis, who travelled out from England.

The publicity that food and equipment manufacturers had acquired by the use of their products on the Everest expedition the previous year made it easier for us to approach some of them for our requirements. Most of them generously made supplies available, either free of cost or at a large discount. Our boots, woollen underwear and outerwear and windproof clothing were similar to those used on Everest and we obtained similar high-altitude food packs which were light-weight and concentrated. Cooking arrangements were simplified by the use of pressure-cookers. We avoided publicity because our efforts on this virtually untried face of Kangchenjunga were to be purely tentative, and we were not a strong enough team to launch a summit attempt even if we succeeded in finding a way. We had no illusions about the limited possibilities open to us, and we felt that if we could reach the great ice-shelf at 24,000 feet on the south-west face, or even open up a route towards it, we would have achieved our object.

If I were to make a list of the personal qualities required for an expedition I would probably place unselfishness near the top, also a sense of humour, an ability to get on with others without being prickly or quarrelsome, being convivial but not gregarious, and shunning the temptation to turn into a recluse. These are the qualities that complement the more obvious ones, such as toughness and staying power, stoicism and patience. So much time is spent waiting and planning, for the weather, the right moment to act, that when the opportunity arrives it must be recognised and grasped, with the mind fully prepared. The qualities that do not fit are pessimism and restlessness, any tendency to be clannish, and, despite human nature, envy which often does not require the spoken word to reveal its ugly symptoms. Though traditionally the mountaineer is said to possess calmness, detachment and emotional stability, these qualities no longer seem characteristic today as they were a generation or two ago. I must confess that I have sometimes found my first impressions proved wrong. Apart from the more common spectacle of seeing the physically robust and athletic type crumple above 14,000 feet, I have watched someone of irreproachable manners fly off the rails after provocation under adverse conditions. Once, the least involved member of the party was able by his calm and sheer ingenuousness to stave off serious personality clashes. When all is said and done, I think that the most vital need on an expedition is for each man to fulfil a clearly agreed role; and if he is capable of loyalty and a certain degree of selflessness he cannot fail to achieve satisfaction for himself and towards others.

The often mis-spelt name Kangchenjunga, literally 'the five treasuries of snow', is Tibetan in origin, and the mountain is situated on the borders of Sikkim and Nepal. It is held in reverence by the Sikkimese, who consider it to be essentially their mountain, attaching to it a special religious significance. Tibet was the ancestral home of the ruling family of Sikkim and the Tibetan derivation of the name, over which controversy once raged, is now accepted. There are five distinct summits, four of which are still unclimbed.* I know of no other mountain group more impressive, and with the exception of Nanga Parbat, I cannot think of any comparable massif. To regard it as a single mountain would convey no impression of its size and structure. Like Nanga Parbat, with its several summits, Kangchenjunga is surrounded by a group of satellites, each one a mountain in its own right, but dwarfed by the main peak. It is the dominating influence from almost any major viewpoint in Sikkim. From Darjeeling it is the presence of Kangchenjunga that adds perspective to the row of high peaks filling the northern horizon for 200 miles from west to east. A mystique had grown round the mountain in the thirties when, as on Nanga Parbat, lives were lost during a series of unsuccessful attempts to climb it. From the climber's

* On 14 May 1973 two members of a Japanese party reached a summit west of the main peak; one of them died during the descent.

viewpoint it was generally regarded as being a tougher proposition than Everest.

The packing of the expedition's equipment and stores was handled in England by Lewis and Tucker, who travelled out with it to India by sea; Jackson travelled out later by air. All of us, except Kempe, who was to follow one week later, reached Darjeeling on 7 April, where we were met by our eight Sherpas headed by Ajeeba. Although Mr and Mrs J. Henderson were away, they generously permitted us to use their home at Rungneet. We spent two days there sorting, re-packing, and selecting coolies for the march to Base Camp. At dawn on our first morning I went outside to catch a glimpse of Kangchenjunga floating above the clouds. Tucker joined me and his initial impression was of disbelief on seeing the shining mass half-way up the sky. We required sixty-five porters to lift our two tons of baggage, and we estimated ten days for the march to the Yalung glacier. We had selected a high-level route along the Singalila ridge and by a series of snow-covered passes to Tseram on the Yalung Chu, in preference to the populated route through the Tamur valley in Nepal. The latter would probably have been more suitable in early spring, owing to the low snowline and the necessity to carry all our coolie-food over uninhabited country. The coolies that we engaged were mostly Sherpas with a small mixture of Nepalese, and there were fifteen women. After Matthews had certified them medically fit they were signed on at five rupees per day, and each of them was issued with a disc showing their name and number, the latter corresponding with the number of their load. All loads were made up to about sixty-five pounds each.

On 10 April we set out from Darjeeling, travelling the first sixteen miles by car to Mane Bhanjan, situated at the foot of the Singalila ridge. The whole caravan got away from there that afternoon, and we reached Tonglu (10,069 ft) in mist and darkness after a climb of nearly 5,000 feet. Between Sandakphu and Phalut we obtained a few glimpses of Kangchenjunga, but we had an undue share of high winds, accompanied one day by a hailstorm. When we reached the alp at Chiabhanjan, disaffection among the coolies expressed itself in their refusal to accept our ration scale. Matters were patched up by Ajeeba and the Sherpas, but the arrival over the passes from Ghunsa of a solitary Nepalese with a report of difficult conditions had an unsettling effect. In good weather the ridge provides striking views of all the major peaks; but we had storms, and there was plenty of trouble in store.

Our camp at Nayathang was situated on an exposed ridge at 10,500 feet. At dusk we were inside our separate tents and most of the coolies were in a large dome tent when a fierce electrical storm began, accompanied by wind and hail. Suddenly there was a bright flash of lightning followed by a crash of thunder and our metal dinner plates were flung out of our hands; Jackson, alongside my tent, actually received a burn on his forearm. At midnight, while the storm continued unabated, a rescue operation had to be carried out when the roof of the dome tent was ripped open by the wind. A seven-hour march to Meguthang (13,100 ft) the next day, mostly on snow, marked the end of the road for twenty-five of our coolies, who balked at the conditions and had to be sent back to Darjeeling. Re-organising the baggage, we made a cache for the return march, and sent a ferry of twenty-four loads towards our first pass the Garakhet La (14,040 ft). Our remaining group of forty coolies seemed now to work more cheerfully. We found the smaller number easier to manage and I think that our overall loss of time on the journey to Base Camp amounted to two and a half days. Bad weather persisted for the crossing of the next three passes; the Semo La (15,300 ft), from which we descended into the Kangla Nangma valley in Nepal, gave us a good deal of trouble owing to deep snow.

On 21 April we reached Tseram at the head of the Yalung valley, sharing our campsite on a meadow with a yakherd family. Daisies and buttercups were beginning to appear and directly ahead loomed the huge terminal moraine of the glacier. Ajeeba was sent to Ghunsa, about 10 miles away, to implement the arrangements which he had made three months earlier for supplies of *tsampa* and rice. He stayed away for ten days and when he returned there were complaints that the *tsampa* was of poor quality. This was probably Ajeeba's first big assignment as *sirdar* and I think that the job was rather beyond him. Most of the rest of his team lacked experience, although I would single out Pasang Phutar, a nephew of Tenzing and part-time jockey at the Darjeeling races. He was quite a live-wire and a potential group-leader, provided his exuberance could be controlled. Angtensing, nicknamed Balu because he was dark and powerful like a bear, was my personal orderly; what he lacked in intelligence was compensated for by his strength. The cook, Ang Dawa IV, needed coaching, and his hygiene was of the scantiest; but he was always cheerful and quite imperturbable. We provided the Sherpas with basic equipment, which they accepted unquestioningly although none of it was new; nor did they acquire proprietary rights, although it was understood that certain items would be given to them at the end in recognition of good service. In the light of present-day demands it is hard to imagine that such a system worked.

Each of us soon acquired a definite role. John Kempe, always impeccable in manner and appearance, was a modest and unobtrusive leader. After all had expressed their opinions, he was usually able to sum up a situation within a few moments of precise reasoning, and would then put his view to the rest of us. Donald Matthews took charge of the mess and was our movie cameraman. Matthews had been pitchforked into this venture, and although he had had some varied adventures in his time, especially in the 'wavy' navy during World War II, I doubt whether he had the vaguest conception about what an expedition to a big mountain would be like; yet he was never once seen to be out of his depth. Ron Jackson, a professional engineer, was general handyman; although he joined the expedition with a high reputation as a rock climber, I think that his contribution was greater as an unflappable, congenial and hard-working member of the team. Jack Tucker, who was responsible for porter's rations and kit, was perhaps best remembered for his ebullience. This had advantages, for he was irrepressible even under the most difficult conditions, but it could sometimes result in a dropped brick at a time when feelings might be rather touchy. Gilmour Lewis, with his understanding and experience of Indian conditions, was ideal at his job which was the co-ordination of transport arrangements; whilst I, with my language qualifications, maintained liaison with the Sherpas.

Jackson and I left Tseram on 23 April with twenty porters to establish a stores dump on the glacier. Following the right bank up an ablation valley, we passed the deserted settlement of Ramser and placed a camp at about 14,500 feet. My first close view of the upper south-west face of Kangchenjunga is an experience I shall not easily forget; the size and the power seemed quite terrifying. A day later we were joined by Tucker and John Kempe, who had just arrived. By the 25th we were installed at 15,250 feet on the left bank at Moraine camp; the crossing of the glacier which was about one and a half miles wide provided three hours of boulder-hopping, which was quite hard work. With one Sherpa sick and another away in Ghunsa with Ajeeba, the next few days were spent moving up the loads, while an advance party of two went ahead to select a suitable site for a base.

It was not until 1 May that all of us were gathered at Base Camp, situated at a conspicuous bend in the Yalung glacier at 16,250 feet. For the first time Kangchenjunga was in full view, situated less than two miles away at the head of the glacier. Now we could study the 10,000-foot south-west face and discuss together the prospect which lay before us.

There appeared to be three possible ways of reaching the ice-shelf. First, the Kangchenjunga icefall, over 5,000 feet high, and evidently in two sections, with the lower part terribly steep and broken. Next, the Talung saddle icefall, from whose upper basin there might be access to a hogsback ridge leading to the lower southern end of the shelf—a long and complicated route. The only other route, partly tried in 1905, began with a steep snow face on the west buttress of the Kangchenjunga ice-fall, from the top of which there might be access to the easier upper part of the icefall. We did not fancy the Kangchenjunga icefall and doubted whether we could make any serious impression upon it. On 3 May Kempe and I went to take a look at the snow face on its west buttress. In four hours we crossed the glacier and climbed to a grassy shelf above the moraine on the other side. We were approaching the foot of the face at about 18,000 feet when we came upon rusty tins and other remains of Dr Guillarmod's camp, untouched for almost half a century; a little below was a wooden cross with an engraved stone marking Pache's grave. The snowslopes above looked steep and at least 2,000 feet high. Two doubts entered our minds; avalanche tracks were clearly visible on the face, underlining the fact that these were the slopes on which Pache and three porters had been killed; moreover, it was impossible to tell from here whether there would be access from the top of the face into the upper part of the icefall. We returned to camp indecisive.

Since the main icefall looked so repellent, we decided to take a look not only into the Talung basin, but also at the rock buttress on the eastern side of the Kangchenjunga icefall. On 5 May Jackson and I moved up with four porters to select a site near the head of the glacier as an advanced base from which to examine both these routes. By-passing an obvious avalanche channel from the face of Talung peak, we entered an area of huge seracs, threading a cautious route through crevasses over which we were relieved to find safe bridges. A feature of this region was the perpetual menace of avalanches. During our residence of over three weeks, hardly ten minutes seemed to go by without the familiar roar of minor or major falls. The mightiest avalanches we saw were those that peeled off the great ice shelf on to the glacier in a single vertical drop of 6,000 feet.

Advanced base was established on 7 May at about 17,500 feet in a snow basin at the head of the Yalung glacier. There was a fairly steady weather pattern, consisting of fine evenings and mornings with snowfalls almost every afternoon. At night temperatures were usually about 10°F below freezing; but in the open sunshine at midday it was not uncommon to record 100°F. Sometimes, in the mellow light of the evening, it was easy to be deceived by an intimate calm reigning over the immense mountain, whose summit stood 10,000 feet above us. During the next few days, separate parties examined the two alternative routes.

In the Talung basin we climbed 750 feet through the seracs before we were stopped by a crevasse ten feet wide. There was no way round and without a ladder we could not get across. This seemed to be the last obstacle at the entrance to an ice cwm, which led apparently without difficulty to an upper basin below the hogsback ridge. All of us, every time we entered the Talung basin, could not suppress feelings of fear; and it is clear that we should have lost no time in deciding to quit this avalanche-menaced area. A massive fall from the ice-shelf one evening, which swept a blizzard across our tents, decided the issue for us, and on 12 May we shifted to a new site 350 feet below and closer to the base of the Kangchenjunga icefall. On this section, for the next few days, we concentrated our energies. Mail arrived from below and more supplies, so there was a contented atmosphere on our first evening at the new camp.

The next day Kempe, Tucker and I made our first acquaintance with the Kangchenjunga icefall. We tackled it directly from its base and were surprised to find that in the first three hours no major obstacle stopped us. In front, I had very little step-cutting to do and I think that we must have gained over 1,000 feet. Beyond, the going looked steeper and more broken before levelling out in a small basin; above that was the icefall's easier-looking upper section. We went up again the next day, Pasang Phutar accompanying us with a load; and we reached our previous high point without difficulty. A short distance above we were faced with a terribly shattered area and progress came to a halt. A near-vertical ice-wall fifteen feet high seemed to be the only way out of the impasse. I began to cut steps up it but noticed that the whole structure seemed unstable. Tucker then had a try, but he was equally repulsed by the feeling of insecurity, and Kempe expressed the view that we should call it off. A closer look at what lay beyond showed that the ice above, scattered with debris, was full of further terrors.

Meanwhile, Jackson and Lewis, who had achieved a measure of success in their earlier examination of the east buttress, could now be seen moving confidently ahead on the rock to our right. They returned to camp late in the evening, having reached the top of a spur forming the eastern wall of the lower icefall; this had enabled them to look down into the basin between the two sections of the icefall. Their reconnaissance was the first step forward; we hoped that it would provide us with the means of setting foot on the upper end of the menacing first section of the icefall.

It was decided to place a camp at the top of the buttress and Tucker, assisted by Pasang Phutar, spent a day preparing the route for a laden party by placing fixed ropes at two points. On the same day, since bridging logs which had been demanded from Ramser had arrived, Kempe, Jackson and I moved over to the Talung basin with six Sherpas bearing the logs. We were due to receive some nasty shocks. Not far above our former camp, the whole area had been swept by an avalanche and our original route into the icefall no longer existed. Threading a way through the seracs we reached the crevasse to find that the place had altered completely. The basin had been shattered by some recent movement, causing a widening of the crevasse, and our logs, which were about fifteen feet in length were insufficient to bridge the gap. There was nothing to be done but abandon the logs and return.

On 16 May the whole party moved up Jackson's rock buttress with eight Sherpas. On a scree slope at the foot of the buttress Matthews, who had come up for the purpose of filming, was struck by a falling stone. This caused a deep cut in a finger of his right hand and as a professional surgeon he was seriously worried about the possibility of permanent injury. He was in a state of mild shock when we escorted him back to camp where he was made comfortable and left in the care of his orderly Ang Dawa. We continued to the top of the buttress where at about 19,000 feet we placed a camp; two Sherpas were retained and the remainder went down. There was low cloud the following morning when we set out to find a way off the buttress on to the icefall. We soon ran into trouble. On two sides there were deep cut-offs; on the third there was a narrow bridge connecting to broken ice-cliffs about fifty feet high. There was an atmosphere of impermanance about the whole place, and Jackson said he was sure that this section had altered during the past two days. Thoroughly disconsolate, we returned to the tents; there we found three Sherpas who had arrived from below with the report that an avalanche had very nearly reached the campsite during the night. In deteriorating weather we packed up and descended. Soon after arriving below we shifted the tents 250 yards further down. Don Matthews seemed better and had given himself strong drugs in order to protect his injury from infection.

The time had come to take stock of the situation. Any further attempt to tackle the main icefall from here seemed futile. The effort involved, if it was indeed merely a question of effort, was frankly beyond us. We did not think that a direct assault on this 5,000-foot obstacle could be recommended to any party. But what was the alternative? I think that there was more of desperation than logic in our half-hearted agreement that a final look should be taken at the Talung approach. We were all agreed that the seracs should be left alone; but it seemed possible to force a passage at the left-hand edge via a gully between the glacier and a conical rock buttress. In this way we hoped not only to avoid the avalanche-menaced area but also to enter the upper basin at a point above the unbridgeable crevasse.

Jackson and I set out on 18 May accompanied by Balu. We were covered by low cloud by the time we had passed our former campsite. Below the gully we put on the rope and climbed quickly in crampons up ice at a moderate angle. Beyond was easy rock, though owing to poor visibility we moved cautiously, one at the time. As we started on a final rock pitch of about fifty feet, snow began to fall. Jackson, in front, made light work of this and called out that the big crevasse was visible below and that we were about five minutes from the cwm. I was tackling the last part of the pitch and was about fifteen feet below Jackson when we heard from above a crack like a pistol shot. We crouched our bodies against the slope; but in an instant I felt a blow on the head as though hit by a sledge-hammer. Judging from the size of the cut in my scalp it was probably a chip of rock weighing no more than a few ounces, but it must have struck with terrific force. Whilst we tried to staunch the flow of blood with ice, I remarked that I seemed to be feeling alright and I asked Jackson to move up a few feet in order to examine the way down into the basin. Balu, unnerved by the incident, was unwilling to advance further. We were getting cold in the continuing snowfall when we turned back. After we had reached the level glacier, Balu raced down ahead of us and Matthews was ready to take me in hand when Jackson and I arrived. He discovered that it was no more than a minor scalp injury and he stitched up the wound without further ado. For years I had prided myself about my immunity from headaches or sleeplessness. Now, as a result of the concussion which followed some hours later, I was afflicted with a real nightmare, the power and duration of which was a totally new experience.

It was decided to evacuate our camp and to make an attempt on Talung peak. By 20 May I felt reasonably well again, so with Matthews and Jackson I descended to Base Camp to join the others. We found that parts of the lower glacier had changed, many of the crevasses having opened up, but good tracks had now been stamped out. Life seemed good again in the warm sunshine, with grass and flowers around Base Camp, and without the constant threat of avalanches. Ang Dawa had a huge tea ready with scones, jam and butter which we devoured with schoolboy relish. Kempe returned with Lewis and Tucker in the afternoon from the lower slopes of Talung peak, where they had made a cache of food. Matthews and I had reached the end of our leave, and since I was not yet considered fit enough to join in the Talung climb, a view which I shared reluctantly, this was the last evening that the party spent together. It was Matthews' thirty-seventh birthday, and we celebrated the event with a tot of rum, talking round a campfire until long after the stars were out.

Although the Talung climb failed, a series of photographs taken from high up on its north-west slopes showed an outlet to the upper Kangchenjunga icefall from the top of the snow face above Pache's grave. This 'ramp', as it was called by Charles Evans'* Expedition in 1955, opened the way to the great ice-shelf. From there, first George Band and Joe Brown, then Norman Hardie and Tony Streather, reached the summit.

In retrospect, I think that before committing ourselves to any route it would have been wise to have climbed high enough on the slopes opposite the south-west face of Kangchenjunga to enable us to make a careful study of the possibilities. Such a step might have avoided some of the errors which followed, and might have given us an opportunity to get within range of the shelf. We worked in a congenial atmosphere as a team, but the performance of the Sherpas was poor largely because they lacked a good *sirdar*. Among other things, Ajeeba was unable to implement adequate supplies of Sherpa food and this resulted in a good deal of pilferage of sahib's food above Base Camp. The presence of a mountain so vast as Kangchenjunga rendered the area impressive but inhospitable. Big mountains have a particular fascination, but they do not always provide the greatest enjoyment.[7]

Matthews and I set out for the return journey to Darjeeling on 21

* Sir Charles Evans, D.SC., FRCS.

May. We began by retracing the route of our outward march; but by now the high passes were mostly clear of snow, while flowers and streams provided a generally more cheerful prospect. We ran into an early monsoon and for six days there was continuous rain. After a night of monsoon rain there is at dawn a special quality about the Himalayan foothills. Beyond the damp grass and the rain-soaked forest there is a background of indigo mountains and blue-grey skies, a moment of ineffable peace before rising mists bring the promise of another day of showers. It was cold at first and everything that we carried was soaked. But lower down, soon after we left the Singalila ridge, we entered steamy tropical forest. From Yarpung we followed the Rimbi Chu to Pemionchi, where we had an early glimpse of Kangchenjunga and paid a visit to the large and ancient monastery. Walking through cultivated fields surrounded by human habitation provided a delightful contrast, and we hungrily eyed unripe fruit on apricot, banana and mango trees. At one village shop we were offered an old beer bottle filled with the local fire-water when what we craved was fresh fruit to satisfy our thirst. On our last night at Rishi, having run out of food, we shared an omelette made from one dozen eggs followed by raw mangoes, un-eatable even after stewing. At Naya Bazar the next morning we hired a decrepit taxi and reached Darjeeling that afternoon in heavy rain.

Two incidents on the return march I recall. I was close on the heels of Balu, speeding down a narrow jungle track, when he halted abruptly, so abruptly that I bumped into him. Before I could speak, I glanced over his shoulder and saw a large black snake sliding across the track, not twelve inches from his feet. The other incident was mystifying and even now I cannot offer an explanation. The abominable snowman was in our minds as this was the year of the Daily Mail Yeti Expedition to Nepal. We had descended through the snowline into a deep forest; it was late in the afternoon and we were rather weary and were becoming cold through our soaked clothing when unexpectedly we came upon a log-hut. Inside it was dry and warm and soon the Sherpas had two fires going. Mugs of tea and soup were followed by supper and within a few hours most of our wet kit had dried. We turned in early, and it seemed luxurious to wriggle into a dry sleeping bag. Around midnight we were awakened by the sound of footfalls outside. They gathered momentum as though some heavy animal were moving swiftly through the sodden forest towards the hut. They were accompanied by an indescribable noise, combining a human shriek with an animal roar and whistle. It was pitch dark inside, as we sat up motionless and speechless in our beds, while the incredible din magnified until it seemed only a matter of seconds before some massive creature would crash through the door. Then suddenly there was absolute silence. We waited in vain for further sounds and then went back uneasily to sleep. On the rain-soaked earth the following morning it was impossible to identify any footmarks. So we shall never know who our visitor was, although the Sherpas had drawn their own conclusion.

When we returned to Darjeeling, Tenzing got in touch with me, asking me to visit his house, which was then on Auckland road below the Mount Everest hotel. He was a charming and exemplary host, shaming me when I thought about his visit to my house in Calcutta on his return from Nanga Parbat four years before. Although he seemed to have lost his youthful unlined appearance, I found him quite unaltered by his worldly success. He introduced me to the American writer James Ramsey Ullman who was then working on his life story.

Charles Evans' party came through Calcutta the following year, and the Himalayan Club Committee had the pleasure of entertaining many of them in our homes. I can still see the youthful Joe Brown, usually taciturn, giving an animated description of his struggle, his oxygen turned on to the full supply, with a twenty-foot vertical rock-crack below the summit of Kangchenjunga.[8]

IV
Kumaon and Garhwal

They had crossed the Siwaliks and the half-tropical Doon, . . .
and headed north along the narrow hill-roads. Day after day
they struck deeper into the huddled mountains, and day after day
Kim watched the lama return to a man's strength.

R. Kipling

The first major expedition to visit the Himalaya from Europe after
World War II was Swiss. It was sponsored by the Swiss Foundation
for Alpine Research, who had launched a successful expedition to
Garhwal in 1939, under the leadership of André Roch. They chose
Garhwal for their second venture in 1947 and Roch was again appointed
as leader. The Foundation, a private body, has among its objects the
extension of mountain exploration to the distant ranges of the world,
with an emphasis on mountain climbing. As it enjoyed the patronage of
a number of wealthy enthusiasts, it was able to encourage several
expeditions and to equip them generously. In Europe climbers were
already beginning to believe that they had solved all the 'last' great
problems. Rightly, therefore, the Foundation directed its focus towards
the mountains of Asia and South America where unlimited opportunities
still existed. The Foundation gained worldwide recognition with its
annual publication, *Berge der Welt*, the first volume of which appeared
in 1946.[1]

Although 1947 was a year of almost unprecedented upheaval on
the Indian sub-continent, the forward-looking Swiss Foundation
succeeded in launching a second venture in that year, sponsoring
a reconnaissance of Rakaposhi (25,550 ft) by a party of four which
included H. W. Tilman and C. Secord. The Garhwal expedition was

organised on a lavish scale and the party was considered to be a strong one. Roch, a professional mountain guide, was considered to be one of the most experienced Swiss climbers and he was at the time attached to the Snow and Avalanche Research Institute on the Weissfluhjoch. He had taken part in an expedition to Greenland and had been a member of G. O. Dyhrenfurth's Karakoram expedition in 1934. Alexander Graven, although past fifty, still enjoyed a reputation as one of Switzerland's top guides. René Dittert was one of the leading amateur climbers at home, though he had not climbed abroad. Alfred Sutter, a wealthy industrialist, and Mme Annelies Lohner, both of whom had contributed substantially to the expedition's funds, had been climbing in the Swiss Alps for several years with Graven. An Indian liaison officer, R. N. Rahul of Delhi, had been appointed, and the Himalayan Club had been requested to nominate a climber to join the party.

I was then one of the Club's newest members and the Honorary Secretary's circular letter inviting applications filled me with tremendous enthusiasm, although also with misgivings. I had recently joined my father's firm in Calcutta, and was still considered to be under training. It seemed rather a tall demand to put in a request for three months' leave in order to go and climb mountains. I tried to appear as casual as possible about the opportunity which had suddenly occurred; but I have never been much good at deception, and I suppose that it was only too clear how much it meant to me to offer myself as a candidate. I was lucky to have had a father who was kind and liberal-minded; although I think this was the first time that his understanding was seriously tested, it was by no means the last. It seemed unbelievably good fortune that my candidature was accepted, and the Swiss invited me to join their expedition.

A good deal of the northern part of Garhwal is pilgrim country, since it contains three of the main sources of the sacred Ganges river, each of which is sanctified by the presence of a temple. Devout Hindus from the plains, youthful and aged, able-bodied and infirm, perform the journey every summer to these ancient shrines deep in the mountains. For the majority of them it is a punishing experience and this is inevitably reflected in the expression upon their faces. One seldom observes signs of revelation or joy, usually evidence of forbearance and much privation, and only rarely an aura of fulfilment. The holiest of the three temples is situated at over 10,000 feet in the village of Badrinath. This is a few miles from one of the sources of the Alaknanda river 'where the Ganges falls from the foot of Vishnu like the slender thread

Kumaon and Garhwal

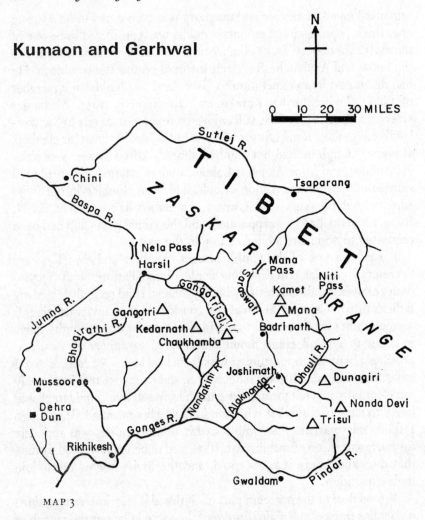

MAP 3

of a lotus flower'. The river is fed by the glaciers below the Chaukhamba group, and by the shapely Nilkanta Peak (21,640 ft). Situated about twenty-four miles away in a direct line to the west is Kedarnath temple. According to legend, the high priest of Badrinath used to conduct services in both temples on the same day, although there is no known route directly linking the two places. In 1934 Eric Shipton and H. W. Tilman accomplished the journey in two and a half weeks, having encountered difficult glaciated country and virgin forest.[2] Gangotri temple is situated eight miles from the Gangotri glacier snout known as Gaumukh (the cow's mouth), from which issues the Bhagirathi river.

The Gangotri region had been selected by the Swiss expedition with the object of ascending as many as possible of its highest unclimbed mountains, which were at the time Kedarnath (22,770 ft), Satopanth (23,263 ft) and Chaukhamba (23,420 ft), the four summits of which comprised the Badrinath group. Between 1935 and 1936 large sections of Kumaon and Garhwal were completely resurveyed; fieldwork was in the charge of G. H. Osmaston, assisted by R. A. Gardiner and R. C. Edge of the Survey of India. This had resulted in the publication of accurate large-scale maps of the mountains and glaciers which form part of the Bhagirathi, Alaknanda and Dhauli river systems, and included the Nanda Devi group. Thus, while virtually no unexplored areas were left in the Central Himalaya, plenty of scope existed for the ascent of peaks. The Gangotri glacier had been visited by two previous climbing expeditions; in 1933 Marco Pallis' party climbed Bhagirathi III (21,176 ft), and in 1938 six German climbers under R. Schwarz-gruber climbed Bhagirathi II (21,364 ft), Chandar Parbat (22,073 ft), Swachand (22,050 ft), and Sri Kailas (22,740 ft).[3]

In the eight years that had elapsed since expeditions from Europe had visited the Himalaya, there had been several innovations in equipment; and to me, after the frugality of the war years, the Swiss expedition seemed luxuriously equipped and provisioned. I arrived in Mussooree in early June to find three wooden boxes containing food and seven kit-bags containing equipment left behind by the Swiss; the abundance seemed almost wasteful. The main party had set out ten days earlier for the 165-mile walk to the Gangotri glacier. My personal Sherpa, Angtensing, had been sent by Angtharkay from Darjeeling and he travelled with me from Calcutta. He was then thirty-five and had been to Gangotri with Schwarzgruber in 1938. He had also been to Everest three times, twice to Kangchenjunga, and he was with Shipton in the Shaksgam in 1937. His experience was valuable, and he made an excellent orderly. With his help I sorted out the items that we should need for the journey to Base Camp, and we departed from Mussooree on 8 June with three local coolies.

I was immediately enchanted by the country. It took us ten days, travelling in easy stages, to reach Gangotri. We followed the Bhagirathi valley through broad areas of cultivation scattered with handsome villages; then we climbed through a temperate forest-clad zone to the narrower and rocky upper reaches of the valley. The people seemed to possess an intimate charm and hospitality that was almost touching. Stopping at a village late one evening, hot and weary after a fifteen-mile walk, a young *patwari* welcomed me inside his hut, insisting that I use his charpoy whilst he occupied a lesser dwelling outside. He embarrassed me further by watching with admiring eyes as I wrote my diary by the light of his lantern placed upon his only table. It was warm for the first two days, marching in the lower valleys; an icy pool below Nakuri bungalow provided me with my first bathe, to be followed by many others, stripping off sweaty clothes to enter the luxury of cool flowing waters. Once, leaving Angtensing to hustle the porters, I reached Dharasu rest-house at dusk so exhausted that I dropped off to sleep almost at once. Angtensing woke me three hours later, when I drank eight mugs of tea and one of soup before going back to sleep. The three porters who appeared shamefaced the next morning were paid off, and we engaged one pony in their place, which solved our further transport problems. One evening in the rain, Angtensing pitched my tent in a small field. When the owner showed up and asked what he thought he was doing, he replied that there was a sahib inside the tent, and the sahib had two guns; this was a resourceful bit of bluff, which persuaded the irate farmer to welcome us as his guests.

There was always evidence that we were on a pilgrim road; the indigent hobbled on sticks, some travelled on ponyback, and a few walked, while the wealthy and infirm rode in baskets or palanquins carried by slender Garhwalis. We were travelling along the route which Kipling had in mind when tracing the journey of Kim's lama who crossed the Nela pass from Chini in the north-west to Harsil. Both Garhwal and Tibet have exercised traditional claims from time to time over the Nelang area which follows the Jadh Ganga north-east of Harsil. Each country used to place boundary pillars on its frontiers, and these were periodically uprooted. The physiography of this region becomes increasingly Tibetan where the Himalayan crest-zone in northern Garhwal gradually gives way to the subsidiary Zaskar range bordering Tibet. The troughs between the Zaskar and the Great Himalaya are drained by the Bhagirathi, Saraswati and Dhauli rivers which join the Alaknanda, the main feeder of the Ganges.

We reached Harsil on 15 June and were directed to a huge wooden mansion built before the Indian Mutiny in 1857 by ex-private Wilson of a Highland regiment. In this rambling house I was welcomed by R. N. Rahul,* our liaison officer, and by our Sherpa *sirdar*, Wangdi Norbu. They had come from Base Camp, to recruit porters. We found

* Now Head of the Department of Central Asian Studies, Delhi; and author of *The Government & Politics of Tibet*, and *The Himalaya Border Land*.

the Harsil men tough, and three of the best of them were retained permanently. We set out with a group of sixty-three porters, moving the last of the expedition's baggage. We bypassed Gangotri village, built around a temple overlooking the river. The goal of hardier pilgrims is Gaumukh, and for their benefit a cairned track extends southwards up the Gangotri valley to the glacier snout. I was impressed by Rahul's efficient control of the army of porters; during the morning, as we walked, he discoursed fluently on metaphysics and on Buddhism, which was his special subject. As soon as we reached the lower moraine of the Gangotri glacier there were views of the three Bhagirathi peaks, their steep north-facing slopes translucent in the sunlight.

On 18 June I reached the Swiss Base Camp and was introduced to each member of the party. They had returned the day before from a reconnaissance of Kedarnath peak and most of them were not fully acclimatised. André Roch lay in his tent with a slight temperature; a rapport grew between us and we were soon able to drop all artificial barriers, a relationship which I found it difficult to acquire with the others. René Dittert, French-speaking like Roch, was probably the best 'expedition man', with a sense of humour, a readiness to take on and to enjoy any task, and making a real effort to win the trust and friendship of the Sherpas. He took part in a climbing expedition to East Nepal two years later, and Roch and he were both members of the Swiss Everest party in the spring of 1952. Alexander Graven kept a good deal to himself. He was probably reserved by nature; I think also that he was unhappy, often expressing regret over the climbing season that he would be missing at home. Being the oldest, he took the longest to acclimatise. When I suggested accompanying him once on the glacier, he was so unsure of his form and so anxious not to reveal any weakness that he apologised profusely and said that he must go alone. Once he found his strength he grew into the giant that he really was. Alfred Sutter and I never found any common ground, partly I think because we had no common language. He was fond of shooting and acquired several head of *barhal*, which provided us with a supply of fresh meat, Graven having constructed a deep-freeze in the ice below our camp. When I met Mme Lohner in Zermatt a year after the expedition, she invited me to dine with her. I think that the gesture was intended as a belated apology, although our relations on the expedition had always been cordial. There was a team of nine Sherpas, and I was delighted to see Tenzing, whom I had last met in Sikkim two years before. Others whom I knew were Thundu and Ajeeba, while Ang Dawa and Ang Norbu were among the best of their kind.

Base Camp was situated below a moraine ridge on the west bank of the glacier at about 14,750 feet. The site chosen was a level stretch of grass containing a stream and providing good views in three directions. Life here seemed pretty luxurious; each of us had his own tent, and hot water was laid on for a morning wash and for occasional baths. Menus were lavish, and with Tenzing acting as cook we ate extremely well. I found the Swiss tents comfortable. They were constructed of a resistant cotton fabric; an entrance bay, that could be used for cooking and for storing kit, left the sleeping quarters undisturbed. Their disadvantages were that they were rather more complicated to erect than a standard Meade, and they weighed more. A great innovation was the modern climbing boot; these were manufactured in Switzerland by Bally and were fitted with the new moulded-rubber soles made in Italy under the trade name Vibram; they were at the time practically unknown in England. I had my own pair of boots fitted with clinker and tricouni nails, which I preferred to wear as a matter of habit, but I could not help remarking upon the amazing lightness and comfort of Vibrams on the glacier and on rock. Wearing them on snow, even at a moderate angle, the Swiss always attached crampons and insisted that the Sherpas did likewise. These observations may appear trite to the modern climber, but at the time the break from traditional practice seemed fundamental.

I was impressed by the size of the glacier, about eighteen miles long and over two miles broad. Half-way up, its medial moraine provided a clearly defined and almost level surface as far as the upper névé, which ended in a wide basin on the western flank of Chaukhamba. At various levels of the glacier Roch took observations with a theodolite in order to measure its rate of flow. In its central section this appeared to be almost one foot per twenty-four hours during the month of June.

On 23 June all the Swiss along with seven Sherpas left Base for another attempt on Kedarnath. I was suffering from a painful tendon and would have to wait. They set up Camp I that afternoon on the north-east face at 17,220 feet. In the evening Mme Lohner and Tenzing returned to Base. Feeling better on the following day, I set out with Angtensing and a Harsil porter. Crossing the névé of the Kirti glacier we ascended 1,250 feet of scree and rock to the campsite, watching the progress of the rest of the party on the long snow slopes above. In the afternoon three Sherpas descended, leaving Wangdi, Ang Dawa and Ang Norbu with four Swiss. Camp II had been placed at about 20,200 feet below a prominent red rock-cliff half-way up the snow face. It took us almost five hours to ascend 3,000 feet to that camp which we reached at noon the next day. Snow conditions were good, but the altitude slowed us. I found that between 19,000 and 20,000 feet I needed to pause for breath after every fifty upward steps, while below that level I could manage 400 steps without having to rest. The route above Camp II led to a snow dome or subsidiary summit at 22,410 feet; from there a narrow ridge, almost a mile long, connected with the highest peak at 22,770 feet. The angle of this face was moderate, but the south side of the mountain was rocky and very steep.

During our ascent to Camp II we were able to follow the progress of the party above who appeared to be moving slowly; at about ten o'clock we saw them approaching the snow dome. It was not until 3 p.m. from Camp II that we saw them again, and only five climbers were visible on the ridge between the two summits. For some while they did not appear to move. An hour and a half later, on the north-west face below the ridge, we could see six figures descending and they were dragging a load. It was now certain that an accident had occurred. We felt utterly helpless because there was no direct access from our camp to the snow face opposite, and by six o'clock cloudy weather blotted out our view altogether. During the night I was unable to sleep; at midnight, thinking that I could hear distress calls, I went outside in order to flash a reply with my torch. At 5 a.m. the following morning I departed for Camp I and on arriving there I despatched three fresh Sherpas to meet the party, following later myself. I met the descending climbers on the glacier. They were without Wangdi Norbu, who was injured and had been left on the snow face, because they were too exhausted to carry him down. My three Sherpas, equipped with rope and hot drinks, were now despatched up the north-west face in order to bring him down.

While Graven and Sutter decided to descend direct to Base Camp, I accompanied Roch and Dittert to Camp I, where they gave me details of the accident. Graven had been in front with Ang Dawa; Roch and Dittert had Ang Norbu on their rope, whilst Sutter and Wangdi were in the rear. During the traverse of the narrow ridge connecting the two summits Wangdi, tripping over his crampons, lost his balance and began to tumble down the north-west face; Sutter, making a vain attempt to hold the fall, had the skin of both hands lacerated before he was dragged after him. The upper part of the face was composed of hard snow at an angle of 50°, and both of them came to rest about 650 feet below in soft snow, where the angle eased above a *bergschrund*. Sutter was unhurt, but Wangdi had a broken ankle as well as scalp and knee injuries. By the time the five others reached them, Wangdi was in severe pain and was given a morphine injection. They succeeded in dragging the injured Wangdi about 500 feet down the face, which was badly crevassed and was threatened by seracs. With darkness falling they bivouacked in the shelter of a crevasse, continuing the descent before dawn the next morning. Wangdi was left inside the crevasse with sufficient warm clothing, and with an assurance that he would be brought down later that day.

In the afternoon, Roch, Dittert and I were shocked to see the three Sherpas returning without Wangdi. They reported that they had been unable to reach him because the sun's heat had rendered the ascent of the crevassed face too dangerous. By now Tenzing had joined us from Base Camp, and before dawn the next day three strong Sherpa teams led by Roch, Dittert and myself left Camp I and reached Wangdi within three hours. He was in an appalling condition, covered with blood and suffering from shock and extreme exhaustion. Watching three figures approaching the day before and then turning back he was convinced that he had been abandoned, and he attempted to end his life by slitting his throat with a pocket knife. The Sherpas were magnificent; they carried him all the way down to Base Camp the same evening. The first steep slopes through the crevasses were very tricky; the operation took four hours and we adopted sledge-technique, with Wangdi's body firmly secured to ten persons. When we reached the foot of the face the Sherpas took it in turns to carry him on their backs down to Base. Wangdi had to be treated with strong drugs for over one week at Base Camp because some of his injuries had turned septic. As soon as he could be moved, a party of coolies was organised to carry him down to Dehra Dun, accompanied by the liaison officer. There, after three months in hospital, he was restored to normal health. Wangdi Norbu did not take part in any further climbing expeditions; and he died in Darjeeling four years later.

Our new Sherpa *sirdar* was Tenzing; he was the obvious choice, since he was head and shoulders above the others in ability and commanded unanimous respect. He seemed to personify many admirable qualities, having tremendous personal charm combined with physical strength, and a keen sensitivity and intelligence. During the expedition I regarded it as a privilege that he often confided in me, feeling able to communicate easily and without any inhibitions.

Returning to flowers and streams after five days at a high camp provided profound contrasts. Forgotten pleasures seemed to flood back; one felt grateful to be alive, to feel the warm sunshine, to hear birdsong and to stretch out one's limbs on the springy turf. At Base, so long as the injured Wangdi was under treatment in the hands of Roch and Dittert, we did not feel free to embark upon any new ventures. As soon as Sutter's hands had recovered, he went out in search of game. Roch would often disappear by himself for an afternoon, returning with a beautifully-finished oil canvas. I spent several hours mostly alone, climbing to various vantage points on the slopes above the glacier. The physical presence of big mountains made a deep impact upon me, and often did I try to translate overpowering impressions into words. Monsoon currents reached us by early July, bringing a rise in temperature and some days of cloudy weather; but there were no heavy storms, and not a day on which rainfall kept us confined to camp.

On 9 July we set out again for Kedarnath peak; there were four Swiss and myself, accompanied by four Sherpas and one Harsil porter. In four and a half hours we reached our former Camp I site. The following day in good conditions it took us five hours to climb to the *Sentinelle Rouge* camp. The next morning we had planned to set out at 4 a.m., but there was light snowfall, so we delayed our start until 6 a.m. I remember Tenzing helping me with my woollen puttees; we still wore them in those days. The snow on the long north ridge was fairly firm and we needed to skirt around a zone of crevasses. The angle steepened towards the top, and within four hours we arrived at the 22,410-foot summit to find ourselves covered by cloud. For the next part of the climb it had been assumed that the Sherpas would not continue; but once on the snow dome, Tenzing was keen to go on. Whilst he tied on with Roch and Dittert, I accompanied the other two Sherpas down. Two ropes set out for the summit at 10.45 a.m. All went well on the narrow connecting ridge, but poor snow conditions on the final face slowed them down. Whilst most of the others were tiring, Tenzing went into the lead on the last stretch. They reached the 22,770-foot summit of Kedarnath at 5 p.m. I had arranged to send Angtensing and Ajeeba up the north-west face to meet them on the descent with torches and hot drinks, and all were back safely at Camp I by 9 p.m. On 12 July we returned to Base. I found that my tent had been pitched and all my possessions carefully arranged inside by Angtensing. A five-course dinner was served that evening, complete with wine; and Tenzing joined us in the Mess tent to celebrate the success in which he had participated.

Northern Garhwal

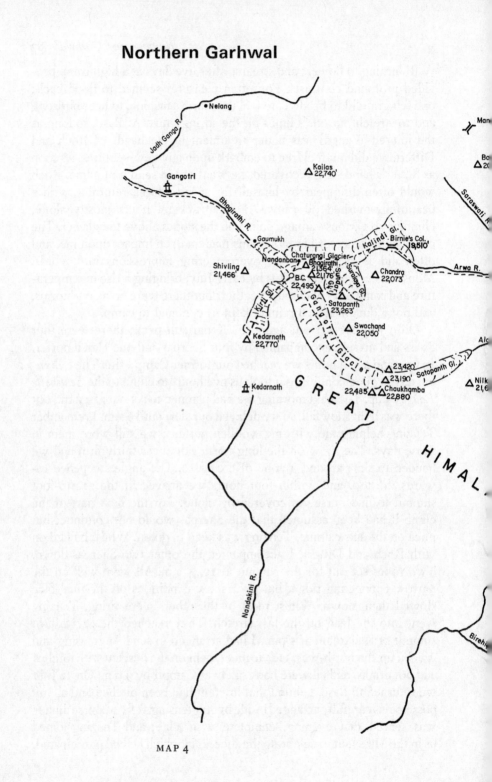

Nelang

Jadh Ganga R.

Man

Kailas
△ 22,740'

Ba
△ 20

Gangotri
⛪

Saraswati R.

Bhagirathi R.

Gaumukh

Kalindi Gl.
Birnie's Col.
19,510'

Arwa R.

Chaturangi Glacier

Nandanban

Bhagirathi
21,364'
B.C. △21,176'

Shivling
21,466' △

Kirti Gl.

Suralaya Gl.

Swachand
Gl.

Chandra
22,073

Satopanth
23,263

Alc

Swachand
22,050

Kedarnath
22,770

Gangotri Glacier

23,420'

Satopanth Gl.

23,190'

Nilk
21,6

Kedarnath ⛪

22,485 △

Chaukhamba
22,880

G R E A T

H I M A L

Nandakini R.

Birehi

MAP 4

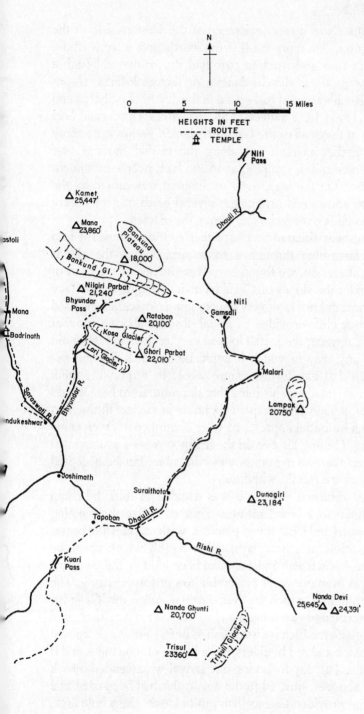

N

```
0        5        10       15 Miles
```

HEIGHTS IN FEET
- - - - ROUTE
⛩ TEMPLE

Niti
Pass

Kamet
25,447'

Mana
23,860'

astoli

Bankund
Plateau

Bankund Gl.

18,000'

Dhauli R.

Nilgiri Parbat
21,240'

Bhyundar
Pass

Niti

Rataban
20,100'

Gamsali

Mana

Kosa Glacier

Badrinath

Lari Glacier

Ghori Parbat
22,010'

Saraswati R.

Bhyundar R.

Malari

Lampak
20,750'

ndukeshwar

Joshimath

Suraithota

Dunagiri
23,184'

Tapoban

Dhauli R.

Kuari
Pass

Rishi R.

Nanda Devi
25,645' 24,391'

Nanda Ghunti
20,700'

Trisul Glacier

Trisul
23,360'

Our next venture was a reconnaissance of the western side of the Chaukhamba group. Attempts made from north and north-east by Schwarzgruber in 1938 and Roch in 1939 had shown that although a route could be found, the avalanche dangers on the north-facing slopes were too great; Roch's attempt had ended in the deaths of a Sherpa and a Dhotial porter. On 15 July, with eight Sherpas, Roch Dittert and I set out for the basin at the head of the Gangotri glacier. Following a route which we had earlier marked out along the medial moraine, we advanced about nine miles, camping at 16,200 feet, near a prominent bend in the glacier. On the way, some excitement was caused by the discovery of bear tracks and droppings; several herds of *barhal* were seen on the steep cliffs over 2,000 feet above the glacier.

Our next camp was situated at 17,450 feet and we reached it in a white-out after struggling through a snowstorm. When the clouds lifted in the late afternoon, we found ourselves situated at the head of the bay, close under the slopes of Chaukhamba. Climbing up the face to our left, the view did not look very encouraging. An icefall enclosed between steep rock cliffs provided an initial obstacle about 2,500 feet high, leading to a terrace; the icefall looked very broken and there did not seem to be any way in which it could be avoided. Beyond the terrace it was felt that two further camps would be required. I think Roch had practically made up his mind that the route from here would not go. However, he and Dittert spent six hours in the icefall the next day, during which his initial impressions were confirmed. Graven came up in the evening. Casting his eye on the prospect with a professional air he pronounced that the mountain was climbable; but he accepted Roch's verdict that we should withdraw.

As soon as we returned to Base it was decided to shift the camp slightly lower down to a broad meadow situated above the meeting point of the Gangotri and Chaturangi glaciers. With our existing porter strength this operation took three days, and on 24 July we occupied the new site. The site, known as Nandaban, had been used by the Germans in 1938 and it was in many ways preferable to our former camp. The striking-looking Shivling, which the Germans had called the 'Gangotri Matterhorn', was situated two miles away to the west. The Chaturangi (four-coloured) glacier, which is distinguished by its moraine composed of grey, white, black and red boulders, has a length of nine miles and is about a mile wide. The day following our arrival we ascended a rock peak marked 17,260 feet, situated to the north; this had been used as a survey-station and provided an excellent outlook over the whole area.

It had been suggested that the unclimbed Bhagirathi I (22,495 ft) could be tackled from the north-east; but it was clear that a greater opportunity existed on Satopanth (23,170 ft) by its north-east ridge and north face. With the assistance of five Sherpas, two camps were set up on the Chaturangi glacier and a southern tributary called the Suralaya. From a final camp on the ridge, two ropes comprising Roch and Dittert, Graven and Sutter reached the summit, taking ten hours to climb the steep 3,000-foot north face of the mountain. The ascent of their first 7,000-metre summit was achieved to their great satisfaction on 1 August, Swiss National Day.

My chief recollections of this period are of days spent alone exploring the ridges on both sides of the valley, gaining confidence and widening my experience. I reached three high points which provided superb views, and I found the loneliness and silence of these big mountains deeply moving. One day, with Angtensing, I walked to the head of the Sundar glacier under a fantastic cirque of six peaks, three of them above 22,000 feet. From the north face of one I watched an avalanche crash 5,000 feet down to the glacier. *Barhal* were plentiful on the upper cliffs. Once I came upon a group of ten animals comprising a handsome male with his entourage, not more than twenty yards away. I whistled and talked to these lovely creatures, who watched me silently with heads cocked and without the slightest sign of fear. Every day I spent in the mountains gave me so much joy that I was scarcely aware of a growing disaffection under an apparently calm surface. But it was becoming evident that, although I felt I could always count upon Roch and Dittert, there seemed to be some resentment over my role on the expedition.

A week after the Satopanth climb, twenty-five coolies reached us from Harsil and we left our camp at Nandanban, on the first stage of the journey over the watershed, which used to divide the former state of Tehri Garhwal from British Garhwal. We made short stages up the Chaturangi glacier, the coolies requiring persuasion through the persistent monsoon snowfall. On the third day, after they had assembled all our loads on the Kalindi glacier at 18,500 feet, they were paid off and released. Our camp was situated below 'Birnie's' col (19,510 ft), which had been crossed for the first time by members of F. S. Smythe's Kamet expedition in 1931. I had decided to part company with the expedition here, in order to spend the next few weeks travelling in the ranges lying between the Alaknanda and Dhauli valleys. In particular I wanted to visit the Bhyundar valley and cross a pass at its head into the Bankund valley, finding a new way home from there.

At 5 a.m. on 14 August Tenzing came to my tent with a mug of tea; since this was usually brought by Angtensing, I was touched by his gesture. At that time Tenzing's English was hesitant; my ability to talk with him fluently in vernacular made it much easier for us to acquire an intimacy which I think both of us felt we would be really sorry to lose. I do not doubt that five years later he was able to achieve a similar relationship with his Swiss colleagues on Everest. With a personality that was perceptive and highly sensitive, he was clearly conscious of his special position, which fitted him so naturally as leader of the Sherpas. I never saw him unoccupied around camp, and anything that he found to do, whether big or small, bore the imprint of his thoroughness, determination and vitality. His marvellous physique and attractive smile gave him the additional human qualities which made him so balanced as an individual.

The damp monsoon clouds that had filled the glacier at dawn seemed to have settled for the day, almost obliterating our small group of tents as we set out. When we reached the top of the col at eight o'clock there was a sudden break in the heavy banks of cumulus to the north-east, which revealed for an instant the summits of Kamet and Mana peak. Beyond the snow crest upon which we stood lay British Garhwal which, within twenty-four hours, would form part of independent India. We descended into a thick mist, Angtensing, Thundu and I each carrying heavy loads. The slopes were moderate at first, but we proceeded cautiously owing to the poor visibility. We encountered some loose rock, and the last 200 feet to the upper basin of the Arwa glacier was steep ice. Initially the icy basin was severely fractured, and we had to prod our way with extreme care, since we possessed one length of nylon rope and no spare rope for a crevasse rescue operation. By mid-afternoon we had reached the lower moraine, and finding a good site at about 16,000 feet, we decided to camp, feeling some relief at having crossed the pass.

The north side of the Arwa valley consists of steep cliffs; on the south side, which we followed, the outflow from six tributary glaciers had to be crossed. In the grey monsoon atmosphere the country looked wild and full of mystery. When we reached the camping ground of Ghastoli that evening, our eyes lit upon the refreshing, half-forgotten colours of chestnut horses grazing on green pastures. The track from here leads north over the Mana Pass (18,400 ft) to Tibet fifteen miles away.[4] Our route lay south, towards Badrinath. When we set out the following morning it felt pleasantly strange after over two months to walk along a path. At Mana village Rahul met us; for a week he had been awaiting the appearance of the expedition. We walked together to Badrinath, passing through ripening fields of barley and maize and villages festooned with flags and banners erected for the recent independence celebrations. Rahul was installed at the temple guest-house in Badrinath, where he had established excellent relations with the local civil and religious officials. Before his departure for Ghastoli to meet the Swiss, I obtained much assistance from him over arrangements for the next part of my journey.[5]

After two days spent in Badrinath in order to obtain porters and food, and thoroughly spoilt by Angtensing's luxurious meals, I set out southwards on 20 August. I had engaged Netar Singh from Mana, who had good chits from Smythe and Roch; he brought with him two wiry and cheerful youths, Bal Singh and Inder Singh. A long descent of the pilgrim road took us through a magnificent belt of conifers and oaks, which provided a feast for my tree-starved eyes. About 4,000 feet below was Pandukeshwar. We left the pilgrim road here and entered the Bhyundar valley, camping the first night in a forest clearing at 8,500 feet. For the first six miles there were signs of quite abundant cultivation, but the habitations are mostly seasonal, and the scattered shepherd communities usually descend to Joshimath and lower towns in the winter. The following day, ascending beyond the last clumps of oak, chestnut and birch trees, we traversed broad meadowlands, where I began to appreciate why Smythe had called this the valley of flowers. There were splashes of colour everywhere. I regretted that I had not come a few weeks earlier when saxifrage, primula, gentian, columbine, polygonum, androsace, now past their best, would have provided an incredible feast.

The hills and valleys of upper Garhwal abound in bears and it is not uncommon for the inhabitants to have encounters with these creatures. It is said that a bear will not attack a man except when startled or angry; since it is the animal who is usually aware first of a man's approach, when it will move away, cases of direct attack are rare. But the villagers have to be wary. Once, when I was walking alone through a winding forest track, I was startled by loud calls; a moment later, when rounding a sharp bend, I saw a man poised with a stick in self-defence. Hearing my footfalls he had assumed that a bear was approaching. The incident gave me a most uncomfortable feeling for the remainder of my walk. Bears have acquired the cunning to avoid the traps set for them by villagers, and a farmer in the Bhyundar valley showed me evidence of recent damage to his potato field, inquiring whether I had a rifle. With him I exchanged an empty ovaltine tin for about five pounds of freshly picked potatoes, and got the feeling that I had made the worse bargain.

We pitched our second camp at 11,500 feet on stony uplands beyond the highest shepherd settlement known as Bamini Daur. Close by was the grave of an English botanist, Joan Margaret Legge, who had a fatal fall in 1939 while collecting flowers from the cliffs above. Harak Singh, a shepherd who had spent twenty-one summers in these pastures, told me that the Bhyundar pass, which I hoped to cross, had fallen into disuse as a shepherd-route in recent years. It provides a high-level crossing between the glaciers on either side of the watershed dividing the Saraswati and Dhauli systems. Our next camp, which was situated below the snout of the Lari glacier, was memorable because it provided me with my first view of a brown bear; a river fifteen yards wide was all that lay between us, but its waters were sufficiently powerful to enable me to make a complacent study of the magnificent beast which had descended for a drink.

The next day was filled with uncertainty. Ascending a tributary north of the Lari glacier we had some misgivings about the route to the pass; the persistent mist and low cloud did nothing to make our search easier, and of tracks there was not a sign. In the late afternoon we came upon a site that had evidently been used before; the height was about 16,200 feet, and although we did not know exactly where we were we decided to pitch the tents.

Before dawn the following day the clouds dispersed, allowing us a brief view of Rataban barely two miles away, and below it the upper Kosa glacier. On the other side was the steep south face of Nilgiri Parbat. It was an exciting moment suddenly to find ourselves in the centre of these lovely mountains. In drifting mists we scrambled up broken rock and scree, and within thirty minutes we found ourselves on top of the Bhyundar pass at 16,688 feet. From it we looked down into the broad sunlit valley of the Bankund glacier. The descent over loose rock on the north side began steeply; there followed a short stretch of smooth ice in which Angtensing and I, wearing crampons, hewed a staircase for the poorly shod porters. After this we descended easily through the moraine of a tributary glacier flowing into the Bankund, with the north face of Rataban visible directly behind. That afternoon we camped in a warm ablation valley at about 13,350 feet, one mile above the terminal moraine of the Bankund glacier. Directly across the glacier we could see the outflow from the Bankund plateau, situated above us at about 17,000 feet.[6]

Our camp was situated half-way between the two highest shepherd settlements called respectively Eri Udiar and Thur Udiar and we had a few visitors in the evening, from one of whom I purchased a sheep for fifteen rupees. Filled with a breakfast of fresh liver, Angtensing and I moved up the valley and that afternoon we placed a camp on a rocky platform at 15,000 feet above a point where the Bankund glacier takes a wide sweep to the north-west. From there, on a cloudless morning, we ascended a rock peak of 18,000 feet, situated on the southern rim of the snow plateau. There were wonderful views in every direction. Nearby, stood the beautiful peak of Nilgiri Parbat (21,240 ft); also Rataban and Ghori Parbat. In the distance were Nilkanta, Chaukhamba and Nanda Devi. The hour spent on that rocky summit was for me one of the most satisfying of the whole expedition.

We started our return journey the next day. Of the descent down the valley to Gamsali I recall the springy turf of the meadows, the sparkling rivulets, and the sudden realisation that this whole enchanting experience would soon end. We camped outside the village. Behind us we could see the peaks of the Bankund plateau; ahead were the mountains of the Lampak group, an area that was still untouched. Why did I need to return? Perhaps I could spend a few days longer wandering among these glorious mountains. The small village of Gamsali had a mixed population which included Tibetans from the nearby village of Niti; with their yak caravans they were mostly engaged in barter trading across the Niti pass into Tibet.

The walk back took eight days, leading at first through rich belts of conifers, including some of the finest cedars I have ever seen. The monsoon had almost ended and the clear crisp air and mellow colours of autumn heightened the natural beauty of the country. At Malari the villagers were celebrating a harvest festival, scattering rice grains in the market place and dancing to the accompaniment of folk-songs. We camped at Surai Thota, above the river, on a meadow scattered with cypress trees; from there, we obtained a pre-dawn glimpse of Dunagiri.[7]

Near Tapoban we glanced into the forbidding depths of the Rishi gorge. Here, leaving the Dhauli valley, our route cut through the grain of the foothills across the Birehi, Nandakini and Pindar rivers. Climbing to the Kuari pass in mist I was joined by a shepherd boy who took over my ice-axe, almost as tall as himself, and led me to the crest. Down a lonely path on the other side I was enthralled by music from an unseen flute; it was probably some shepherd improvising on a folk-melody, but the performance had a magical quality embodying the brilliance and the pathos an untutored art. At a village near Pana I was given a touching reception by the masters and boys of a school who vacated their building and begged me to occupy it for the night. I was happy later to be able to present the school with its first clock. From the forest bungalow at Gwaldam, on 7 September, I had my last glimpse of the Garhwal Himalaya, crowned by the peaks of Trisul and Nanda Ghunti. The next day the three porters who had been my cheerful and uncomplaining companions began the journey back to their homes near Mana, whilst I boarded a bus to Ranikhet.

I had spent over three months in these mountains. Two years before, on my first visit to Sikkim, three weeks had seemed long enough; but now the time had gone by all too quickly. No other Himalayan region has provided me with deeper enjoyment. Was this because of strong youthful impressions aroused by the solitude of large glaciers and unspoilt valleys; or had I felt some subconscious affinity with the simple charm of its attractive inhabitants? Longstaff has described the Central Himalaya as the grandest and most beautiful part of the whole range. It was Garhwal that the Hindu sage had in mind when his traditional words were written: 'In a hundred ages of the gods I could not tell thee of the glories of Himachal.'

8. Dunagiri seen from near the Kuari pass (3 September 1947)

9. Typical landscape in the Spiti valley (14 September 1955)

V
Kulu and Spiti

This business of discovering passes and minor peaks is a most fascinating form of Himalayan mountaineering. The climber who cares only for capturing a big peak necessarily knows exactly where he will get to if he is successful, for the top is a blatantly obvious goal. On the other hand, the explorer of passes is often shielded from the commonplace certainty of knowing where he is likely to come out.

C. F. Meade

It is a principle of geology that where areas of the earth have sunk the deepest they also rise the highest. These sunken belts, or geosynclines, have played a large part in the revolution of the earth's past geography, giving rise to its features such as the continents, mountains and oceans as we know them today. The Himalaya probably comprise the largest individual geosyncline on the earth's surface, representing a system of mountain ranges 1,500 miles long and from 150 to 200 miles broad. Geological research has proved an essential unity of structure and composition in these mountains from Kashmir to Assam, showing that the vast tract north of the Indian subcontinent was under the waters of a Mediterranean Sea known as the Tethys, from the end of the Carboniferous period to the end of the Eocene, that is, between 300 million and 50 million years ago. Thousands of feet of marine sediments which have been laid down with their characteristic fossils indicate the successive ages of the deposits. The uplifting of the Tethys floor, compressed between the two continental plates of the Tibetan plateau to the north and peninsular India to the south produced the youngest and highest chain of mountains in the world. In the geologist's view the Himalaya are a living organism, since the gigantic movement of the crust which began 53 to 54 million years ago has not yet come to rest.[1]

The Himalayan system follows a persistent gently curved alignment in a south-east to north-west direction terminating with knee-bends in the west with Nanga Parbat (26,660 ft) and the deep trench of the Indus river, and in the east with Namcha Barwa (25,445 ft) and the Brahmaputra river. The inflexion of the Great Himalayan Range west of Nanga Parbat affects the trans-Himalayan ranges of the Karakoram and Hindu Kush, which follow a similar alignment extending to the Pamir plateau. The disappearance of the High Karakoram towards Tibet, one of the most striking features of the relief of Central Asia, has probably not yet been fully explained by geologists. In 1932 the geologist Dr H. de Terra of the Yale expedition found outside Leh in Ladakh a locality of fossil plants in the Tertiary rock formation between sixty and seventy million years old which he collected from greenish-coloured shales: 'An entire petrified forest appeared before me; palm leaves, swamp plants, leaves of a great variety of trees which must once have clad the slopes of an ancestral range.'

In the autumn of 1954 I received a letter from Peter Holmes. He was in his final term at Cambridge and was working on plans for a visit to the Himalaya; he had also just married. His letter seemed to underline an unusual self-confidence; he was obviously not one of those easily deterred by the obstacles strewn across the path of all who aim to realise the dream of a Himalayan journey. He was interested in cartography and geology, and he was a member of the Cambridge University Mountaineering Club. Deciding that he could combine these interests in Spiti, he discussed his ideas with Dr Richard Hey*, a geology don at the university. Hey had recently been on a geological expedition to North Africa, and the idea of searching for marine fossils in the Himalaya appealed to him. The rock-shales of Spiti, at 12,000 to 15,000 feet were known to contain deposits of several species of ammonites and belemnites, probably more than any other rocks of comparable age; and only small numbers of these had been sporadically collected. Hey not only agreed to join the expedition but obtained special grants for the project from the Sedgwick Museum and from the Royal Society.

Peter Holmes' ideas extended further. North of a line of mountains forming the main Kulu watershed the existing map, which showed very little detail, indicated two rivers, the Ratang and Gyundi, draining into the Spiti valley. Both were unexplored, and were believed to flow through deep gorges. It seemed interesting to try to penetrate these valleys in order to examine the glaciers and peaks forming their head-

* R. W. Hey, MA., PhD., Founder Fellow of Churchill College, Cambridge.

waters. Alastair Lamb,* who was reading for his doctorate at Cambridge, readily fell in with Holmes' plans. He was making a special study of Central Asia and was interested in conducting an ecological survey in the little-known Spiti region. Holmes was looking for a second climber to join him in the exploration of the gorges. My plans for the summer of 1955 were tentative. Garhwal was the country that appealed to me most strongly, but political restrictions had drawn a curtain across most of the interesting areas. My second choice was Kulu, where A. E. Gunther and also K. Snelson and Graaff had recently carried out pioneer ventures on the watershed mountains.[2] Spiti seemed a good alternative. The party comprised Richard Hey, Peter and Judy Holmes, Alastair Lamb and his wife Venice.

Spiti (the name literally means 'the middle country') comprises an area of 3,000 square miles. It is bounded on the south and west by Kulu and Lahul; Ladakh, or little Tibet, lies to the north. The Spiti river, whose headwaters rise near the Kanzam La in the west, later enters the Sutlej; the Chandra river, rising near the Baralacha pass in northern Lahul, becomes the Chenab; and the Beas river has its source near the Rohtang pass at the head of the Kulu valley. These are three of the five main rivers that flow through the Punjab. Practically the whole of Spiti is a barren plateau above 12,000 feet. The glacier and snow-fed waters, entering the main valley via gorges and torrents, have carved deep features into the dessicated soil. In this isolated and backward country a population of about 3,000 follows a way of life that has probably remained unchanged for over 1,000 years. The villages, situated several hundred feet above the river on eroded cliffs of shale and conglomerate, are small and scattered—tiny oases surrounded by fields of barley, peas and mustard cultivated at subsistence level from an uncompromising soil by means of carefully devised irrigation channels. Spiti has a Tibetan climate, receiving practically no rainfall. The summers are hot, but the winters are severe and the valley is virtually isolated from October to April because all the approach passes are snowbound.

The resemblance to Tibet extends to the inhabitants, who originate from Ladakh, Spiti having formerly comprised part of Ladakhi territory. Pasturage is limited, domestic livestock comprising yak, dzo, sheep and goats have to be kept small. Trade is conducted mostly by barter, the local pottery and wool being exchanged for tea, salt and

* Author of: *Britain and Chinese Central Asia*. Routledge and Kegan Paul. London 1960. *Asian Frontiers: Studies on a Continuing Problem*. Pall Mall. London 1968, and other works.

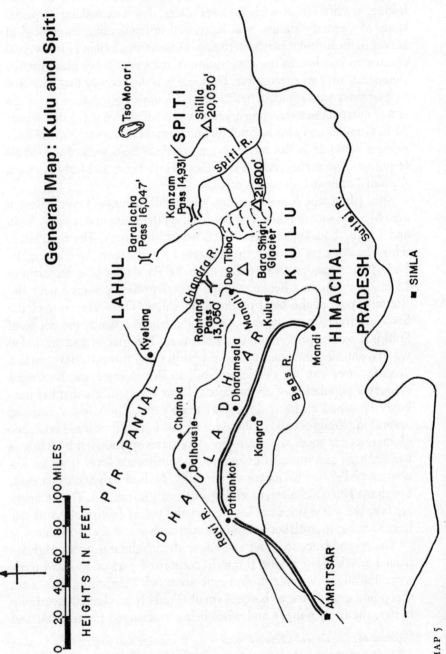

General Map: Kulu and Spiti

N

HEIGHTS IN FEET

0 20 40 60 80 100 MILES

PIR PANJAL

LAHUL

Kyelang

Baralacha
Pass 16,047'

Chandra R.

Rohtang
Pass
13,050

Kanzam
Pass 14,931'

Spiti R.

SPITI

Tso Morari

Shilla
△ 20,050'

△ 21,800'

Deo Tibba
△

Bara Shigri
Glacier

CHAMBA

DHAULADHAR

Dharamsala

Manali

Kulu

K U L U

Chamba

Dalhousie

Kangra

Beas R.

Mandi

HIMACHAL

PRADESH

Sutlej R.

Ravi R.

Pathankot

AMRITSAR

SIMLA

MAP 5

tobacco. Each village possesses a monastery and it is here that all the younger sons of a family must enter at the age of nine, and where they must live in celibacy for the remainder of their lives. Only the eldest sons are permitted to marry and to raise a family. This social system, existing from time immemorial, provides a method of birth-control in a country where the limitations of soil and crops would never meet the demands of increasing mouths to be fed. That the system has worked is proved by the census figures, which have shown a fairly constant population over a period of fifty years. One feels that the unquestioning faith of these simple people has developed fundamental beliefs and attitudes, symbolised in the story given to the brothers Theodore and Kermit Roosevelt during their travels through Turkestan in 1928. They had noticed many instances of idols and gods neglected and broken and on enquiring the reason were told in the interpreter's pidgin language: 'people ask god for something, kill chicken for him, god not do it, break his arm off'.

I travelled to Kulu on the overnight train from Delhi to Pathankot on 2 August, and from there by bus 132 miles to Mandi, which is a pleasant town, once the capital of one of the former Punjab Hill States. From there another bus took me to the delightful hamlet of Kulu in the heart of the Beas valley. This was my second experience of a bus journey through Himalayan foothills and it turned out to be much more alarming than my first. The driver would stop indiscriminately by the wayside in order to pick up passengers, and when he brought the vehicle to a halt the engine would usually cut out. His mate, a youth in oil-stained clothes, would struggle with the starting handle in front, the driver's feet would shift between the clutch, the accelerator and the brake pedal, the hand-brake being unserviceable, whilst the vehicle would slide dangerously downhill near the edge of the track. But the moment of greatest terror came when, about eight miles from our destination, the driver discovered that his steering gear was out of action. In the absence of any spares, I watched in amazement while the tie-rod ends were bound together with scraps of wire, and the journey continued with a load of distraught passengers reverently reciting prayers every time the vehicle negotiated a bend.

The Kulu valley, as this tract is called, is a rich alpine region situated below the uplands of Lahul and the plateau of Spiti, its western limits extend towards the Pir Panjal and Dhauladhar ranges bordering Kashmir. It is one of the greenest and most fertile valleys I have seen. Around fields of rice and maize are scattered forest belts of walnut, oak and elm and a wealth of apple orchards. The people look healthy and attractive, and their homesteads are solid wooden constructions reminiscent of Swiss peasant dwellings. At the travellers' bungalow in Kulu I discovered Judy Holmes and Venice Lamb recovering from the exertions of their 7,500-mile overland journey. They regarded the landslide-ridden road between Pathankot and Kulu as one of the worst sections of the whole journey; an impression to which I was able to add further points of emphasis. The male members of the party had left for Bombay in order to collect the expedition's baggage which had travelled out from England by sea.

On 5 August three of us arrived in Manali, where we stayed at Sunshine Orchards, a guest-house owned by Major H. M. Banon. The Banon family were well known throughout the Kulu valley, Major Banon, whom General Bruce had mentioned having met in 1912, had been local Secretary of the Himalayan Club for a number of years. Now in his eighties he was a popular father-figure and exercised a good deal of genial authority. On retirement from the British Army he had settled in Manali, building a wooden chalet and marrying a girl from the valley. His tall bronzed figure blended with the red-banded Kulu hat he always wore, and he was invariably surrounded by importuning relatives of all ages. His orchard produced apples, pears and plums famous throughout India; and I can picture him, seated at one end of his store-room, sorting the freshly picked fruit and supervising its packing into wooden boxes. Sunshine Orchards was attractively situated about a mile above Manali village. Through the fruit trees we could see fields of brown and gold dotted with cottages, and to the north there was a view of the snow-covered ridge dividing Kulu from Lahul. Our bedrooms, filled with the scent of pine wood, looked out on to blue forest-clad slopes.

Peter Holmes and Alastair Lamb arrived on 8 August bringing all the luggage, and we spent the next day arranging ponies for the journey over the passes into Spiti. We engaged eighteen altogether, they cost us four rupees per day and carried 120 pounds each.[3] They were accompanied by six ponymen, a cheerful hard-working group, who were often ready at the end of a day's march to assist with various chores around the camp. After setting up a base in Spiti we retained six ponies and three men on half-pay for the return journey; this arrangement worked very well. The main caravan, comprising the Holmes' and the Lambs with fifteen baggage animals and their drivers, left Manali on 10 August. I stayed behind to recruit a few Ladakhis as camp porters and to await Richard Hey, who was travelling out by air from England. When Hey arrived a day later he was full of amusing anecdotes about the last lap of his journey from Delhi to Manali, during which he had his first encounter on train and bus with the local population, who were embarrassingly eager to indoctrinate him into Indian customs and manners. I think that I saw Richard's equanimity upset only once during the expedition; he was a model of sanity and sobriety, taking in his stride elation and disappointment, and revealing only on the last day a minor worry that had rankled apparently from the start: 'Now I wouldn't mind', he said, 'if an appendicitis came on.'

Two days went by pleasantly in Manali while we explored the forests and some of the homes which had been built by early British settlers. One of these was Duff Dunbar, once an elegant country mansion, now slowly decaying in the embrace of an overgrown garden. We were able to engage two Ladakhi porters returning from an earlier expedition, and Hey and I got away from Manali on 15 August. On the way out we waved a greeting to Major Banon, who was seated at the centre of a large reception in the village celebrating India's eighth anniversary of Independence.

Ascending boulder-strewn slopes in a Scotch mist the next morning, we reached the crest of the Rohtang pass (13,050 ft). Here we left the monsoon behind and looked down into the brown sunlit Chandra valley, with the mountains of Lahul beyond. We had entered a different world. On the track we ran into Mr and Mrs H. McArthur and Mr and Mrs F. Solari, returning from a journey to Lahul. It was agreed that their two Ladakhi porters would double-march back from Manali to join us at a camp below the Kanzam La within three days. The next day we reached a cross-roads. The Chatru stream entered from the north; we were on the south side, and ahead of us was the much-swollen Hampta torrent, which we would have to ford. Road-building was in progress to Chatru and nowadays a jeep track follows the north side of the valley. Beyond the Hampta stream we saw our caravan encamped, but owing to the roar of the waters, conversation was impossible.

We made our first acquaintance with Spiti streams at dawn the following morning; these were to become a regular feature of our forthcoming journey. Fording the icy waters, often waist-deep, required skill only slowly acquired, and on a few occasions the excitement came rather too near to disaster. On that morning a doubled rope was thrown across as a handrail by the ponymen on the opposite bank; then, held by a waist-rope, our two ponymen and their animals crossed over, at

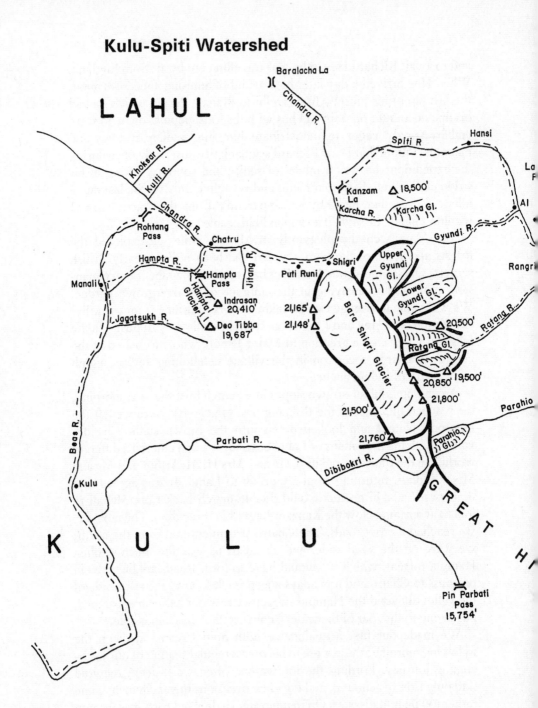

Kulu-Spiti Watershed

LAHUL

Baralacha La

Chandra R.

Khoksar R.

Kulti R.

Chandra R.

Spiti R

Hansi

Kanzam La

△ 18,500'

Karcha R.

Karcha Gl.

La

Al

Gyundi R.

Rangri

Rohtang Pass

Chatru

Shigri

Upper Gyundi Gl.

Hampta R.

Jitang R.

Puti Runi

Lower Gyundi Gl.

Manali

Hampta Pass

Hampta Glacier

Indrasan 20,410'

21,165' △

21,148' △

Bara Shigri Glacier

△ 20,500'

Ratang R.

Jagatsukh R.

Deo Tibba 19,687'

Ratang Gl.

△ 20,850' 19,500'

△ 21,800'

Beas R.

21,500' △

Parahio

21,760' △

Parahio Gl.

Parbati R.

Dibibokri R.

G R E A T   H I

Kulu

K U L U

Pin Parbati Pass 15,754'

MAP 6

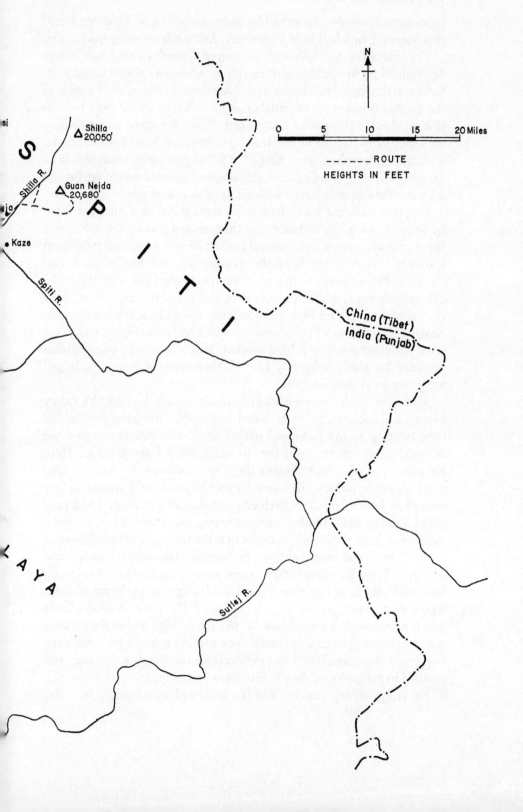

S

P I T I

Shilla
20,050'

Guan Neida
20,680'

Kaze

Shilla R.

Spiti R.

Sutlej R.

L A Y A

N

0   5   10   15   20 Miles

- - - - - ROUTE
HEIGHTS IN FEET

China (Tibet)
India (Punjab)

times almost wholly submerged by the rushing waters. Later we learnt that Venice Lamb had been very nearly lost while crossing this stream.

For three days we followed the barren Chandra valley, our stages determined by the existence of meadows where the ponies could feed. Once our day's progress ended at midday because the swollen waters of the Jitang stream were unfordable and a crossing would only be possible at dawn. The ponies shared our dislike for these streams; they were persuaded across after a leading animal had been drawn into the water, then the others were hustled in accompanied by loud cries from the pony-men. A wide detour on moraine took us over the stream issuing from the Bara Shigri glacier, with views of its nearer peaks.

Our two Ladakhis had joined us by now and with a third recruited by Holmes below the Rohtang pass they made a good team. Rinzing, a lad of twenty, seemed their natural leader; he was tough and intelligent and very keen to learn. With the training we gave him on snow and ice, I rated him equally with a good Sherpa. Sonam was something of a clown; only once, when he nearly drowned in the Ratang stream, did I ever see him at all worried. He was given some elementary training in cooking by Judy and Venice and was quick to learn. Jigmy, small and wiry, acquired merit as a hard worker, ready to accept any situation provided he was intelligently led. All three carried heavy loads and never once did they complain.

Ascending to the Kanzam La (14,931 ft), we left the Chandra valley behind and moved east from Lahul into Spiti. Our pony men added their offering to the festooned prayer walls[4] on the summit and we dropped down about 2,000 feet to camp on a lush meadow. Here the men persuaded us to have a day's rest, because the next grazing place was over twenty miles away. Peter Holmes and I spent that day ascending a mountain of 18,500 feet, south-east of our camp, which provided an enjoyable training climb; Rinzing came with us. Crossing a small glacier we ascended 1,000 feet of scree to a col and then followed a mixed rock and snow ridge to the summit cone which was icy and corniced. From the summit there was a view to the south of the Karcha basin, which was at that time unexplored, being one of the many areas where there were gaps in the existing maps. The position of this basin was later found to be north-east of the Bara Shigri and of the Gyundi systems. Existing maps were based upon surveys made in 1921, and very few peaks were marked. Later surveys filled in most of the gaps and resulted in major corrections to the alignment of the glaciers.

Two days of long marches across a brown plateau brought us to the village of Al (13,000 ft), situated at the entrance to the Gyundi valley. Richard Hey and Alastair Lamb left us here, crossing to the east bank of the Spiti river in order to explore the area around the Laguadarsi La. Hey's comments on the country were always refreshing; after a sleepless night encamped outside a Spiti village, bothered at all hours by the chatter and curiosity of the local population importuning around our camp, he peered bleary-eyed out of his tent and muttered, 'Can you imagine seven years in Tibet?'

Having arrived at our first objective, we asked our pony *sirdar* to accompany us on a preliminary excursion up the Gyundi valley. As always, I sought whatever information I could obtain from the local population; this is generally a useful exercise, provided one can strike a balanced assessment between their tendency to exaggerate and their desire to tell you what they think you would like to hear. It seemed that the only two periods of the year when the Gyundi river is not considered too treacherous are early spring and late autumn. Herds of yak are driven some way up the valley for grazing before the melting of winter snow-bridges across the river; they are brought down again when winter freezing has begun to reduce the flow of water. Shepherds from the Karcha valley were said to take their flocks over a pass into the upper Gyundi from the other side, which, at the time, seemed to us a little surprising. The length of the Gyundi river from its source near the Kulu watershed to its junction with the Spiti was estimated to be about thirty miles.

Near its mouth the Gyundi river is over a mile wide and we followed a thin track on its north bank, observing another track on the opposite side. In two hours we gained about as many miles, following crumbly slopes a few hundred feet above the river. Later we descended to the stream bed, but were soon blocked by a wide flood with cliffs above. We returned the next day with a rope to explore the other bank, accompanied by Rinzing and two ponymen. Judging by the size of the initial path, we were green enough to think that we had found a pony track when the first two miles did not give us undue trouble. Within the next mile we crossed and re-crossed the stream three times, then we climbed a steep slope for about 1,500 feet. From there we could see the next six miles up the gorge; the view was of steepening cliffs in a narrow valley and it seemed obvious that the difficulties would increase. The round trip of eight hours was followed by a discussion in camp that evening. We decided to leave the Gyundi alone for the present, and to move over to the Ratang.

A pleasant walk took us through three small villages, very similar in character, bringing us to Rangrik. One of the larger villages in Spiti with a population of about 200, it contained a school, a post-office and a picturesque monastery perched on a hill. We were given an unusual welcome by a village youth who handed us garlands of fresh peas. About one and a half miles beyond we entered the Ratang valley and found a sheltered site on a shelf at about 12,500 feet, overlooking shingle flats; there was a fresh water stream nearby and we decided at once to make this our base. We paid off three ponymen who departed with their twelve animals; the remaining ponies were released to roam over the area for the next two-and-a-half weeks, grazing on any scanty vegetation which they could find.

Richard Hey and Alastair Lamb returned pleased with their exploration, and there was much still unexploited to keep them busy. As soon as Hey had got through to the locals what he was seeking, a flood of specimens was produced. After a while his examination of these became more critical and only the best were accepted. But his own finds were more rewarding. Searching in dry channels and streambeds above 14,000 feet, he seemed to possess an intuitive knack for picking the right stone; a crack with his hammer would reveal fossilised sea-shells inside, to me a source of perpetual wonder. He managed to fill three wooden crates with specimens, which were shipped to England after the Bombay customs had been persuaded that ammonites were not the preserved remains of some Biblical tribe.

Alastair Lamb found much that was to hold his interest for the next few weeks. With his traditional English background, I felt that he nourished some ideas that had grown out of date. One of these was a single-minded assertion of authority despite the absence of any conventions in the environment. I think also that he was sometimes impatient of the separate roles that each member of the party was called upon to play. Lamb satisfied some of his inquiries through the Rangrik schoolmaster, an unhappy exile from the Punjab plains, who complained of the snow-bound winters lasting six months; also from the monastery; and through the friendly Nono whom he visited at the nearby village of Kibar, formerly his seat as hereditary ruler. The Indian Government had deprived the Nono of his powers and he was reduced to the status of an honorary magistrate. A small outpost of Indian armed police was stationed at Kaze; and an itinerant Indian doctor, who told us that he dispensed mainly goodwill and epsom salts, wandered through the area each summer.

Venice Lamb's calm and relaxed temperament made her appear quite at home in an atmosphere that must have seemed entirely alien to her background. She and Judy Holmes set up a kitchen in the mess-tent where hygiene and cleanliness, a source of amusement to our Ladakhis, were given priority. Judy was a trained occupational therapist and from time to time she was called upon to treat the local population, who demonstrated unfaltering faith in the power of a few pills to cure chronic complaints. Judy Holmes seemed to possess exactly the right qualities required for an expedition. Congenial and adaptable, with a kind word and a smile for everyone, it was to her that we usually turned for an answer to problems over food and health. Perhaps it was not surprising that her temperament complemented Peter's so well, being entirely different from his which tended to be hustling and restless, always trying to look over the next hump or around the unseen corner.

Peter Holmes and I scrambled to the top of a spur 2,000 feet above the camp to gain a glimpse of the Ratang valley. The map showed it to be about twenty miles long, it looked narrower than the Gyundi, but contained cliffs of equally forbidding aspect. We were encouraged by a view of three snow peaks seemingly only twelve miles away, which looked quite climable provided they could be reached. In the other direction, north-east of Rangrik, stood a beautiful peak above the Shilla *nala*. The moment we saw it we were both filled with the desire to climb it. Could this be Shilla peak? A legend had grown around that mountain, which was first ascended in 1860 by a *khalasi* of the Survey of India. Some doubts had been raised about its height of 23,050 feet, because of the recent discovery that it had been calculated from a single observation and not by the accepted principle of three intersections. The Ratang gorge claimed our immediate attention and Holmes and I decided to spend about one week exploring it with a light party. Local information revealed that in 1940 a British District Commissioner had tried to enter the valley, but was turned back by flood-waters; an attempt had also been made by J. O. M. Roberts in 1939. At our camp the sound of boulders crashing down the stream bed provided sharp warning of the force of the water.

It seemed advisable to secure a couple of local men in order to assist us with route-finding through the gorge. The schoolmaster offered to help, and negotiations were conducted in his house situated in the village. The house was typical of the region, a rectangular mud-walled dwelling on two levels, with the ground floor used for cattle and for storage of fuel and fodder, and a narrow stairway leading to an earthen-floored room above. Since there was only one opening, two feet square, to provide light and ventilation, working, cooking, eating and sleeping takes place in the room in perpetual twilight. The room becomes a virtual prison during the long snowbound winters, filled with the smoke and the pungent odour of yak-dung fires. A hole in the floor of the verandah outside serves as a privy. Whilst the schoolmaster regaled us with cups of sweet tea, it was settled that two villagers would accompany us in return for a daily wage of five rupees each. But we did not realise until two days later that this arrangement had been concluded without proper authority.

When our caravan of six set out from Base, it seemed bulkier than intended with Rinzing, Sonam and the two local men carrying heavy loads. Our guides' plan was to traverse the face high above the river, whereby they said the north side of the valley would provide a direct passage up the gorge. After a short first day, we were attracted by cries from the slopes above before we broke camp the next morning. Soon we were joined by Hey, Lamb, and Jigmy who had travelled all night to reach us following an uproar in Rangrik demanding the return of their two men. The trouble had arisen because the schoolmaster had despatched the men without having first obtained the consent of the headman and his council of elders. Within a short while two villagers had arrived to ensure their release. The two truants offered to show us over the next bit before leaving. But our real problem was one of transport, and we decided to cut down the loads a good deal. Jigmy joined us, and our three Ladakhis now carried about fifty pounds each. The local men were not a great loss; it was amusing to watch them depart, not by the route up which they had led us, but by fording the stream to the opposite bank. They simply removed their pantaloons drew up their woollen robes waist-high and strode into the water.

During the next four days we advanced up the gorge gaining from two-and-a-half to five miles a day, feeling at the end of eight to ten hours of effort that we could only tackle the next obstacle after a night's rest. Disregarding the villagers' advice about keeping high above the river, we followed the stream bed as far as possible, taking to the cliffs of crumbling rock and conglomerate only when forced to do so. For a whole day we were enclosed in the sunless depths of the gorge, with sometimes no more than a stone's throw between the containing walls. Three times were were faced with a traverse of 50° slopes a few hundred feet above the river; we prepared these passages as best we could, but there was no real security because a rope could not be fixed, and a slip would have landed us in the rushing waters. Rinzing performed magnificently on these occasions, and he possessed complete confidence when dealing with the stream. On the third day the valley opened out and the going became easier; not far ahead were our three peaks rising above a small glacier. To approach them, we had to cross the Ratang river, which even here not far from its source was swollen. Rinzing as usual was across first with his load, returning unladen to lend a helping hand.

At this point, where the Ratang took a sharp bend to the north-west, we left it to enter a subsidiary valley in the south, where we placed two camps. From the second, at 17,000 feet, Holmes and I with Rinzing climbed a peak of about 19,500 feet. This was the highest of the row of three peaks which we had seen in our first view up the gorge. Though our mountain was not situated on the watershed, from its summit a whole new vista was revealed. Monsoon clouds were heavily massed over Kulu, contrasting with clear skies over Spiti. The source of the Ratang river was clearly not more than five or six miles away; and we could see now the long line of peaks on the Kulu watershed. A glimpse to the north showed the outline of the Gyundi gorge, whilst below us to the left was the Parahio valley, leading to what looked like an easy snow pass over the watershed. We were looking at fragments of an un-explored area, like a geographical crossword into which none of the known pieces seemed to fit. Later exploration of the Bara Shigri glacier revealed that its boundaries were commonly aligned with the Ratang and Gyundi systems; there had been no hint of this on existing maps where the main peaks, though correctly triangulated, were wrongly placed. The topography of these areas has now been cleared up, and many of the watershed peaks have been climbed from the Kulu side.[5] To us, after travelling for four days up an unknown valley, it was a view filled with thrilling possibilities.

That evening we descended to a meadow where Sonam had set up the tents. The peaceful atmosphere by the glow of a campfire under a sky filled with stars seemed to capture our mood exactly. The return journey took two days. Our tracks were still intact on the traverses, and we were much more confident with the stream, which we crossed and recrossed several times in order to avoid the cliffs. Becoming over-confident, Rinzing slipped on a smooth boulder in mid-stream and the weight of his load very nearly carried him down. Later, Sonam lost his balance and in trying to hold him both he and I were almost swept away by the rushing waters before support came quickly from Rinzing. We were back at Base Camp on 7 September, reasonably satisfied with the week's adventures. Peter Holmes had made up his mind to return to the Ratang.⁶

After a day's rest Holmes and I set out for the mountain which dominated the Shilla valley. It was known locally as Guan Nelda, literally Snow Moon in the Sky, and the map showed its height as 20,680 feet. Shilla itself was behind, at the head of the valley. We did not know at the time that in 1939 Roberts had climbed Guan Nelda. Since Richard Hey had not yet explored the Shilla valley he joined us. By contrast with the journey up the gorge we travelled luxuriously, accompanied by two baggage ponies, with Rinzing and Sonam acting as orderlies. below Rangrik there was a fragile footbridge across the Spiti river; our misgivings, I noticed, were shared by Rinzing who mumbled a brief prayer before venturing across. The Shilla valley provided a delightful walk for five miles along good tracks to Langja, a small settlement at about 13,500 feet, surrounded by cultivated fields. About 1,000 feet above this we reached rolling hills with an occasional cover of scrub, provoking Richard to remark, 'Just like the Pennines'. He must have been overheard by the weather, which now turned cloudy and grey, and in the evening, after we had set up the tents, we had a rare and quite sharp thunderstorm. Before sunset the skies cleared to reveal Guan Nelda shining under a fresh mantle of snow.

While Hey stayed at this camp because the area looked promising, the rest of us moved up the next day. We had to cross a deep ravine, where we saw a herd of ibex. Then a long traverse brought us round to the foot of Guan Nelda, where we began toiling up scree slopes. The ponies required some persuasion, but they did extremely well to reach by mid-afternoon a site at about 17,500 feet, where we placed two tents. We were situated a few hundred yards below a tongue of ice at the foot of the south-west face of our peak. From this camp we were able to study the course of the Ratang gorge, picking out the peak which we had climbed. The two ponies stood disconsolate around the camp all night while the temperature dropped to 26°F.

Before dawn there was a sharp flurry of snow, not uncharacteristic, and signifying the approach of winter. Though there was a belt of cloud halfway up the face, Peter Holmes and I set out with Rinzing at 6.15 a.m. We were able to kick steps easily up the firm snow. When we judged in the poor visibility that we were nearly level with the west ridge, we traversed the face below it because of the cornices which we

10. Guan Nelda, 20,680 feet; Rinzing in the foreground (11 September 1955)

11. Near the junction of the Bara Shigri glacier and the Chandra valley (17 September 1955)

had observed from below. The angle of the face was seldom less than 45°, and we ascended cautiously, each of us battling with his will and his lungs. When we reached the foot of the summit cone the slope steepened and steps had to be cut up the last 200 feet. Suddenly the angle eased and there was a glimpse of the sky. We knew now with certainty that this beautiful peak was ours. Rinzing—this was his third climb—moved confidently and he acknowledged my smile as I edged him out into the front. We waited on the summit for thirty minutes hoping for a break in the clouds which would reveal Shilla. But the curtain withdrew only briefly to reveal the long ridge which we had traversed and a small glacier curling out of sight into the brown and gold valley below.

Late that afternoon we reached a sunny hollow at 16,000 feet, where Sonam and the ponyman had shifted our camp. The evening was clear, and basking in the glow of contentment we were able to admire our peak, lit by the changing colours of sunset. We spent a day at Hey's camp, where he was still busy with new discoveries. From there we travelled round our mountain to the west for a glimpse up the main valley. The day was clear and we were granted a view of a snow mountain behind ours with a long ridge gently inclining towards a domed summit. This could only be Shilla, and we judged its height to be no greater than that of Guan Nelda. Eight years later a modern survey officially established the height of Shilla as 20,050 feet. Whilst it was gratifying to have our observations confirmed, I must admit to some disappointment over the demolishing of the legend concerning the *khalasi* of the Survey of India. The error in calculating the height of his peak in no way diminishes one's admiration for his courage in climbing to the top, seeking neither acclaim nor reward. In those days a *khalasi*'s salary was six rupees per month.

We returned to Base Camp and began preparations for the journey back. When we hinted that we had some surplus food we found ourselves surrounded by eager buyers; so our six ponies set out lightly laden when we finally left Rangrik on 14 September. Accompanying us was Nono, a Tibetan terrier two weeks old, presented to Alastair Lamb by the Nono of Spiti. About a year later I saw Nono at the British Embassy in Berne, a great favourite of Lamb's parents, who had taken him over.

The march back to Manali took just over a week and was as enjoyable as any I can remember. We covered fifteen to sixteen miles every day. We were much fitter, and the weather was cool, with characteristic Tibetan winds sweeping across the exposed plain. One evening a group of 'Pitoons' from a nearby village arrived at our camp with pipes, drums and a young female dancer; then there was a social call from four youthful monks with a gift of peas. Until our last day in Spiti, villagers would seek our Richard Hey, offering him fossils; their bush telegraph system, we thought was very efficient. We crossed the Kanzam La in cold and blustery weather, camping on the Shigri flats beyond. All the streams had shrunk considerably and had altered in colour from slatey-grey to blue. Fording them, despite the icy temperature, was a tame affair compared with our experiences a month before. At the Hampta stream, where Venice had nearly come to grief, our decision to divert over the steeper Hampta Pass was not popular with the ponymen; so we sent most of the caravan back over the easier Rohtang pass in the care of Rinzing and Sonam, and the rest of us turned south. Skirting the Hampta glacier, we climbed up to the pass of 14,027 feet, obtained good views of Deo Tibba and Indrasan. The latter looked vicious from the north, with a steep hanging glacier. We had a warmer camp that evening on grass at 9,500 feet, and on 21 September we descended through luxuriant forests to Manali.

Hey had to leave, and the Lambs departed also. The Holmes and I, having a few days to spare, decided to travel up the Jagatsukh valley in order to take a look at the south side of Deo Tibba and Indrasan. A number of attempts were made to climb Deo Tibba before the first ascent was made in 1952; it has been climbed several times since. Indrasan was first climbed in 1962. The Jagatsukh looked an attractive valley, but after two camps in bad weather we spent a third night in a cave which seemed to provide the best shelter from rain and sleet. Though the cave had a clearance of only three feet, it was sufficiently large to keep all of us warm and dry. When we emerged the next morning to find the snowline down to 13,000 feet we decided that it was time to go home. After a day feasting on delicious fruit at Sunshine Orchards we left Manali on 28 September. Our three Ladakhi porters had served us as well as any Sherpas. They were tough and cheerful and, unlike many Sherpas, they were utterly unspoilt. We felt that Rinzing was likely to become a future leader.

The Kulu valley must have changed much since those days. Its climbing potential was well exploited in the sixties and a Mountaineering Institute has been established near Manali. In recent years Lahul and Spiti have been closed. One is left wondering what changes will have taken place in those forbidden areas once there is sufficient stability on the borders for the resumption of further travel.

VI
Karakoram

*We are all travellers in what John Bunyan calls the wilderness
of this world . . . and the best that we can find in our travels is
an honest friend. He is a fortunate voyager who finds many.
We travel, indeed, to find them. They are the end and the reward
of life. They keep us worthy of ourselves; and when we are alone,
we are only nearer to the absent.*

R. L. Stevenson

The Great Karakoram range extends for over 200 miles along a crest-
zone between longitude 74°–78° E. and latitude 35°–36° N. It is the most
heavily glaciated region outside the polar areas and contains nineteen
mountains above 25,000 feet, six of which are over 26,000 feet. These
latter, comprising K2 (28,250 ft) with the four Gasherbrum peaks and
Broad Peak, all rise within a proximity of fifteen miles of each other
above the Baltoro glacier. The range south of this crest zone is known to
geographers as the Lesser Karakoram, which contains the Rakaposhi,
Haramosh, Masherbrum and Saltoro groups, among others. Rakaposhi
(25,550 ft), or Dumani as it is called locally, occupies a dominant position at the western end of this range. Forming a part of the Rakaposhi
group, and connected to it by a ridge over ten miles long is Minapin
(23,861 ft), known locally as Diran. From an ice-basin below the north
face of this mountain drains a glacier which is very broken and winds
steeply through a narrow gorge into a valley that lies fifteen miles
west of Nagar town. This glacier made an extremely rapid advance in
1892 and was at its maximum flow until about 1912. Since then it has
gradually retreated and in 1958 its terminal moraine was about four
miles above Minapin village. This village, like other villages in the state
of Nagar, forms a tiny oasis in terrain that is essentially barren and
mountainous; on a rocky soil, irrigated by glacier-fed streams, cereal
crops and a variety of fruit trees flourish. Nagar lies south of the main

river, with its bigger neighbour Hunza facing it on the north. A traditional rivalry has existed between the two.

It is said that the population of Hunza is descended from five soldiers of Alexander the Great who were left behind when his army passed through on their way south to India. This belief is supported by the predominantly Aryan features and complexion of the Hunza race, many of whom possess fair hair. The history of the state, together with that of Nagar, can be summed up as one of petty wars and brigandage. Gilgit, which once comprised part of the territories of the Maharaja of Jammu and Kashmir, came under British administration when the Gilgit agency was established in 1889. Gilgit town was the meeting point of a trade-route for caravans between India and Central Asia; this was the old Silk Road that linked Peking and Sinkiang.

The two independent states of Hunza and Nagar subsisted to a large extent on armed plunder of the merchandise carried by these caravans which unavoidably passed through their territories. In 1891–2 a campaign was launched against the two warring states in order to put an end to these wild raids and also to their general attitude of defiance towards the British garrison at Gilgit. The battle was commanded by Colonel Durand and its culminating point was the siege of the fort at Nilt, which lasted for eighteen days. The fort, held by a very determined group of Hunzas and Nagaris, was eventually captured when a small force led by Lt. Manners-Smith* succeeded in ascending a cliff 1,200 feet high, thus storming it from the only direction in which it was undefended. Manners-Smith was awarded the Victoria Cross for this exploit.[1] After the campaign the ruler of Hunza, Mir Safdar Ali, went into exile in Chitral, and the two states of Hunza and Nagar passed under the overall control of the British through the Political Agent at Gilgit. A levy force was raised by Cockerill† and Younghusband in 1892, known as the Gilgit Scouts, which was commanded by British officers.[2]

Though survey work now began it was not until 1931 that the Survey of India completed detailed maps of the Gilgit agency, including Hunza and Nagar, the Astor region in the south, and as far as Yasin and Ishkuman in the west. Being situated near the point where the three empires of Russia, China and India once almost met, this region has always been politically sensitive, and even at the height of British rule travel restrictions applied to all except military and civil officials on duty.

* As Lieut-Col. J. Manners-Smith, vc, cvo, cie, he was British President in Katmandu, Nepal from 1905–16.
† Later Brig.-Gen. S. R. George Cockerill, cb, mp for Reigate, Surrey.

Formerly Gilgit was approached through Kashmir over the Burzil pass, a journey of about 240 miles that took rather more than two weeks. Alternatively, starting from Abbottabad in the Hazara district, one travelled via the Kaghan valley and over the Babusar pass into Chilas, situated on the Indus about eighty miles below Gilgit, an overall distance of nearly 250 miles. A newly-opened motor road along the Indus valley, which can accommodate heavy traffic, has cut the journey time to about thirty hours, starting from Rawalpindi or Peshawar; but the use of this road is restricted to official traffic.[3]

On 28 March 1929 four Wapiti aeroplanes of the Royal Air Force left Risalpur, near Peshawar, at 7.30 a.m.; four hours later, including a re-fuelling halt at Chakdarra, lasting an hour and twenty minutes, they landed in Gilgit. They flew at a height of about 12,000 feet across Indus Kohistan and they followed the Indus gorge partly over country where no European had ever penetrated on foot. Their maps of the gorge were based upon a journey made by one of the *pundit* explorers in 1876 from Attock to Bunji. When they touched down, there was immense excitement among the inhabitants of Gilgit, none of whom had ever seen an airplane. Whilst some placed fodder by the nose of this monster, others wanted to know what sort of creature was hidden inside, turning the *punkah*.* A second flight, also by the RAF, did not take place until two years later. Today it is considered usual to approach Gilgit by air and there is a daily flight which does the journey from Rawalpindi in an hour, providing extensive views of the Karakoram and passing close by the south-western cliffs of the isolated Nanga Parbat massif.

Early in 1958 I received an invitation from E. C. G. Warr to join an expedition to the Karakoram, whose aim was the ascent of Minapin peak. The objective was a relatively modest one, and it appealed to me because the mountain had never been attempted; indeed the glacier had been briefly looked at only twice before, by a survey team in 1939 and a German party in 1954.[4] It seemed to me that the venture had been carefully planned, and the party of four, none of whom had climbed outside Britain and Europe, had raised the necessary finances almost entirely out of private resources. There is probably no clear choice as to the best time for climbing in the Karakoram. In May the snowline is often at about 11,000 feet, which entails heavy work in establishing a base suitably high for attempts on the big peaks; on the plus side, crevasses are firmly bridged and the higher slopes are composed of

*punkah=fan.

compacted snow. June and July are probably the most suitable months. The monsoon is not as continuous an influence as in the eastern sectors of the Himalayan range; but moist currents generally help to retain an adequate snow cover except on the steepest faces, where bare ice is exposed.

Typically, up to the time of the expedition's departure from England at the end of March, permission had not been received from the authorities in Pakistan, although an application had been submitted several months in advance. Warr's time-schedule covered a period of two-and-a-half months, and I accepted his invitation to join the team for a period of six weeks. Ted Warr was partner of a London-based firm of suppliers of mountaineering and skiing equipment; he was the leader, and at forty-two he was also the oldest in the party. Dennis Kemp a professional photographer was deputy leader. Chris Hoyte aged thirty-one, was a thoracic surgeon from Liverpool; and Walter Sharpley, from Edinburgh, was an electrical engineer.

Following two weeks behind the main party, it was my intention to join them at Base Camp on the Minapin glacier. I reached Rawalpindi on 9 May, having journeyed by air from Calcutta via New Delhi and Lahore. It was a relief, travelling with only light mountaineering equipment, to be spared the rigorous physical search to which all passengers between India and Pakistan were subjected at that time. The airport facilities at Lahore and Rawalpindi consisted of canvas huts, reminiscent of amateur flying clubs of the thirties, with toilets which contained a thunder-box and an enamel water-jug and basin. One of my co-passengers between Delhi and Rawalpindi was Colonel Roger Bacon, who had been the last British Political Agent in Gilgit and was then operating Pakistan's largest sugar mill, situated at Mardan in the north-west tribal area. His conversation was fascinating, and he provided me with much useful information. At Rawalpindi I was accommodated at an army mess on the Mall, where others of the party had stayed. The building looked rather run down, but I was content to be lodged and fed economically, especially as my stay turned out to be much longer than expected. Permission for my visit to Gilgit had not yet come through.

For twelve days I walked every morning to an ornamental bungalow called Shahzada Kothi, which had known better days; it was now the office where such matters were decided. Whilst day after day of my precious leave drained out, an apathetic, vacillating bureaucracy, which worked for five half-days a week, pored over, dissected and ultimately passed judgment upon my file. Visits to the army swimming-pool and to

'Buster' Goodwin's house partly relieved my boredom and frustration. Major Peter Goodwin had been the last local secretary of the Himalayan Club in Rawalpindi, but he had recently left Pakistan. His elder brother Eric, a retired Colonel of the Indian army, had settled in Rawalpindi after a lifetime of service spent mostly on the north-west frontier amongst the Pathan tribes.[5] The garden of his bungalow was filled with fruit trees, ornamental plants and a fish pond. The verandah walls were decorated with hunting trophies, and inside there was an impressive library and a grand piano. With his extensive knowledge of the north-western region, Buster Goodwin seemed to be exactly the right person to represent the Himalayan Club in Rawalpindi, and I was happy when he agreed to my suggestion that he should do so. His home has since been, for several years, a caravanserai for climbers and travellers from Europe visiting the Karakoram and Hindu Kush. 1958 was an unusually active year in the Karakoram. On the Baltoro glacier three expeditions set up their Base Camps within a few miles of each other achieving three major first ascents; the Americans on Gasherbrum I, the Japanese on Chogolisa, and the Italians on Gasherbrum IV. Two other first ascents of big peaks were made during that summer, by the British army on Rakaposhi and the Austrians on Haramosh.

Dawn on 23 May at Rawalpindi airstrip. After some head-shaking by the pilot, clear weather being essential for the flight, I found myself airborne for Gilgit. The DC-3 aircraft was used basically as a freight transporter, and the whole length of the fuselage was laden with cargo strapped to the floor. Three other passengers besides myself filled the four seats behind the pilot's cabin. Photography was prohibited; but on this first flight merely to witness the astonishing spectacle of Nanga Parbat and other peaks across the wingtips was thrilling enough. Stepping down on to the sandy plain at Gilgit airfield produced a feeling of having entered a different world. The commandant at Gilgit was departing for Rawalpindi by the aircraft on which we had come, and the Gilgit Scouts provided a march-past complete with massed bands, a smart and colourful ceremony. Our liaison officer Lieut. Jaffery, who had been seconded to the expedition from the Pakistan army, was travelling to Rawalpindi by the same flight. It was unfortunate that at that time liaison officers were attached to mountaineering expeditions without regard to their background or interests. It was only much later that officers were appointed from a panel of volunteers set up for the purpose by the Pakistan army. A large proportion of those who were attached to the early expeditions appeared to lack enthusiasm, some even showing an

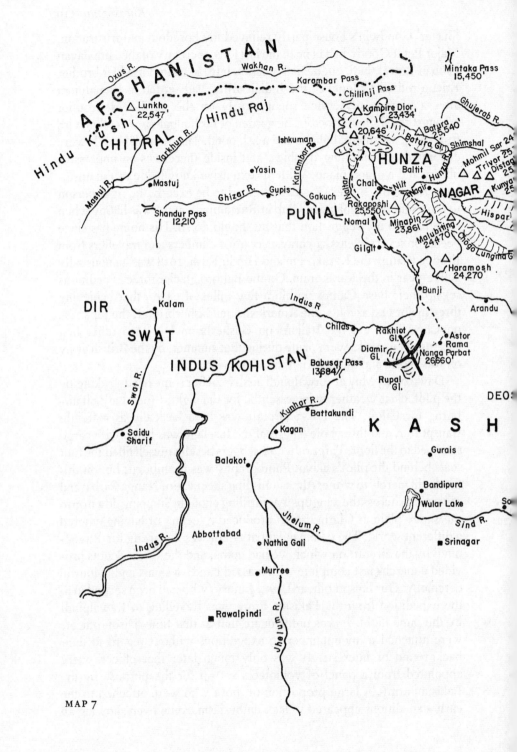

MAP 7

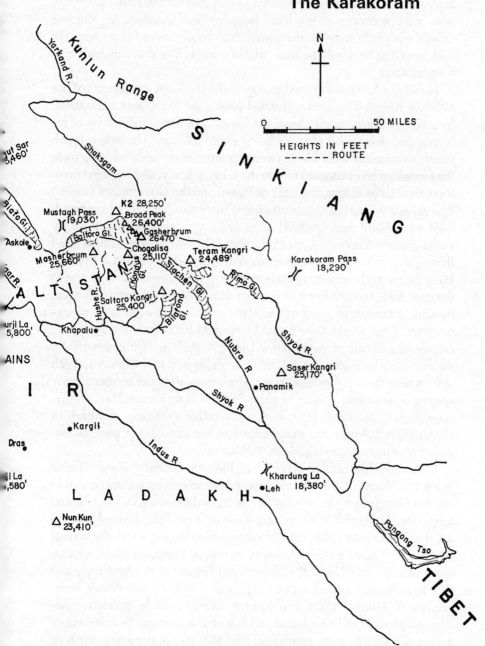

The Karakoram

N

0   50 MILES

HEIGHTS IN FEET
------ ROUTE

Kunlun Range

Yarkand R.

SINKIANG

Shaksgam

Jut Sar
5,460'

Biafo Gl.

Mustagh Pass
19,030'

K2 28,250'
Broad Peak
26,400'
Gasherbrum
26470'

Baltoro Gl.

Askole

Chogolisa
25,110'

Teram Kangri
24,489'

Karakoram Pass
18,290'

Masherbrum
25,660'

nar R.

Hushe R.

Kondus
Gl.

Siachen Gl.

Rimo Gl.

B A L T I S T A N

Shyok R.

urji La
5,800'

Saltoro Kangri
25,400'

Khapalu

Biafond
Gl.

Nubra R.

Saser Kangri
25,170'

AINS

I R

Panamik

Kargil

Shyok R.

Dras

Indus R.

ji La
,580'

Khardung La
18,380'
Leh

L A D A K H

Nun Kun
23,410'

Pangong
Tso

T I B E T

active dislike for the job. Lieutenant Jaffery had left our four-man party, who were ignorant of the local language and customs, in Minapin village without having implemented their requirement for porters. He told them that he would be back within a week. We saw him again one month later.

In Gilgit I had been invited to stay at the Residency as a guest of the Political Agent. The house, situated above the town, was surrounded by a beautiful garden. My host, Mr Kiyani, possessed a diversity of interests and discoursed eloquently on many subjects. He held a lunch party that afternoon for about twenty guests; many were visitors from the feudal enclaves situated within the Gilgit agency, and amongst them were the Mir of Nagar, the Raja of Punial and the Governor of Gupis.[6] The meal consisted of one meat course after another, all richly spiced, until everybody had gorged; then fruit was served, followed by sweet green tea scented with cardamom. The Mir of Nagar, then aged thirty-two, was only fourteen years old when he succeeded his father. He drew me aside, enjoining upon me to engage Nagaris for work above the snowline, and not Hunzas as other expeditions had done. His men, he said, were just as good as the Hunzas and were eager to gain experience. Four weeks later I could have told him that the Nagaris we employed had earned a reputation for petty theft and pusillanimity. In the evening, the Political Agent drove us in his jeep to the lower Kargah *nala*, where there is a trout nursery. Higher up, this *nala* contains many species of wild life. As the trophies in the Gilgit Scouts Mess testify, snow-leopard, *ovis poli*, bear, ibex, and *markhor* were once plentiful. In recent years Pakistan has made efforts to ban shooting in parts of this area which have been set aside as wild life reserves.

Certain idyllic notions have been built up recently about Hunza being the Shangri La of the modern world, whose inhabitants dwell in an area of surpassing beauty and are possessed of prodigious vigour and longevity. At the risk of debunking some of these ideas it is only fair to say that I have seen valleys in Chitral as well as Nagar where the natural environment bears a close similarity to that of Hunza, while in certain areas of Kulu and Nepal the exceptional beauty of the landscape and the attractiveness and charm of the people combine to produce a stronger appeal. Hunza's claim to uniqueness rests I think in its relative isolation, a product of its secluded position near a strategic frontier where access has always been restricted; and also to the presence north of Baltit of big mountains, most of which are still little known and many of which are unclimbed. If the Hunzas are healthier and more virile than the Nagaris it is because, until recently, of their comparative lack of contact with the influences of civilisation. Pakistan is very conscious of the tourist appeal of Hunza, having itself played a part in fostering it; but persisting political instability has continued to keep the area virtually closed to visitors, perpetuating the idyllic legend. The writings of the earliest travellers certainly show nothing to indicate that the area possesses a special quality beyond the overall aura of remoteness that undoubtedly encompasses the whole region. A fellow-guest at the Residency during my stay there was a camera-laden American, representing an enterprising concern in California, whose assignment it was to capture the life and the folk-lore of the region for television screens at home. Having received the blessing of the authorities in Rawalpindi, he was given generous treatment by the Political Agent who went out of his way to provide facilities that nowadays would be rather frowned upon.

A jeep-road following the Hunza river and linking Gilgit with the Hunza capital Baltit had been opened recently. It was still something of a novelty and was subject to sudden closures following landslides or swollen torrents. Petrol was scarce and very expensive, supplies having to be replenished mostly by air. Every jeep leaving Gilgit for the journey to Hunza or Nagar carried twice as much as seemed prudent or safe. When I left Gilgit by jeep on 24 May, seven passengers and about 650 lbs of baggage were loaded on to the groaning vehicle. The forty-five miles to Minapin took seven and a half hours. Halts were made at Nomal and Chalt for the diversion of the driver or his passengers, when gossip might be exchanged about the result of a recent polo match; and there were three halts along the hot and dusty road for repairs to the vehicle, one battle-worn inner tube receiving its fourteenth patch. The route was sometimes spectacular, passing under rocky overhangs or traversing steep cliffs above the river. I have seldom driven through country that seemed more desolate or barren, with only an occasional glimpse of the big peaks towards which we were advancing. After a series of vicissitudes the driver deposited me at Minapin village towards dusk and I suggested that he might like to pay me for the journey, a remark which he was human enough to enjoy.

I entered the small white-washed rest-house to find Ted Warr and Walter Sharpley plunged in gloom. They had been held up here for about two and a half weeks whilst negotiations for the fifty porters required to lift loads up the glacier were deadlocked. A recalcitrant *lumbardar*, taking advantage of the liaison officer's departure, had refused to co-operate. He was summoned in the night and my recent conversation with the Mir of Nagar was used as a bargaining counter. If the Nagaris wished to obtain employment with us, they could have twenty-four hours to make up their minds. Since our requirements thus became a point of honour with the *lumbardar*, he made us a solemn promise that they would be met without further delay.

The *lumbardar* kept his word and at 5.30 a.m. on 26 May an army of biblical-looking characters was assembled outside the rest-house. We got off to a surprisingly good start, following narrow tracks between irrigation-channels for almost three miles. When we had passed the last fields of the village, under crops of wheat and barley, we crossed a shrunken stream issuing from the glacier; then we began to climb up the right-hand slopes, following good tracks. At about 11,000 feet we emerged on to a moraine ridge. This soon petered out and we saw below us an ablation valley, white and wintry-looking. The porters so far had done very well, but as soon as we struck snow they laid down their loads. No amount of cajoling would encourage or shame them into advancing one step further. Selecting seven of the strongest, whom we issued later with basic equipment, we paid off the others on the spot and sent them home. Our ton and a half of baggage had been carried hardly one-third of the distance up the glacier, which looked badly broken beyond, and we were still about seven miles from the foot of our mountain. It seemed as though a good deal of work was in store before we would be able to set up a suitable base. It was cold, and the weather looked stormy. On a typical first evening in camp, everything seemed highly disorganised.

The next day we crossed the glacier; Dennis Kemp and I set out ahead in order to prospect the route, whilst a ferry party formed by seven laden porters followed in our wake. We found the going surprisingly easy because of the consolidated snow which provided firm bridges over the crevasses. The weather was clear, and we were able to study Minapin Peak, which now filled the head of the valley. The Batura peaks rising to over 25,000 feet in the north looked quite spectacular; the highest summit of the group, 25,540 feet, is still unclimbed. After three hours we reached the summer alp of Kacheli, a wide plain at 12,250 feet on the northern albation valley, now heavily snow-covered. This seemed a good place for our Base Camp. During the following week our seven porters left Depot Camp each morning, and after depositing loads at Base they returned to their encampment below for the night. The initial ferries up the glacier were escorted by one of us;

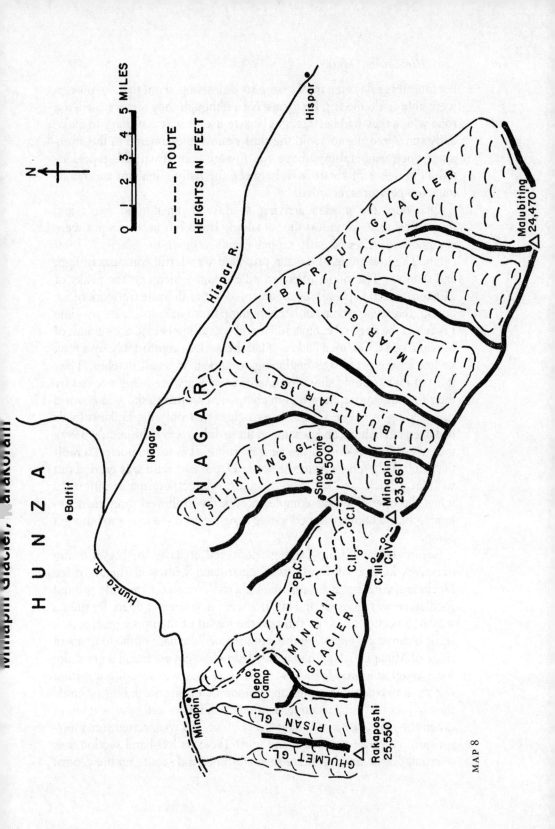

Minapin Glacier, Karakoram

N

0 1 2 3 4 5 MILES

---- ROUTE

HEIGHTS IN FEET

HUNZA

NAGAR

• Baltit

• Nagar

Hispar •

Hispar R.

BARPU GLACIER

Malubiting
24,470'

MIAR GL.

BUALTAR GL.

SILKIANG GL.

Snow Dome
18,500

Minapin
23,861'

C.I
C.II
C.III
C.IV
B.C.

MINAPIN
GLACIER

• Minapin

Depot
Camp

PISAN GL.

GHULMET GL.

Rakaposhi
25,550'

Hunza R.

MAP 8

but after three days the tracks were so well stamped out that the porters were able to do the trip by themselves, although they always carried a rope which they had been taught how to use. It was necessary to make early starts in order to avoid the slushy snow encountered in the afternoon when temperatures above 100°F were quite usual; this represented a difference of about 80°F between the daily minimum and maximum temperatures recorded.

One day, the porters arriving at Base dumped their loads and threatened to strike unless the remaining items left at the Depot were re-organised. After an early supper I walked down the glacier to their camp. The low angle of the sun provided wonderful contrasts of light and shadow. The ridge, over ten miles long, whichjoins the peaks of Minapin and Rakaposhi was ornamented with a delicate fretwork of ice fluting, reflecting a constantly changing pattern of colours. By the time I reached the porters' camp a full moon was rising behind the summit of Minapin peak. The men had installed themselves comfortably by a rock shelter where grass was beginning to appear in small patches. They insisted that I should share the *chapattis* which were being cooked by their fire; the atmosphere was in complete contrast to the white world surrounding our Base Camp. It was clear that only the bulkiest loads had been left behind, and as some of these did appear to be unduly heavy they were soon re-sorted the next morning. It is to the porters' credit that their daily ferry-service between Depot and Base was carried out without a hitch, and we were unable to detect any major pilferages when the operation was completed. We then relieved three men, retaining four whom we hoped would assist us with the move to our next camp.

Meanwhile, with our baggage delivered at Base, we began to dig ourselves in. A cook-house was constructed with walls made of ice blocks and with a canvas tarpaulin for a roof. An elaborate underground food-store was devised; and latrines were dug ten feet deep. By then a way had been prospected through the icefall of the upper glacier to a snow basin; a col enclosing the latter formed the base of the long north ridge of Minapin. About half a mile below the col we found a good site for a camp at 15,000 feet. It seemed clear that we were faced with a choice of two possible routes on our mountain. The north ridge seemed the obvious way, and its upper section certainly looked easy; yet lower down the existence of a broken crest of ice and rock raised some misgivings. The alternative was the north face; its left-hand section was overhung by seracs, but there seemed to be a safe route up the central portion of the face to the west ridge and from there to the summit. In order to study both routes before committing ourselves, we decided to ascend a snow dome marked 18,510 feet rising above the other arm of the north col.

The first task was to stock Camp I and this we proceeded to do by forming our own daily ferry-parties of two, having flagged a safe way through the upper icefall. Owing to extremely unpleasant snow conditions by day, we adopted a routine of alpine starts. Leaving Base by torch-light at about 2 a.m. with loads, we moved up the frozen glacier under starlit skies, reaching Camp I just as the summit of Rakaposhi was set aflame by the sun's first light. Returning unladen down the glacier we were back at Base by 8.30 a.m. Ski-running on the slopes above Kacheli was a favourite sport during this period, Ted Warr and Dennis Kemp being the most competent performers. A regular weather pattern seemed to have been established, with a few days of sunshine followed by snowfall lasting for two or three days.

The attempt to climb the Snow Dome was not successful owing to soft snow, but from high up on its slopes, both the routes on Minapin were examined. We decided that the technical difficulties on the lower part of the north ridge were probably too great, especially as its other side looked icy and steep. We scanned the north face very carefully for evidence of avalanches, and concluded that by keeping well to the right a route could be found that was free from any objective dangers; once the west ridge of the mountain was gained there seemed to be no difficulty in reaching the summit.

By 10 June almost everyone had moved to Camp I, whilst the four porters ferried loads up from Base under escort. Ted Warr had returned from a three-day rest below the snowline. He was slow to acclimatise, and had been troubled by a persistent cold. He was tremendously enthusiastic and rather highly-strung; he had practically no personal faults, except a tendency to push himself too hard. Chris Hoyte, physically tough and a sound climber, was one of those likeable people whose honesty and unselfishness shine through when the going gets hard. For Dennis Kemp the impact of the atmosphere and the situation was obviously deep and lasting; if the goal was impressive, so were the obstacles and the dangers. Walter Sharpley lightened a number of the day-to-day problems; whether a crampon needed mending or an ice-cave had to be designed, or as a guide for the porters, he was both able and willing to do the job.

On 11 June Chris and I left Camp I before dawn to trace a route up the north face. It was necessary to descend below the basin in order to reach that part of the face which we had judged to be safe; indeed no avalanche was seen to fall in this section during the next four weeks. The snow was firm and we ascended rapidly, following a pre-determined line. At about 16,000 feet we were slowed down by soft snow. When we reached a point about half-way up the face we were stopped by a crevasse. It seemed possible to work a way round this obstacle, and the following day, assisted by Dennis, we returned to set up a tent. This was pitched at about 17,000 feet and soon afterwards snow began to fall, continuing for the rest of the afternoon. As a protection against avalanches the site we had chosen lay directly below an ice-cliff, but dripping and hissing sounds throughout the night gave us an anxious time. At dawn Chris and I, thinking exactly the same thoughts though refraining from expressing them, packed up without further ado. We carried everything to a point below the big crevasse where we made a cache. We had made up our minds that before we spent another night on the face an ice cave would have to be built. We struggled down through deep snow to Camp I and then to Base for a brief rest.

Meanwhile Ted Warr and Dennis Kemp went up the face to start work on an ice-cave. Two days later, when a party of four moved up with loads to the cave, the prospect looked encouraging. Chris and I were left behind to open a route to the west ridge. After the others had departed, we spent the afternoon enlarging and improving the ice-cave. This could sleep four comfortably and the temperature inside was stable at 32°F. Shelves were hewn into the walls for food storage and excellent cooking and lighting arrangements were devised; but an air-mattress was essential if one valued a dry sleeping bag. In the evening heavy snowfall began, and we had to work hard with the shovel to prevent drifts from blocking the entrance. By the next morning twelve inches of new snow had accumulated, and as there seemed little advantage in consuming food at this camp, we returned to Camp I, where we had to sit out two days of stormy weather.

We occupied our time organising the porters into digging parties in order to convert Camp I into an Advanced Base. The four porters after moving sufficient loads from Base, were asked to assist us with the carries to Camp II. They refused at first; after a patient discussion we thought that we had almost won them over, when, at a critical moment, an avalanche broke away below the summit of Minapin, thundering 6,000 feet down the face in a massive cloud of ice dust and debris. It

12. On the way to Camp I, which was placed in the basin at the head of the Minapin glacier; the north ridge is on the right skyline with the north face below to the right (31 May 1958)

13. The snow dome, 18,510 feet, seen from near Camp II on the north face of Minapin peak. The route went directly up the face to the saddle on the left (12 June 1958)

14. The summit of Minapin peak seen from Camp III (*photo D. Kemp*) (5 July 1958)

seemed futile to argue that our route lay over one mile to the right; the men could no longer be persuaded to venture up the face. We then released two of them; a week later the remaining two made a few journeys with loads to Camp II. By volunteering to do so they demonstrated how small was the percentage of men from this region who could be counted upon to act as mountain porters.

The arrival of our liaison officer at Camp I coincided with three days of snowfall. We considered it prudent to allow the new snow to consolidate before launching a fresh advance beyond Camp II.

On 21 June Dennis and I prepared for a 2 a.m. start in order to climb Snow Dome (18,510 ft); but snowfall and flashes of lightning sent us back to bed. We set off at the same hour the following morning. The temperature was 12°F and by torchlight we followed tracks which we had prepared earlier to the foot of our mountain. We tackled its south face direct, which had an average angle of 45°, cramponing easily up the frozen snow. Towards the top of the 2,500-foot slope the angle became much steeper and handholds had to be cut. After climbing in shadow for almost four hours, we arrived on a saddle below the west ridge of the Dome, where we were greeted by the sun. There was a wonderful view of the Batura peaks, and we could pick out other big peaks to the north-east—Disteghil Sar, Mohmil Sar and Trivor, all of which were then unclimbed. Beyond, we looked out on to a lunar landscape formed by countless multitudes of peaks to the north, their jagged outlines emphasised by the harsh light and the deep shadows. Above 17,000 feet we broke through a wind-crust which slowed our progress to the summit. From the top of the Dome, making a comparative study of the ridge and the face routes on Minapin, we were convinced about the soundness of our original choice. A close study of the north face revealed two large crevasses above Camp II, whilst the uppermost part of the face promised to be steep. We had to proceed very cautiously on the descent because the snow had turned soft, revealing ice twelve inches below. In these dangerous conditions it was fortunate that the tumble which I took when attempting a sitting glissade lower down ended harmlessly. We returned to camp, well satisfied with our twelve-hour day, to find Chris and Walter back from the north face of Minapin; they had battled through a morass of powder snow in an attempt to prepare fresh tracks to Camp II.

Despite these conditions it was felt that after so many delays the advance up the face to the west ridge should be carried out by a party of two the next day. My time was up, and it seemed incredible that I could play no further part in these plans. On 23 June I had to leave Camp I. Spring had advanced into summer and our inhospitable Depot Camp had been transformed into a colourful meadow strewn with primulas and gentians. When, late that evening, I arrived at the Minapin rest-house I was so thirsty that I swallowed the contents of three tins of Guinness which had been opened with the pick of my ice-axe. I was unaware that I was being watched by a curious group of villagers, who concluded that my beverage was 'English milk'. The following day I waited on the road outside Minapin village for a jeep to take me back to Gilgit. The sky was clear but I could see streamers of snow blowing from the summit of Rakaposhi, unaware that Mike Banks and Tom Patey of the British army expedition were probably approaching the highest point at that moment. My general feelings of frustration at having to leave made the journey from Gilgit through Rawalpindi and Lahore seem long. It came as a sickening shock to learn from a newspaper report three weeks later that two of my companions had failed to return.

On 24 June Ted Warr and Chris Hoyte reached the west ridge of Minapin; Camp III was placed there at 19,200 feet. Another spell of bad weather followed and it was not until 4 July that all four climbers occupied that camp. The next two days were spent setting up a fourth camp at 21,500 feet, situated on the ridge about one-third of the way between Camp III and the summit. On 6 July there were bad-weather signs in the sky at sunset, but the 7th dawned clear, with a high wind. Ted and Chris left Camp IV for the summit; Dennis Kemp and Walter Sharpley, who ferried loads between III and IV, watched them ascending until they were close to the summit dome at about eleven o'clock; then storm clouds descended. When Dennis and Walter went up to Camp IV again the following morning it was clear that the tent had not been occupied. They followed the upward tracks on the ridge beyond the camp, hoping that a high bivouac might have caused the late return of the summit pair. For two days they searched the slopes in vain; then, in deteriorating weather and snow conditions, they descended to Advanced Base on 11 July.

The disappearance of Ted Warr and Chris Hoyte was tragic and mystifying, especially as there seemed good reason to believe that they climbed to the summit of Minapin Peak. My own feeling is that during the storm, which must have struck them in the summit area, they strayed off their tracks on to the steep north-east face. Had they waited for one day at Camp IV they would have been granted perfect conditions for their climb. Surprisingly, the mountain resisted three subsequent attempts, all of which were made by our route. In 1968 three Austrian climbers, placing their last camp at almost the same point where Warr and Hoyte had placed theirs, were successful.

VII

Swat and Indus Kohistan

*In the first place consult all the highest and most reliable
authorities you can find. In the second place read every book good
bad or indifferent that has been written upon the country you
propose to visit . . . In the third place take no superfluous
baggage. In the fourth place realise that travel has not only its
incidents and adventures but also its humour. And in the fifth
place never expect any encouragement from the government of
your country.*

Lord Curzon
(Speech to the Royal Geographical Society 1895)

For three years, living in London and elsewhere, the Himalaya seemed
very far away. I sometimes wondered whether there would be another
opportunity to go back; and how much I would be able to make of the
opportunity if it ever came. There were occasional compensations when
I could get away briefly to the hills and was able to reassure myself that
I had lost nothing of my capacity to absorb from them strength and contentment. There were twelve-hour walks on Lakeland fells in all
weathers; or a solitary dawn on Helvellyn when all Grasmere was
still abed. Traverses of the Snowdon Horseshoe with cloud blotting
out every vestige of the way. Walks with friends on sunny Appalachian
ridges across the summits of Mts. Jefferson and Washington down to the
Lake of the Clouds for lunch. Alleyways behind the centre of Athens,
and a lonely path winding up in the moonlight to Likavittos; overlooking, from a small church-door on the summit, the bright lights of a
modern city which had outgrown its traditions. But these were
occasional moments during a period of my life that was essentially one

of upheaval from the past; and filled with uncertainty over my decisions concerning the future.

In early 1961 I found myself again on the Indian sub-continent, having taken up an appointment in Pakistan. Practically every major Himalayan mountain had been ascended by the end of the 1950s, and with the race for the giants over, there seemed to be a brief pause in the search for fresh ideas. For a while South America appeared almost to replace the Himalaya as a playground for climbers from Europe. To some extent this may have been owing to difficulties of access caused by a tightening of entry restrictions into Nepal, Pakistan and India. The climbing of the Mustagh Tower, Gasherbrum IV and Jannu began to alter conceptions about what was technically feasible in the Himalaya and Karakoram; but a few more years were to elapse before it became fashionable to look for severe routes on the major peaks.

With evolving mountaineering practices and ideas, and with a vast expansion in the number of those who indulged in climbing as a pastime, a new approach to Himalayan climbing gradually began to emerge. The first manifestation of change was the invasion that took place during the early 1960s by small groups from Europe and Japan. Each season as many as fifteen to twenty parties, often numbering fewer than four and seldom more than six climbers, spent short climbing holidays in every sector of the range. They sought out areas that had not been fully explored and made first ascents of peaks between 20,000 and 23,000 feet. Nepal became one of the most popular regions; another was the Chitral and Afghan Hindu Kush.

Plans for a Karakoram trip in the summer of 1962, discussed with friends in England before my departure for Pakistan, had to be postponed. In early January of that year I approached the authorities in Pakistan for permission to travel through Swat and over the Shandur pass to Chitral and Yasin. After several months of correspondence with four separate ministries who at various times claimed or disclaimed responsibility, I began to feel that to retain any hope would be unrealistic. I had been in touch with Major E. J. E. Mills who while stationed at the Staff College in Quetta had visited upper Swat, and had hinted about the possibility of finding a mountain in Indus Kohistan, the existence of which the old Survey maps did not indicate.[1] The prospect appealed to me strongly, although I expected to obtain leave for only three weeks and was unlikely to find anyone to join me.

Following a chance encounter during a visit to Peshawar in May I was given an introduction to the Waliahad* of Swat State, Miangul Aurangzeb Khan. He was most hospitable, and it turned out that he had been educated at the Doon School Dehra Dun, three of whose masters had climbed in Swat by his invitation in 1940. He showed an interest in my plans and assured me of any assistance which I might need, suggesting that I should engage an armed escort which the State would provide. I did not know at the time that he was very shortly to be married to a daughter of the President of Pakistan, Field-Marshal Ayub Khan. His father the Wali, Miangul Jehanzeb Khan exercised an autocratic rule over his subjects. But it was a benevolent autocracy in which every dispute was dealt with promptly, and every citizen was assured of a completely impartial judgement personally decreed by his ruler. Poverty, crime and tyranny had become increasingly rare in the state.[2]

The history of Swat is one of warring religious and political elements; and of endless tribal rivalries and vendettas. The country was the scene of a campaign in 327 B.C. when the inhabitants savagely resisted the invading armies of Alexander, threatening to block their passage to India. Between the fifth and eighth centuries A.D. Buddhism thrived, to be crushed later by the rise of Islam. The Yusufzai Pathans occupied Swat towards the close of the fifteenth century. While resisting any outside influence, the people were torn by centuries of internal feuds and bloodshed. The founder of the Miangul family, hereditary rulers of Swat state, was known as the *Akhund*, or religious teacher, who died in 1877. His grandson, Miangul Gul Shahzada, by achieving political cohesion between the tribes, created the modern state of Swat, which was granted recognition by the British in 1926. He ruled for thirty years as a feudal though enlightened leader bringing about peace, security and progress. In 1948 he handed over power to his son Miangul Jehanzeb Khan in order to devote the remainder of his life to meditation and prayer.[3]

With an agreeable climate and adequate rainfall Swat has always been immensely fertile, and a variety of fruit and cereal crops flourish, both on the wide green plains in the lower part of the valley and on the terraced slopes above. Until 1947 the state was virtually closed to Europeans. The Survey of India had done some mapping in the early 1920s, but detailed map-sheets of the upper mountain ranges had not been prepared. Indus Kohistan, comprising the areas to the north and east, was virtually unknown. Between 1958–60 the Survey of Pakistan carried out some field-work in the area. For security reasons, their map has not been made available; it is said to show a peak of 20,528 feet,

*Heir-apparent

though no mountain of this height has been observed by climbers and travellers. The highest peak in the state is still believed to be Falak Ser (19,415 ft), which was first climbed in 1957.[4]

A summer spent in the Punjab plains with temperatures of 118°F is not the best preparation for mountain climbing. Besides, four years had passed since my last visit to big mountains. On 13 August after an overnight railway journey I arrived at the old-world station of Nowshera at dawn. In due course, a branch-line train moved out leisurely towards the railhead at Dargai, situated at the foot of the Malakand hills. On arrival, three hours later, all the passengers made a frantic rush for two buses waiting outside. How everyone was eventually accommodated is one of the mysteries of travel in the east. As a sahib I was accorded the honour of a front seat beside the driver, which was fortunate because the 48-mile journey took about three hours. From Dargai the road winds steeply up a hill, on the top of which Malakand fort is situated. On a visit made two years later I was invited inside the fort; on the mantelpiece of the officer's mess Lieutenant W. S. Churchill scratched his name in 1897. The Malakand pass forms the southern boundary of Swat state. After descending into the broad valley of the Swat river, the road, lined with avenues of poplar and eucalyptus trees, runs through a green landscape containing fields of rice and corn and dotted with fruit trees. On sale everywhere by the roadside were freshly picked peaches, pears, grapes and raspberries. Not far from the state capital is the small town of Barikot where Alexander's army halted on its way through Buner to the Peshawar plains.

I spent a comfortable night in Saidu Sharif at the Swat hotel, owned by the ruler, and departed by car the next morning for the sixty-five-mile journey to Kalam. Instructions had been passed to state officials about my visit, and seldom in my travels has my path been made so smooth by the courtesy and assistance of all whom I met. At Bahrain the *Bara Hakim*, or administrative head of the district, offered me tea and apples picked from his garden. While we talked in his house, which was reminiscent of a Swiss chalet, he telephoned instructions to the authorities at Kalam regarding my transport requirements. I reached Kalam in the early afternoon. Situated on a plain about 500 feet above the village were two timbered bungalows and a fort; Falak Ser and other peaks were visible to the east and the valley was overlooked by snow-covered mountains in every direction. It was a perfect Alpine setting, possessing the rare peacefulness of untouched valleys. The next day the *subedar* offered me a ride in a jeep to his fort at Matiltan

Swat, Kohistan and Kaghan

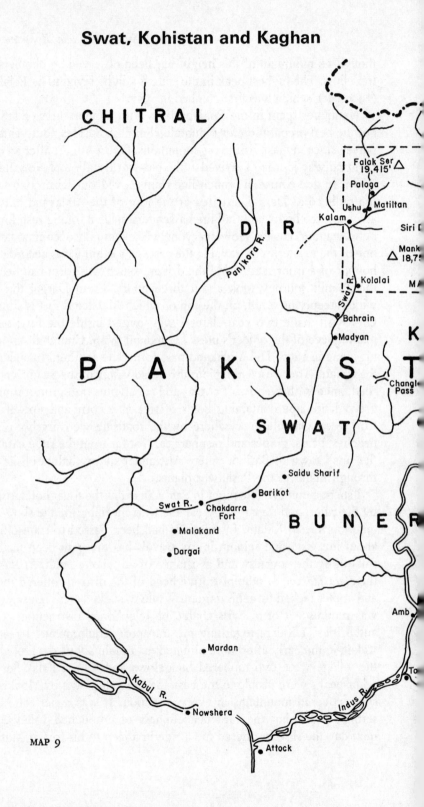

MAP 9

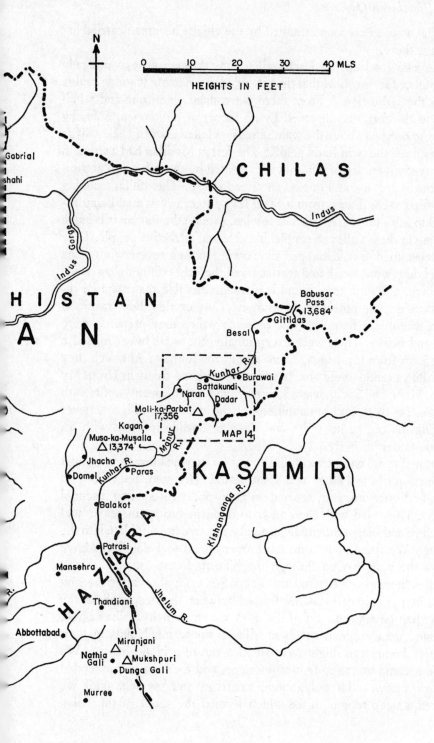

six miles away. Five men arranged by the village headman carried my baggage there.

The jeep road up the Ushu valley runs through an exceptionally beautiful cedar forest. At that time it ended at a narrow wooden bridge across the Ushu river.[5] From there we walked about one and a half miles to the fort, accompanied by an escort of militiamen. Standing almost 10,000 feet above the walnut trees and meadows of Ushu village we could see the twin Batin peaks.[6] The fort at Matiltan had a strength of thirty-six men, six of whom were selected by the *subedar* to accompany me as porters, and one as an armed escort. The militia manning these forts were drawn from a State levy force, every man being required to fulfil up to five years of service. I found the Pathan tribesmen dwelling in these valleys a simple, likeable and attractive people. They are accustomed to cold and privation owing to their severe winters. As porters they were tough and fearless, and they cheerfully followed me anywhere, although they found it incomprehensible that material reward was not the object of my journey. They carried their own food which was maize flour, and the *chapattis* which they prepared were thick and heavy. They were exceptionally honest; I never missed a single item from my baggage throughout the journey. Although they spoke Pushtu, they were able to converse with me freely in Urdu. My escort, Mohmand Sadiq, was a serious young man of twenty-four; with his rifle, bayonet, and ammunition-belt he was very diligent, never allowing me out of his sight, and sleeping outside my tent with his weapon under his body.

Our first camp was on an idyllic flower-strewn meadow situated near the junction of the Paloga and Ushu rivers. The men, full of boyish spirits and good humour, created an atmosphere resembling a school holiday. They vied with each other to perform various duties around the camp, and sang contentedly around a massive fire until late into the evening. We spent about one week over a visit to Falak Ser. Above Paloga the path wound through magnificent forests of pine. About six miles beyond we entered the Falak Ser *nala*; soon after we saw the white pyramid of Falak Ser framed between the steep walls of the valley. Just beyond the last of the trees, a narrow belt of silver birch, we came upon a small shepherd village whose inhabitants in their primitive homestead might have stepped out of a biblical scene. We placed a camp at 11,500 feet on moraine, and the next day ascended hillsides strewn with polygonum, saxifrage and gentian, until we reached a steep tongue of ice which formed the snout of the Falak

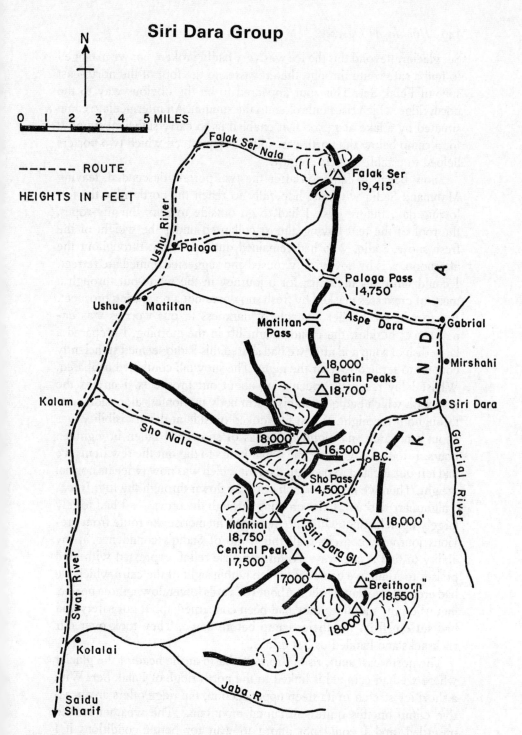

Siri Dara Group

N

0 1 2 3 4 5 MILES

- - - - ROUTE

HEIGHTS IN FEET

Falak Ser Nala

Falak Ser
19,415'

Ushu River

Paloga

Paloga Pass
14,750'

Ushu　Matiltan

Matiltan
Pass

Aspe Dara

Gabrial

K A N D I A

Mirshahi

Batin Peaks
△ 18,000'
△ 18,700'

Kalam

Siri Dara

Sho Nala

△ 18,000'　△ 16,500'

B.C.

Sho Pass
14,500'

Gabrial River

Mankial
18,750'

△ 18,000'

Siri Dara Gl.

Central Peak
17,500'

△ 17,000'

△ "Breithorn"
18,550'

Swat River

△ 18,000'

Kolalai

Jaba R.

Saidu
Sharif

MAP 10

Ser glacier. Beyond this the ice was very badly broken, but we managed to find a safe route through the crevasses to the foot of the north-east spur of Falak Ser. This spur appeared to be the obvious way to the north ridge which rises unbroken to the summit. An intermediate camp situated by a lake at 13,500 feet enabled us to carry sufficient supplies for a camp below the north-east spur at 15,500 feet, which two porters helped to establish on 20 August.

Snow began to fall soon after the two porters descended, leaving Mohmand Sadiq with me, hopefully to reach the north ridge the following day. Before dusk I had to go outside to refix the guy-ropes, the roof of the tent having almost collapsed under the weight of the fresh snow. Sadiq, who had remained dutifully silent throughout the afternoon, was by now visibly roused and suggested immediate retreat. I could sense his thoughts, for a journey in the white-out through a maze of crevasses masked by fresh snow was not a reassuring prospect. But to add the further obstacle of darkness to our worries was unnecessary; besides, the clouds might lift in the morning. I prepared a large dish of soup and after we had shared this Sadiq seemed sufficiently content to settle down for the night. The snowfall continued unabated. Whilst I lay restlessly speculating about our prospects, I envied the ease with which Sadiq slept, his warm body motionless alongside mine throughout the night. When we looked outside at dawn visibility was about ten yards and eighteen inches of snow had fallen in eighteen hours. It took us over one and a half hours to dig out the few items we had left outside and to pack up the tent which was now twice its normal weight. Then we began to inch our way down through the fog. It was a nightmare descent. Criss-crossing through the crevasses I had to rely largely upon instinct while attempting to memorise the route from previous journeys, conscious all the while of Sadiq's confidence in my ability to find a safe way. To his immense relief, expressed with loud praises to Allah, we came off the ice within sight of the cairn which we had erected two days earlier. About 500 yards lower down, three porters met us on the moraine; they had been concerned about our safety and had set out from the lower camp before dawn. They took over our rucksacks and handed us hot drinks.

The north-east spur, rising from the basin at the head of the glacier where we had camped is linked to the north ridge of Falak Ser. With a short icy stretch in its steep upper section, the ridge offers an attractive climb on this quite substantial mountain.[7] The weather looked unsettled, and I could not afford to wait for better conditions if I were to allow myself sufficient time for the next part of my journey. So we packed up for the return to Paloga. On the way back we halted at a small village in order to recruit a porter. Everybody crowded round offering to help, and various charades followed. One man picked up the load as though it weighed a few ounces, demonstrating to a young victim that easy money could be earned. When the victim declined and Hercules was invited to join us he could barely find the strength to lift the load off the ground. His bargaining instincts had been aroused in order to extract a better wage. The militiamen, their eight-day spell of duty completed, had to be replaced.

On 25 August, with a motley crew recruited from nearby villages, I set out again from Paloga heading east up a valley towards Indus Kohistan. I found my new porters slower and much less willing than the tough and cheerful levies. The valley was steep and narrow at first, widening into a broad plain where we crossed a stream issuing from the south side of Falak Ser. I was looking for the Paloga pass, but was not sure in which direction it lay; the map showed a blank here, the area of Indus Kohistan having not been surveyed. Although I was keen to press on until the pass was within sight, the porters tried to persuade me to halt at every likely-looking site on the plea that it would be the last. We eventually camped on an alp at 11,500 feet in the late afternoon. A group of shepherds dwelling in caves not far off, brought us a brass urn filled with warm and frothy milk, which my men relished.

The next day, five hours of fairly continuous ascent across scree slopes and moraine, misled by one false pass after another, brought us to a dividing ridge. I raced up the final slopes, full of anticipation. There was a striking view of the Batin peaks, barely four miles away, but it was the view beyond which attracted me. I saw a large group of mountains rising from an ice plateau, and between drifting clouds it was intriguing to try to guess the size of the area. I wondered whether one of these peaks could have been Jimmy Mills' elusive mountain in Indus Kohistan, or whether I had come upon something quite unsuspected. The prospect of exploring the plateau, indeed of locating it, seemed immensely exciting. The porters had arrived at the foot of the water-shed ridge where I returned to join them, and while we put up the tents light snow began to fall.

Our pass, about 14,750 feet, bore no cairn or other signs of human passage; but we met a solitary shepherd from whom we learnt that it was occasionally used as a summer route by Kohistani herdsmen. The Aspe Dara river flowing through Kandia, as this region of Indus

Kohistan is known, was visible about 2,500 feet below. The next day one of the porters, a trouble-maker, thought that the descent from the pass looked too steep, so I got rid of him on the spot. The other porters gave an excellent account of themselves that day. On reaching the Aspe Dara valley we struck the main track linking Matiltan and Gabrial across a pass about three miles south of the one we had crossed. The going was pretty rough, with the descent first of a rocky defile, followed by two river fordings. That evening we camped on a bouldery plain at about 10,750 feet near a deserted sheepfold.

After the gentle landscape of Swat, Kandia seemed wild and rugged with steeper valleys and scant signs of cultivation. The porters rather tended to treat the Kandiawals as a distant tribe, regarding with amused disdain their coarse dialect and manners. The people certainly looked backward and indigent; yet to me they seemed to possess all the charm of a community isolated from the corrupting influences of civilisation. I did not observe any sign of discontent, but an uninhibited friendliness and courtesy. With their fields yielding crops barely sufficient for their needs over the long winter, their requirements of corn have to be supplemented from outside; wool is bartered in lower Swat for cereals and salt, using human transport.

Early the next morning we set out for Gabrial, one of the larger villages in Kandia. I recollect the eight-mile walk there because of an incident that unsettled me at the time. I was walking ahead of the porters with my armed escort, Mam Seth, a stocky youth of about twenty-two. The track entered a dark belt of walnut trees, then passed through a narrow gorge. There was an eerie silence in which Mam Seth who was in front announced that it would be better if we changed positions, explaining that we had entered an unsafe area and from behind he could protect me more easily against any attack. For one mile we walked in this fashion, Mam Seth two paces behind, his rifle loaded and his bayonet fixed, whilst I could not suppress a strong feeling of uneasiness about the armed tribesman at my back. Later it shamed me that I should have entertained such unjust and unwarranted fears.

We climbed up to Gabrial fort, constructed in the picturesque manner of the country with turrets, peepholes and a drawbridge. A most unlikely-looking *subedar*, hirsute and paunchy, invited me into his domain. Seated there, unshod and crosslegged, I was entertained to a meal. The *subedar*'s contact with the world was a telephone line to Saidu Sharif and a transistor radio. He was full of eager questions. I gathered that apart from a visit two years before by an Italian scientific group under Prof. G. Tucci, no other European had visited this valley. I found it difficult to break away from my host, grateful though I was for his assistance and kindness. We were able to leave by mid-afternoon, when a new porter and some freshly milled maize flour had been made available, also a welcome gift of sixteen eggs. We had scarcely left behind the last maize field when I was beckoned imploringly by an old man from some distance away. He had cut his finger with a sickle ten days ago; when he removed a rag covering the wound I was revolted by the sight and the smell of a gangrenous finger swollen to twice its size. I could hardly tell the poor man, who was obviously in pain, that a surgeon's knife was the only cure. I dosed him with antibiotics, his profuse thanks heightening my feeling of helplessness.

In the evening we camped on a patch of tall grass one mile short of Mirshahi. To the south-west the plateau and its peaks filled the view, much closer now but still elusive and full of mystery. Would we be able to find an approach from this direction? My first real clue was given by a white-bearded man in flowing robes who walked by our camp the following dawn. With great dignity he offered me not only the hospitality of his village near Mirshahi, but also his company on my journey to the Siri Dara mountains; for that was the name of my objective, gleaming there in the sunlight. We parted after he had extracted my promise that I would call upon his assistance if it were needed. At noon we arrived at a village containing meagre patches of cultivation surrounded by a dozen huts; its name was Siri Dara. Below it, a crude bridge led across a torrent that joined the main stream from the west. I decided to enter this valley, still nagged by doubt; until, rounding a corner, I glimpsed the edge of an icefall and above it a rock feature that had stood out prominently in the view from our last camp. I was certain now that we were heading in the right direction.

There was a fair track, and for the first few miles we climbed through forests of oak, walnut and juniper scrub; then we were confined in a gorge, where all evidence of the icefall was obscured behind the winding walls of the valley. By late afternoon we reached a small opening containing scattered cornfields and a handful of crude huts. We camped on a meadow at 8,000 feet where a small boy presented welcome gifts of grapes and spinach. In the evening three descending Kandiawals passed by, claiming that they had left Kalam the day before. I made a mental note of their easy short-cut for our return journey. In a misty drizzle we continued our ascent the next day, passing two summer settlements which were occupied by groups of shepherds. From time to time there were brief glimpses of the icefall. Beyond the highest settlement, where a striking archway of ice overhung a fall in the river, the valley began to steepen sharply.

We began a long climb, zigzagging up diminishing pinewoods until we emerged above the trees when a ladder, with crude footholds hewn in a pine log thirty feet tall, led us up a rock cliff out on to an exposed spur. It was a thrilling moment. We turned a corner and suddenly a wide vista was spread out before us. An icefall, not less than three miles wide, stretched across the entire valley forming a barrier of cliffs and seracs poised 3,500 feet above the glacier floor which consisted of a broad stretch of dark-coloured moraine streaked with the silver of small streams. From our outlook it was not possible to see what lay beyond this barrier; but a single peak stood out above the centre of the icefall draped with snowslopes that led invitingly up to twin rocky summits. One could only guess at the opportunities that this unsuspected plateau would provide, for my view from the Paloga pass had revealed the presence of at least half a dozen mountains. The porters were unable to share my excitement. Instead, casting about in the desolate waste of boulders and stones below they searched in vain for the grassy meadows upon which the cheerful Kandiawals had promised them they would be able to camp. A steep descent followed, and a rough journey across the moraine; if the Kandiawals had cairned a route, we were unable to find it. About a mile below the glacier snout, on a bouldery plain devoid of grass or scrub, we pitched our tents. I felt like Moses when he led the children of Israel into the wilderness. But neither the murmurings of the porters, nor the overcast weather could dampen my joy over having arrived.

It was a magnificent prospect and the scale seemed unexpectedly large. From this camp at 10,500 feet I would be amply satisfied if I could reach the plateau and climb one of its peaks. The icefall, from which avalanches were discharging regularly, bore signs of recent retreat. It seemed clear that its true right or eastern edge was steep and threatened by avalanches from a subsidiary hanging glacier. It did not appear possible to find a safe passage through any part of its central section. The only hopeful approach seemed to be from the western side where slopes of grass and rock should provide a relatively easy climb to the upper edge of the ice.

I had some difficulty in finding volunteers to accompany me the next day. Rahimatulla the strongest porter, complained of backache;

15. Falak Ser from the upper Falak Ser glacier showing the north-east spur on the lower sky-line, leading to the north ridge and the summit (19 August 1962)

16. Our first view of the Siri Dara icefall showing the upper part of Central peak (30 August 1962)

17. The eastern end of the Siri Dara plateau showing the 'Breithorn' (2 September 1962)

Sobhan, the third and least venturous of my armed escorts, thought that he had better guard the camp. I set out with the youngest of my group of four men, a trusty and surefooted lad of seventeen. We skirted the glacier snout, a sixty-foot high cavern echoing the almost noiseless waters of a stream; then we struck upwards over moraine scattered with yellow ragwort and purple river-beauty. Within four and a half hours we reached a point where no more than a 500-foot ice-slope seemed to separate us from the plateau. Near the foot of the ice-slope we located a good campsite on a level patch of scree. We returned the following day, setting up a tent there at just under 14,000 feet. Rahima-tulla stayed with me at this camp while two other porters descended.

It was my intention to reach the plateau early the next morning and climb the central peak, whose lower slopes seemed barely one mile away. From this peak I expected to be able to study the whole area, and to try to relate the plateau and its peaks to the few summits whose height and position had been fixed on existing maps. Reconnoitring that afternoon I cramponed about half way up the ice slope ahead of our camp but was stopped by an insurmountable ice-wall. So at dawn the next day Rahimatulla and I moved off instead towards the left. This turned out to be a major error. Very soon afterwards we found ourselves involved in a labyrinth of seracs and crevasses. For over two hours we struggled to find a way through this unstable and threatened zone. We tried three lines of approach, all of which led nowhere. It became increasingly clear that we were barking up the wrong tree. I was sure that the plateau was only a short way above, and we could see the lower slopes of Central peak which looked tantalisingly close. It was frustrating to have to retreat, especially because retreat meant failure; there was simply no time left for a detailed study of the problem.

Utterly dejected I packed the tent, instructing the porter to descend; then I spent some hours examining the icefall for a possible line of weakness. The more I looked, the more I was convinced that we had been right to try from this west side. Two days later, when I stood on the watershed ridge that divides Swat from Kandia, the solution seemed obvious; had we traversed to the right of our camp a passage would have been found to the western edge of the plateau, free from difficulty or danger. Apart from Central peak, two other peaks appeared to dominate the cirque of mountains rising from the plateau. One of them provided a steep rock curtain enclosing its west side; the other situated near the eastern boundary of the plateau resembled the Zermatt Breit-horn. In between were half-a-dozen smaller peaks. I committed the common error of over-estimating the height of these peaks, considering the highest to be about 20,000 feet, taking the upper level of the plateau to be 15,500 feet. I was guilty of an error of the order of 1,500 feet.[8]

On 4 September we began our return journey. The porters denied any knowledge about the Kandiawals' short-cut, and my suggestion that we should make an early start in order to reach Kalam by nightfall was greeted by them with derision. Surely I was not ready to believe the claim of the Kandiawals? We climbed out of the Siri Dara valley towards the west, ascending steep slopes which became increasingly rocky, until the path was often no more than scratches between boulders. Six hours of ascent brought us to a crest dividing Kandia from Swat; from there we looked down into a small glacier flowing west. We were standing on the Sho Dara* (14,500 ft); the Sho *nala*, fed by three subsidiary glaciers, joins the Ushu river about one mile above Kalam. An hour later, having descended about 1,000 feet over steep snow and moraine, we reached an unexpected meadow where we camped. Rock slabs and boulders in the neighbourhood bore distinct signs of old glaciation. To the south was a group of peaks and two small glaciers; north of us were two peaks, the lower of which attracted me as a suitable outlook point. The porters including Sobhan, for once devoid of his humorous pranks, appeared to be in the dumps. I could not tell whether they had really had enough as they claimed; or whether, with the end in sight, their spirits had deflated. At any rate, two of them went supperless to sleep.

As there were no eager faces ready to join me on the climb the following morning I set out alone at 6.30 a.m. Ascending a glacier I was startled by a sudden crack, and noticed a split in the ice under my feet. Since the crevasses were mostly concealed I had to keep my senses sharply alerted. Above the glacier was a long south-facing slope; it was of well-compacted névé, and I was able to make rapid progress reaching the top of the peak in three hours. This summit, about 16,500 feet, is a high point on the ridge that falls to the Sho Dara dividing the Siri Dara and Sho valleys. It gave me just the perspective I needed to complete my picture of the Siri Dara plateau, most of which was now visible, including the lower valley through which I had approached the area. It seemed fascinating to inquire how far the plateau extended to the east; whether it fell away steeply on that side, and what lay beyond. I thought of Mills' elusive mountain and the high peak of the Survey of Pakistan, wondering whether both their observations had been made towards this direction. After half an hour on the top I noticed that

* Dara = Pass.

clouds were gathering; by the time I was back in camp at 11 o'clock the weather had closed in.

The porters started the descent at once in the gathering mist; I followed later with Sobhan. We had hoped to make Kalam that evening, but it was a long descent down the moraine, and towards dusk we found ourselves still on the edge of the tree-line. We camped on a patch of grass beside a birchwood. The men attempted to make up for their poor performance on the march by putting on a farewell entertainment around the campfire; it was impossible to be displeased with them. After an enchanting descent through forests, meadows and ripening maize fields, we reached Kalam by noon the next day.

I visited Swat again three years later. During a winter weekend we drove our Land-Rover just beyond Bahrain. Then we walked six miles to a forest hut at 9,000 feet, struggling through knee-deep snow for the last two miles, and shovelling away a four-foot drift before we could enter the hut. Later we visited Changla where Pakistan army engineers had recently commenced work on the new road to Gilgit. From a rest-house perched on the crest of the Changla ridge I had my first view of the Kaghan mountains, a long line of peaks dominated by one large and shapely mountain with which I later made a close acquaintance.

There have been many changes in the Swat valley since my first visit. The region has since become an integral part of Pakistan, and Saidu Sharif is no longer a quiet isolated capital of state. A scheme to build a ski resort, sponsored by the Austrian government when Fritz Kolb represented his country as ambassador in Pakistan, has foundered in the vast shallows of bureaucratic inertia and indifference; although, ostensibly, there is a desire to attract tourists to the area. Some mountaineering parties have been allowed to travel through Swat to Northern Kohistan and the mountains that lie south of the Hindu Raj; but in recent years applications to visit these areas, though far removed from strategic frontiers, have been refused. The main road to Kalam, which was often blocked in winter, has been widened and improved. Kalam itself has entirely altered in character. The peaceful uncrowded plain on which stood two timbered chalets and a fort is now filled with an array of tourist rest-houses and ancillary buildings, attracting crowds of visitors in their cars each summer; the more enterprising can venture in their vehicles through the magnificent cedar forest to Matiltan and Paloga. Although the highest peaks in Swat have been climbed, scores of unclimbed mountains await the climber and explorer in Kohistan.

VIII
Nepal

Mais les vrais voyageurs sont ceux-là seuls qui partent
Pour partir, coeurs légers, semblable aux ballons,
De leur fatalité jamais ils ne s'écartent,
Et, sans savoir pourquoi disent toujours; 'Allons'.

Baudelaire, 'Le Voyage'

The first Europeans to enter Nepal were probably the Jesuit fathers Johann Grueber and Albert d'Orville on their journey overland from China to India. Leaving Peking in April 1661 they travelled via Lhasa to Katmandu reaching India in March 1662. In 1767, in response to an appeal from the Raja of Nepal, a small expedition under Captain Kinloch brought back sketches of the country's southern border. The country was then nearing the end of a twenty years' war waged between the leader of the small state of Gurkha, one of twenty-four hill states known as *Chaubisia Raj*,* and the Newar Kings for the possession of Nepal. In 1769 the Gurkha leader, Prithvi Narayan Shah, finally triumphed, establishing control of the whole kingdom. The Gurkhas later carried out several armed expeditions in an effort to extend their dominion north into Tibet. In 1792 they had to acknowledge ultimate defeat against an army of mixed Tibetans and Chinese. They had also spread their influence as far west as the borders of Chamba and the Punjab and east towards Sikkim, but were halted by British and Indian forces. During the Gurkha war of 1814–16 they were eventually pushed back from the areas of Garhwal and Kumaon to their present territory east of the Kali river.[1]

Various unofficial surveys of the country were carried out by British officers between 1801 and 1804; also during the Gurkha war. But it was not until 1873 that more detailed survey could be done. In that year,

* *Chaubis* = Twenty-four.

Hari Ram, one of the *pundit* explorers of the Survey of India, crossed the Bheri valley south of Jumla, and following the Barbung Khola, crossed north-east of Mukut Himal. He also visited Muktinath and crossed the Kali Gandaki; in the northern reaches of this valley, near Mustang, ammonite fossils were found. Until 1950 no European had passed along the valley of the Kali Gandaki; indeed, with very few exceptions, the mountains of Nepal were closed to outsiders. In 1924 the Prime Minister of Nepal approached the Survey of India for their co-operation in carrying out a survey of the country with the object of preparing maps. Field-work, which occupied three years and covered 55,000 square miles, included practically the whole of the country except for three gaps; sixty square miles north of Manang Bhot in Central Nepal; an area by Rasua Garhi on the Tibetan border; and 150 square miles north of Jagdula Lekh in west Nepal. The survey was carried out by Indian officers of the Survey Department with the assistance of the Nepalese army.

With the presence of twenty-five mountains over 25,000 feet, two of them over 28,000 feet and three over 27,000 feet, Nepal contains the greatest concentration of high peaks throughout the Himalayan range. The trenches carved by three main rivers which break through the crest zones, subdivide the Nepal Himalaya roughly into three sections. In the east from the Sikkim border to the Langtang is the Kosi, containing Kangchenjunga, Everest, Makalu and Cho Oyu; with the Arun gorge separating the massifs of Makalu and Kangchenjunga. The Po Chu which flows on the north side of the range draining a large area in Tibet becomes the Sun Kosi. The Gandaki with its various tributaries, Kali, Seti, Buri, Trisuli, comprises the central section which contains the Ganesh, Himalchuli, Manaslu and Annapurna ranges. The western section, Karnali, forms a trough between two crest-zones containing the Dhaulagiri massif in the east with the Saipal, Api and Nampa groups in the west. Situated in the middle of this section were the unsurveyed ranges north of the Jagdula Lekh, which included Kanjiroba Himal. The most easterly of the three main sections contains the largest peaks and a gradually diminishing trend is apparent towards the west where the Nepal Himalaya merges into the Indian ranges of Garhwal. In the mid-1950s surveys were carried out in order to reassess the height of Mount Everest and other major peaks. The height corrections made were only minor, testifying to the accuracy of the observations made over one hundred years before from distant stations in India. More recently maps of several of the main mountain groups have been extended and corrected, with official approval, as a result of work carried out by various private expeditions.[2]

Probably the first expedition to receive permission to visit the Nepal Himalaya was H. W. Tilman's party in 1949. So little was known about the country that this, as well as Tilman's second venture in 1950, was concerned more with orientation and exploration of some of the main groups than with specific climbing objectives. In the wake of the French Annapurna ascent in 1950 permission was granted to explore the south side of Everest. The Everest Reconnaissance Expedition of 1951 opened up a completely new phase for mountaineering in Nepal. But the spate of expeditions that followed almost came to a halt when the initial liberal attitude of the Nepalese government encouraged an unfortunate lack of courtesy by some who trespassed over the borders into Tibet. In their embarrassment it seemed for a while that the Nepalese authorities would resume their policy of isolation and would ban all further mountaineering expeditions. At present Nepal welcomes tourists. Royalties are imposed on climbing expeditions, and there is an insistence upon the attachment of liaison officers seconded from their army or police force. This is a logical precaution; though unfortunately it is sometimes defeated when the persons chosen fall short of the requirements and are unable to provide effective assistance or control in the field.

Insistence also that Sherpas should be recruited only from Nepal created anomalies at first with many of the experienced Sherpas then permanently settled in Darjeeling. Of course the result of this has been a gradual shift of the Sherpa population back to their homes in Nepal, with Darjeeling no longer the focal point for their recruitment. A good deal has been said about Sherpas and they have justly earned so much praise that the fact that there are, as in every community, good and bad among them often tends to be overlooked. When I made my first acquaintance with them, outstanding men like Tenzing, Angtharkay, and Pasang Dawa stood head and shoulders above the rest as leaders in their community. Apart from these there were many men who had an excellent record. But the community was by and large backward, lacking both training and security of employment. The pattern has changed very rapidly over the years commencing after 1953 with the setting up of the Himalayan Mountaineering Institute in Darjeeling. There the best among them are given opportunities to develop their technique and to qualify as guides and instructors. Increasing demand for their services has given birth to a new breed of Sherpas, more competent and much more conscious of their rights and privileges. If the old undemanding loyalty to the employer appears to have dimmed the reasons can sometimes be found in the changing attitudes of the employers themselves. Very few of them, I suppose, have really tried to understand the Sherpas. Bred in high mountains they are among the world's natural climbers; and the skill and experience which many of them have acquired qualifies them to lead on difficult climbs. Lately there has been a regrettable tendency to use them as beasts of burden on routes involving advanced modern techniques. When their respect has been won, and they have been given a confident lead under the most demanding conditions, only then will all their fine qualities rise to the surface.

In 1961 John Tyson spent three months exploring and mapping in one of the few untouched areas left, north of the Jagdula Lekh in West Nepal. His party of three set up survey points in the Jagdula valley and areas to its south and west where they plotted and triangulated mountains of the unknown Kanjiroba Himal whose highest peaks exceed 22,500 feet. In 1958 and 1959 unsuccessful attempts had been made to approach the Kanjiroba massif from the east by Japanese and American parties. Tyson's party who attempted to do so from the south via the Jagdula Khola was frustrated by a difficult and lengthy gorge. Tyson planned a second expedition to the area in 1964. A later start was proposed in order to ensure clear post-monsoon weather for survey work. The plan included an attempt to reach the Kanjiroba mountains from the south, above the section of the Jagdula gorge which had been found impassable in 1961; and an alternative approach was also tried from the north, via the Langu valley.

John Tyson, then geography master at Rugby School, was good enough to invite me to join him. His party included James Burnet, who had been with him in 1961, besides two younger climbers, Dr Bob Kendell and John Cole who had recently been members of an expedition to the Peruvian Andes. Since the expedition was scheduled to last well over three months I could give only a qualified acceptance to Tyson's invitation, because the maximum period of leave I could obtain was for two months. In order to reach the Kanjiroba region a long approach was involved and it occurred to me that almost two-thirds of my time would be spent on the journey there and back. But it seemed a good opportunity to learn something about a fairly large section of West Nepal, and possibly to glimpse at unexplored mountains.

In Delhi on 15 August Tyson received the disquieting news that our expedition's permit was likely to be withdrawn. It was feared that the

KUMAON & GARHWAL

Gurla Mandhata

Talakot
Lipu Lekh Pass
Garbyang
Api
Nampa
Saipal
Simkot

Humla R.

Seti R.

Silgarh

Karnali R.

Mugu R.

Dalphu
Jumla
Kaigaon

KANJIROBA HIMAL
Langu R.

Jagdula
Charkabhot

Dailekh
Hiunchuli
Patan

Jajarkot

Thuli R.

DHAULA GIRI
IV III I
II Tukuche

Mustang

Jomossom

Muktinath

ANNAPURNA HIMAL

Gogra R.

Bheri R.

Sallyana

Tatopani

Macha
Puchare
Pokhara

Baglung

Kali Gandaki

Marsiandi

Seti Gandaki

Great Gandaki

Rapti

T
I
B
E
T

N

MAP II

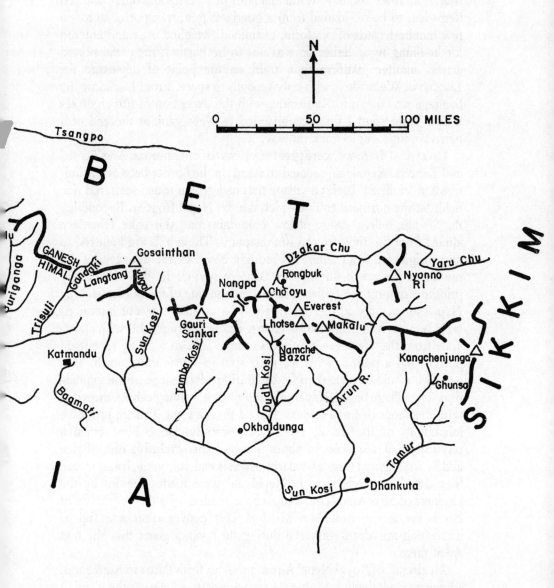

Nepal Himalaya

N

0   50   100 MILES

Tsangpo

B E T

Juriganga

GANESH
HIMAL.

Gandaki

Langtang

Trisuli

Gosainthan

Jugal

Sun Kosi

Gauri
Sankar

Nangpa
La

Cho oyu

Rongbuk

Dzakar Chu

Yaru Chu

Nyonno
Ri

Everest

Lhotse

Makalu

Tamba Kosi

Dudh Kosi

Namche
Bazar

Arun R.

Kangchenjunga

Ghunsa

Katmandu

Bagmati

Okhaldunga

Sun Kosi

Tamur

Dhankuta

I A

S I K K I M

Nepalese authorities might impose a ban following their embarrassment over a recent trespass across the border into Tibet. John Tyson departed the next day for Katmandu to sort out this problem with the assistance of Colonel Charles Wylie who was then Military attaché at the British Embassy. James Burnet arrived with the expedition's baggage on the Mail train from Bombay. Within an hour fifty crates and other assorted items had to be off-loaded from a goods wagon, transported across a few hundred yards of platform, examined, weighed over and entered for booking by a clerk who was not to be hustled; then transported across another platform to a train on the point of departure for Lucknow. We made it with only seconds to spare. From Lucknow the baggage was flown to Katmandu, with the exception of fifteen crates which Burnet and I first accompanied to Nepalganj, at the end of a narrow gauge single-track railway.

On arrival there we were greeted by two of our Sherpas, Ang Temba and Kancha. Nepalganj seemed to stand on the border between primitive and 'civilised' India; a village that had grown round scattered rice fields, at the northern end of which ran the Nepal frontier. Beyond lay the Siwalik hills, a range of low mountains that skirts the Himalaya almost from the Indus to the Brahmaputra. These hills are believed to have originated from sediments brought down by the upheaval of the ranges to the north during the Tertiary period. In this attractively primitive outpost the Indian customs on one side of the border and the Nepalese customs on the other had to be satisfied that our intentions were honest. Ang Temba took charge of the baggage, and with assistance from the Nepalese officials we were able to arrange seventeen porters and a police escort for their sixteen-day journey north. This baggage would be picked up for use during a later stage of the expedition. The village on the Nepal side was quite a thriving centre, crowded with the shops of small traders. Here I first saw the Tharus, primitive inhabitants of the Terai; their black scantily-clad bodies reveal a physical weakness brought about by an almost exclusive diet of rice and by a malignant form of malaria which is endemic in the tracts where they dwell. Our two days in Nepalganj were made pleasant by the kindness of Miss Anna Tomaseck who extended to us the hospitality of her home at the American Mission. Her conversation was full of interesting anecdotes gathered during the twenty years that she had spent there.

An aircraft of Royal Nepal Airlines took us from Patna to Katmandu. Flying at a relatively low altitude we were very soon over the Terai, a dense purple carpet starting abruptly from the plain and merging into the lower hills; until suddenly visible ahead was the vale of Katmandu; an incredibly green and fertile plain, which was once a lake, encircled by hills. On 21 August our Sherpas joined us there. Kancha, the youngest, had accompanied us from Nepalganj. The others were Mingma Tsering, who had been with Tyson before; and Dannu whom Jean Franco had praised on the French expeditions to Makalu and Jannu. There were also two less experienced and younger men, Phutare and Ang Dorje. The liaison officer attached to our expedition was a smart and well-mannered police officer, brother-in-law of Katmandu's chief of police. He was on the whole a useful member of the party.

Katmandu seemed to embody an extraordinary mixture of Hindu and Buddhist influences, with temples and monasteries existing happily side by side, each ethnic and religious group retaining its separate culture and identity. Little more than a decade had passed since the revolution which had toppled more than a hundred years of autocratic rule by the Rana family as hereditary Prime Ministers, restoring power to the King who now rules the country heading a council of ministers. The city is full of palaces of the former Ranas, immense stately buildings some of which have been converted into government offices or hotels. We visited the Buddhist temple of Bodhnath whose stupa is topped by two all-seeing eyes which, for 1,000 years, have gazed out towards all four points of the compass; also the Hindu temple of Pashupati Nath where kings and sages are cremated. Katmandu, even then, possessed a large floating population of travellers and visitors from Europe. For many years tourists have provided an increasing flow of revenue to the Nepal government. Their Department of Tourism now publishes various colour brochures on the tourist delights of the country. A trek to the Everest Base Camp contains a route-map showing a 'trial' [*sic*] which can be followed all the way to the summit of the mountain.[3] Charles Wylie, our host, was immensely helpful to us with his intimate knowledge of the country and people.

On 23 August John Tyson and I flew to Pokhara; the others followed two days later. During the flight there was a brief view of peaks through monsoon clouds, and we touched down forty minutes later on a quiet meadow from which cattle had to be cleared. Beyond a foreground of huts and rice fields there was a view of the Annapurna range, dominated by the striking peak of Machapuchare. It was interesting to see the cheerful and healthy faces of the Nepalese in their homes. If they seemed less prosperous they were certainly less sophisticated than those who had emigrated to places like Darjeeling. I soon began to distinguish differences between the tribes, each speaking their own dialect. The Tamangs of the lower valleys, the Chettris from whom most of the Gurkha soldiers are drawn, the Gurungs of Central Nepal and the Newars of the upper and trading classes. The people of the north, dwelling under more rugged conditions, belong ethnologically to the Tibetan region.

We began our outward march on 26 August, our caravan comprising thirty coolies. The three Sherpas walked like sahibs, the only difference being that they were better dressed than we were and carried less; a decade had gone by since I had travelled with Sherpas, and this was a revelation to me. Beyond Pokhara village, we reached an open plain where the Mission Hospital stands. It was staffed at the time by fourteen British doctors and nurses and was an asset to the region. An inconvenience commonly accepted when travelling through western and central Nepal is the need to change coolies at every main village, the local inhabitants jealously guarding the rights to their own immediate area. We were relieved therefore to have made an arrangement whereby our Pokhara coolies undertook the eight-day march to Tukuche for a consolidated wage. For the first two days at altitudes below 4,000 feet we walked through the upper Terai belt, rendered excessively humid by flooded rice fields. The next three stages gave us an experience of monsoon conditions in the tropical rain-forest. I did not mind the gloom, occasionally lit by flashes of colour from some exotic plant, nor even the heavy and persistent rainfall; but one felt defenceless against the mass assault of leeches. I think that the morale of the expedition reached its nadir one evening in the pouring rain when, wet and hungry, five of us bedded down on the verandah of a squalid hut, having lost sight not only of the coolies but also of the Sherpas.

At the small village of Sikha in West Nawakot we accepted an invitation from a soldier on leave from a British regiment stationed in Hong Kong to attend a party at his home; the occasion was a celebration of the lord Krishna's birthday. From early in the evening until long after midnight an entertainment of folk-singing and dancing was provided by half-a-dozen young girls, some of whom performed with great skill and charm. After we had drunk the first few cupfuls of home-brewed *rakshi* (rice-beer) we had to be careful to avoid draining our cups, whereupon they were immediately refilled. When we got up to leave, our host, a suave youth in the daytime, was too far gone to usher us out.

After passing the hot spring at Tatopani, where we bathed, we crossed the Kali Gandaki over a suspension bridge and climbed up towards Lete. We had entered a different zone; the country seemed more rugged with black cliffs rising on either side, spectacular waterfalls, and the river now a rushing torrent. It was not difficult to visualise that we were passing between the two great massifs of Annapurna and Dhaulagiri, whose highest summits rose 18,000 feet above us. We met a party of Tibetans from the south-eastern province of Khamba working on the road. The Khambas had a reputation as warriors and armed brigands; large numbers of them resisted the Chinese armies which occupied Tibet after 1950. For several years they kept up armed skirmishes and later many of them escaped across the borders to Nepal and India. The group we met had left their homes many years before and were now employed on a semi-permanent basis by the Nepalese Government.

On the eighth day, as our porters had promised, we reached Tukuche; the approach had been along gravel flats with the Kali Gandaki moving swiftly through broad channels. Two days were spent waiting here for transport, whilst we investigated this large and curiously Tibetan village. It used to be an important centre on the Tibetan trade-route over the passes from Mustangbhot; but little was left of its traditional trade and the wide stone-paved streets looked deserted. The monastery, about 200 years old, appeared to be well looked after although we saw few permanent monks; from it there is a view of Tukuche peak, situated on the edge of the Dhaulagiri massif.

With a caravan of fourteen dzos we left Tukuche on 5 September. Crossbred from yaks and cows, dzos are used as pack-animals at altitudes from 8,500 feet to 13,000 feet. They are less intractable than yaks, and are capable of quite heavy work. At Jomossom the trade-route leads north to Mustangbhot. Hospitably though we were received here for a baggage-check at the Nepalese army post, our rifle and ammunition were withheld because we did not possess a permit which we learnt for the first time we needed to produce. A Sikh soldier operating the wireless line to Katmandu was unable to get an intelligible message through, so we had to forego the rifle, a brand-new one; and the prospect of fresh meat supplies. From this village there was a striking view of Nilgiri Peak (23,452 ft), highest of a group situated north-west of Annapurna. We now turned west across green uplands and rolling hills on the edge of the rain-shadow; and after two stages we crossed the first of a series of high passes that took us north of Mukut Himal and into the Barbung Kola towards Charkabhot. On 9 September from a camp situated near an unnamed peak of about 21,500 feet, we crossed the Khog La (16,300 ft) in heavy fog, meeting a group of armed Khambas dressed seemingly in Chinese army uniforms. One could not help wondering what they were about; and under whose authority. We learned later that parties of Tibetans occasionally strayed across the border, indulging in armed plunder. Perhaps our caravan was luckier than we realised, to have escaped from one of their raids. Later the same day we crossed the Thije La (17,300 ft), the approach to which was steep. We were thankful for an easier descent on the other side to a meadow at 16,000 feet, where we camped.

Charkabhot village, a huddle of buildings perched on a domed hill at 13,500 feet, possessed all the characteristics of a Tibetan settlement: the sights and the smells; the archaic way of life belonging to a former era; and the curious inhabitants who invaded our campsite. This was a relatively prosperous village surrounded by ripening fields of buckwheat and barley. A fortnight's walking had brought us about half way to our destination. Here we paid off our dzos, and arrangements had to be made for yak transport. The yak with its bushy coat and heavy stature really comes into its own above 13,000 feet. It is an inspiring sight to watch these powerful animals, who can carry up to 250 pounds, steadily ploughing a track through knee-deep snow above 18,000 feet, oblivious to weather conditions. It is interesting to watch yak drivers, woollen homespun wrapped around their sturdy bodies, setting about loading a reluctant beast. With one man stationed on each side of the animal it is a battle as much of wits as of strength, which the yak often wins.

From Charkabhot we crossed the Charka La (17,000 ft), and for the next six days our tracks, heading westwards, led across the scantily-populated villages of this northern region. If the landscape bore little geographical resemblance to the southerly regions of Nepal it differed also, with its rocky and often verdant character, from Tibet. I found the journey through this country full of interest. The inhabitants, though obviously unaccustomed to seeing frequent passers-by, seemed so pre-occupied with their seasonal tasks of harvesting and collecting winter fuel, that they took only a mild interest in us. I recall at least one idyllic camp, situated at 14,150 feet on a thick carpet of grass, with a small stream issuing from a glacier, and an unexplored group of 20,000-foot peaks filling the head of the valley; an ideal base for small climbs. Our

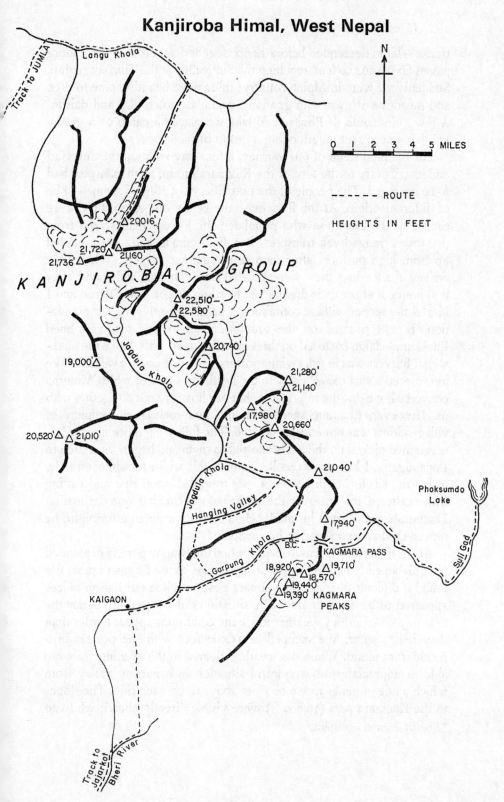

Kanjiroba Himal, West Nepal

N

Track to JUMLA

Langu Khola

0 1 2 3 4 5 MILES

- - - - - ROUTE

HEIGHTS IN FEET

△ 20,016

△ 21,720 △ 21,160'

21,736' △

K A N J I R O B A   G R O U P

△ 22,510'
△ 22,580'

△ 20,740'

19,000 △

Jagdula Khola

△ 21,280'
△ 21,140'

△ 17,980' △ 20,660'

20,520' △ △ 21,010'

Jagdula Khola

△ 21,040'

Phoksumdo
Lake

Hanging Valley

△ 17,940'

Garpung Khola

B.C.

KAGMARA PASS

Suli Gad

18,920' △ △ 19,710'
△ 18,570'
△ 19,440'

KAIGAON

△ 19,390' KAGMARA
PEAKS

Track to Jajarkot

Bheri River

MAP 12

tracks seldom descended below 14,000 feet and we crossed three more passes above 16,000 feet, reaching the Suli valley in the Tibrikot region. Suddenly we were in Alpine country; there were beautiful pine forests, and meadows strewn with gentians, primulas, potentillas and daisies. A few miles south of Phoksumdo lake we placed a camp on a grassy knoll at 12,000 feet, overlooking a group of snow peaks.

For the final stage of our journey, a four-day walk up the Suli Gad and its tributary to the foot of the Kagmara group, fresh transport had to be arranged. The people of the two villages of Ringmi seemed to be of different origin. At the first, one mile below our camp, they were similar to the Nepalese who populated the lower villages; and from them we arranged yak transport. But their animals had to be rounded up from high pastures after months of summer grazing. When they arrived for loading they were spirited and unmanageable; and after two hours of effort their drivers had to admit defeat. John Tyson and I visited the second village containing a predominantly Tibetan population. It was situated on the southern shore of the turquoise-hued Phoksumdo lake, enclosed on three sides by steep cliffs. Since the buckwheat harvest was in full swing, porters were not easily available. We interrupted a vast *chang** party in the headman's house; whilst Mingma conversed, we got the impression that our host was not altogether with us. However, the time spent with the semi-inebriated company of village elders was not entirely wasted. The following morning twenty-seven men picked up the loads allotted to them and began the march to Pudamigaon. I have two recollections of this walk; for almost a mile, under the shade of apricot trees, we trampled upon ripe and rotting fruit scattered thickly over the path; before reaching our destination Dannu Sherpa twisted his ankle. Henceforth, for about a fortnight, he represented an extra load to be carried.

At our next camp a dispute began when the Ringmi porters demanded not only an early halt but an extra day's wage to the Kagmara pass. We found it difficult to adopt an adamant posture when our liaison officer appeared to be on their side. The situation did not get any better the next day when snowy weather made the conditions appear harder than they really were. We camped at 15,500 feet with the porters in a recalcitrant mood. When the weather cleared in the evening we were able to appreciate our wonderful situation in a narrow valley from which a line of peaks rose 2,000 feet above us on each side. The slopes to the Kagmara pass (16,860 ft) were visible directly ahead; whilst to

* Locally brewed rice-spirit.

18. Prayer wheels and prayer flag at Tukuche; Nilgiri Peaks behind (4 September 1964)

19. Loading a yak at Charkabhot (13 September 1964)

the left were some of the peaks of the Kagmara group, rising to over 19,000 feet.

The next morning there was heavy mist following a night of snow-fall. The porters were slow in starting; it was intended that they would continue over the pass and down to a suitable camping place on the other side. The top of the pass was a broad snow saddle which we reached in about one and a half hours. While we waited there for an hour heavy cloud gathered and snow began to fall. On their arrival the porters downed loads and demanded payment for four days' work, although the fourth day had just begun. Aware that they were in a strong position to press their point they refused to budge until the money was handed over; then they carried our loads to a shelf about 750 feet down on the other side where we camped, relieved to see the last of them. The next two days were spent by us relaying loads with the aid of one available Sherpa to a camp-site at 13,500 feet in the Garpung Khola. It was decided from this camp to split the party into groups for survey and exploration.

We were situated at the foot of the Kagmara Lekh, comprising a line of peaks eight miles long. Lha Shamma (21,040 ft), which had been climbed in 1962, faced us to the north. A ridge running south from that mountain formed the eastern containing wall of the lower Jagdula gorge. It was our intention to cross this ridge in order to gain the upper section of the gorge and to look for a way from there to the foot of the Kanjiroba mountains. Bob Kendell, James Burnet and I carried out this operation. John Tyson and John Cole set up a number of survey stations on the Kagmara ridge taking observations to the north and north-west. Both groups set out on 27 September. But before we were able to do so, a serious disagreement arose with the Sherpas. I found myself quite out of sympathy with their demands, which were for brand-new wind-proof and down jackets and sleeping bags in place of the used ones which they had received; also with the manner in which the demands were made. In my estimation this incident lowered them to the level of the porters on the Kagmara pass, because they were apparently pre-pared to leave us and go home if their demands were not met. That they did not do so is a tribute to the good sense which prevailed in the end. I think it is doubtful whether this incident would have arisen at all if the *sirdar* Ang Temba, who was then escorting the advance baggage, had been present.

Our party of four, which included Kancha Sherpa, crossed the dividing ridge at 17,000 feet over the southern shoulder of Lha Shamma peak. Three days spent exploring a valley to the north-west brought us to the confluence of the Jagdula gorge over a route that seemed mostly unsuitable for a laden party, and too far extended from any possible base. This approach looked a forlorn hope; especially as we could see from our furthest point that the highest Kanjiroba peaks were still over ten miles away. Disappointment over this abortive venture did not diminish in any way the excitement of entering a basin containing a large hanging glacier and two peaks over 21,000 feet. A perfect base camp site could be found here, with unlimited scope for exploration in every direction; possibly even an unsuspected exit to the upper Jagdula gorge and the unvisited southern side of Kanjiroba.

Bob Kendell returned with Kancha by the same route; but James Burnet and I diverted down a valley to the south called by Tyson in 1961 the Hanging valley. Our object was to find an easier and perhaps shorter route back, and we carried food sufficient for two days. After placing our first camp amidst azalea scrub at 14,500 feet we ran into serious trouble. The lower part of the west side of the Jagdula gorge contains a track, and about seven miles above its junction with the Garpung Khola there is an alpine meadow on which Tyson's 1961 party had camped. On descending our 'hanging' valley we found ourselves on the east side of the Jagdula gorge, which comprises a wall falling steeply from 17,000 feet to the river at about 12,500 feet. This wall divides the Garpung and Jagdula valleys, and consists of cliffs, rock-gullies and dense belts of azalea, birch, and pine. During our five-day struggle through the gorge, we seldom gained more than one mile a day; and not once did we observe signs of former human passage. By the fourth day morale had fallen so low that we began seriously to doubt our ability to find a way out, knowing that to fight our way back would probably have been much more difficult. I think that our depressed spirits resulted from physical weakness, for we had virtually run out of food after the third day.

On the fifth morning our breakfast consisted of a dexedrine tablet each, which neither of us had ever taken before. It affected us in different ways, making James Burnet over-cautious, almost hesitant in his steps, and providing me with complete relief from the effects of hunger and thirst. That morning we climbed almost 1,000 feet to the crest of the ridge where we were granted an extensive view which included the Kanjiroba summits, the whole Kagmara range, and in the distance to the south the Dhaulagiri group and the striking-looking Hiunchuli Patan. To our immense relief we looked down into the

Garpung valley and saw the track that would take us back to Base. But it was a long descent, and an inky darkness overtook us when we were still three miles short of Base Camp. The next morning whilst James Burnet made his way there, I turned my weary steps three miles down the valley to recover my camera which I had left behind during a way-side halt the previous evening. Dehydrated and weakened by hunger, I found myself lightheaded and moving very slowly. Ang Temba met me with food and drink during the long struggle back, and we reached Base Camp in the afternoon.

The final stage, the search for a northern route to the Kanjiroba peaks, now began. John Tyson descended to Kaigaon on 8 October to make arrangements for transport. Marching from Maharigaon to Dalphu on 22 October the expedition entered the wild Langu country, a gorge in which three days' travel yielded six miles of progress. The Sherpas excelled themselves here, particularly with their skill in constructing bridges over the Langu stream. Striking south, a stage too early as it turned out, Cole, Kendell and Tyson climbed on 31 October a peak of 20,016 feet from which looking south-east they were able to identify the two highest summits of the Kanjiroba range (22,580 ft and 22,510 ft). These were six miles away and separated by a complicated system of high ridges and glaciers. John Tyson, accompanied by three young climbers, returned to the Kanjiroba in 1969.[4] As a result of survey carried out during the course of three expeditions John Tyson has filled large blanks in the map of the Kagmara, Jagdula and Kanjiroba, plotting and fixing the heights of all the main peaks in these ranges. I think it might be said that whilst the north side of the Kanjiroba range has now been thoroughly examined, the southern approach has not yet been traversed by man. The latter would undoubtedly be an interesting though difficult journey; and could provide the key to the ascent of the two highest summits.[5]

On 9 October I descended with Ang Dorji to Kaigaon. I was accommodated with John Tyson in a disused school-house situated in the shade of apricot and walnut trees. The village sparkled in the autumn sunshine; its entire population of 200 appeared to be harvesting corn in their fields, in which a profusion of wild amaranthus lent added colour. Tobacco and sun-hemp are amongst the crops grown on small patches in almost every settlement; the cultivation as well as consumption of the latter being without any restriction. Bidding farewell to John and Ang Temba, I started my return journey on 10 October. The 175-mile walk during twelve days took me through a great variety of the

Nepal landscape from passes, meadows, and pine forest to rice fields and terai at the foot of the hills. For almost one week I followed the valley of the Bheri river, in its higher reaches passing through narrow walls; and lower down through broad flats supporting fields and prosperous homesteads. Climbing through forests of walnut and pine resounding with cowbells and the steady rhythm of the woodcutter's axe, I reached the top of a 10,000-foot pass which formed a dividing ridge or Lekh. From there the colours were grey and brown to the north with shades of blue and green in the south; there was a view of the Hiunchuli group containing steep-sided peaks with spiry summits. The maize and rice harvests were being gathered everywhere; and *Dussera*, the highlight of the autumn festivals, was being celebrated.

We left the Bheri river below Jajarkot, turning south towards Sallyana and the plains. I had started my journey with two Kaigaon porters of mixed Tibetan descent, with ruddy complexions, and dressed in their woollen homespun. The porters at the end of my journey were the slim scantily-dressed dwellers of the lower hills, sallow-complexioned and nimble in their bare feet. There were changes in the men after every two days, sometimes even after a single stage. Under this system, the *mukhiar** of each village provides porters from a number of volunteers. For my small needs, very little delay or inconvenience resulted and I was able to acquire some familiarity with the varying inhabitants at different levels of the foothills as we descended. The Government have posted at each village a *panchayat*† development officer, whose job is community welfare work; these were mostly young men, some of whom were intelligent and dedicated workers. As I descended into a warmer atmosphere I had an increasing craving for fresh fruit, relishing the green bananas that I was offered; also the large jugfuls of yoghurt that were frequently produced.

For the two last stages I engaged a pony. The pony-boy, Puran Dhar, a lad of eighteen, appeared outside my tent door at 4 a.m. We loaded the animal by candle-light and walked for five and a half hours before halting for breakfast. The next morning, another early start provided one of the nicest walks of the whole journey. Misty starlight gradually merged into daybreak with a cloud sea stretching north, and a view from a 6,500-foot pass towards Dhaulagiri and the Annapurnas. That was our last pass; on the other side there was a view of the plains. The villages here were spotlessly clean; the cottages had whitewashed

* Village elder; literally, spokesman.
† Village council.

walls, thatched roofs and painted doors and windows; displaying cannas, marigold, cosmos and other blossoms. Within two hours we had left behind the last bouldery incline and were treading upon the level trough at the foot of the Himalayan range from which rises the Siwalik hills. It was a long and hot walk to Tarigaon airfield.

On arrival there I was taken in hand by the headman's son, the warmth of whose welcome was quite overwhelming. Travel-stained and about twelve pounds underweight I must have seemed in need of care. I was accepted at once into the village community and I had to be careful at times to conceal feelings of real embarrassment; for in a society that was innocent of any inhibitions it was naturally assumed that I had none. The following morning, declining with some reluctance an invitation to extend my stay, I boarded a Royal Nepal Airlines ferry service, finding myself the only passenger amid crates of village produce and other cargo. Flying low over the Terai, we landed thirty minutes later at Nepalganj.

IX

Chitral

*When the traveller leaves Badakhshan he goes 12 days' journey
east-north-east up a river valley . . . where there are towns and
homesteads peopled by a warlike race who worship Mahomet.
After these 12 days he reaches a country called Wakhan, of no
great size for it is 3 days' journey every way. The people . . .
speak a language of their own, and are doughty warriors. When
the traveller leaves this place he goes 3 days' journey towards the
north-east, through mountains all the time, climbing so high that
this is said to be the highest place in the world.*

Travels of Marco Polo, 1272

With the passage of the years I found my interests beginning to show an
increasing shift in emphasis. A decade ago any holiday spent in Europe
would have been regarded as wasted unless I had done some climbing
in the Swiss Alps. But with widening activities I found it possible now
to derive satisfaction and enjoyment from the mountains in different
ways. Physical achievement had never been of primary importance;
that was really no more than a desire to measure one's strength. I think
that I had reached a degree of self-knowledge where no further tests of
that sort were essential. Involvement with the mountain environment
in the widest sense had always had a greater appeal. Days spent alone
on the hills in all weathers were nearly always more rewarding than a
particular climb made with a party, irrespective of the extent of physical
effort. Cesare Maestri once said that he was compelled to invent new
methods for attacking mountains because no known mountaineering
problem could give him the satisfaction of achievement which he
needed. To me it seemed that an extension of this principle would
ridicule our relationship with the mountains, reducing mountaineering
to an exercise for exhibitionists. I could appreciate, though I could not
accept, that enjoyment of the mountains was impossible without the
stimulus of victory.

During a spell of leave in the summer of 1966 I was attracted by the idea of climbing a volcano. On Demavend, two of us bivouacked below the snowline on the north-east side; and in a high wind we climbed to a col on the east ridge searching for a new route. A week later I spent a night at the Italian Alpine Club hut situated at 2,900 metres on Etna. Before dawn I climbed to the crest to see a fantastic fireworks display from the north-east crater, and walked along the edge of the quiescent north-west crater with steam rising under my feet and half-choked by sulphurous fumes. As the sun rose the tall shadow of Etna stretched across an unruffled sea forming a perfectly shaped pyramid at the apex of which I was standing. Later I saw Stromboli, a dark shadow from the ferry-boat, during a night-crossing from Palermo to Naples; there was no more than a delicate orange glow from its cone. Then I visited Pompeii, situated under the shadow of the almost extinct Vesuvius. Walking between the wrecked pillars of the Roman forum, I could not help recalling the day of wrath when the forces sweeping down those eroded slopes engulfed an advanced and complacent civilisation.

Meeting Sally and Michael Westmacott in England after an interval of three years I found them full of their recent climbing exploits, and I began to feel rather out of the swim. Before I had gone out to Pakistan there had been serious talk of our organising an expedition to the Karakoram. Various reasons had brought about what we hoped was only a postponement. The idea, stored for many years, was now revived. Entry restrictions seemed to be one of the main obstacles. I knew that there was little hope of permission being given to visit either Hunza or Nagar in which we were especially interested, because the Gilgit Agency, which included Ishkuman and Yasin, was closed. Chitral occurred to us as a good alternative. There had been almost unrestricted entry into the Hindu Kush in recent years. Although this had been mostly from the Afghan side, Pakistan, whose interest was growing towards promoting tourism, had begun to allow parties of tourists into the mountains north of Chitral.

In 1960, when Noshaq (7,492 m) was climbed by two separate parties from Japan and Poland, the invasion of the Hindu Kush had already begun. For climbers from Europe, many of whom travelled out overland, this became one of the easiest ways of launching an expedition to the trans-Himalayan ranges, at a time when many of the better-known mountain areas in Pakistan, India and Nepal were closed. The major appeal of these attractive mountains was that they were then completely untouched. The opening up in the 1960s of this new phase

PAMIR

Ab-i-Panj (Oxus)

Shakhaur

WAKHAN

H I N D

Hushko

Udren
Zom
7131

Roshgol Gl.

Saraghrar
7349

N

Mandaras
Gl.

Upper Udren Gl.

Darban Gl.

Ros

Lower Udren
Gl.

Udren Gol

Noshaq
7492

Istoro Nal
7398

Upper Tirich' Gl.

Atak Gol

Shekhniyak

Tirich North 6732

Lower Tirich

N.
Barum
Gl.

Tirich Mir
7706

Dirgol Gl.

S. Barum Gl.

Owir Gl.

Owir Gol

Barum

River

Reshun

Owir An

Mastuj

Barenis

Dorah
Pass

Lutkho River

Maroi

Koghozi

Chitral

MAP 13

Pegish An.
Wakhikan 5681
Wakhikan Rgh
Chutidum 8405m
269
Khandut Gl.
Lunkho Gl.
Lunkhoi 5952m
Lunkho I 6868
Uparisina Gl.
Anoshah An.
6530
6535
Phur Nisini An
Phur Nisini Gl.
Anoshah Gl.
Kotgaz Glacier
B.C.
Chutidum Gl.
Snahgologh
605m
6442m
Shah Jinali Pass
Kotgaz Zom 6681
Noghor Zom 5935
Chikar Gl.
Uzhnu Gol
Sararich Zom 6216m
Phurgram
Ziwar Gol
Rich Gol
Morich

K U S H

Uzhnu
Wasisch
Burzum
Hindu Raj Mts. →

Turikho Gol
Shagram
Deosir
Rain
Brep
rich Gol
Warkup
Mulikho Gol
Istaru
Kargum
Mastuj River
Mastuj
Buni
Miragram

N

0   10   20KMS

----- ROUTE
HEIGHTS IN METRES

Chitral

in the Hindu Kush was brought about by a reorientation of the expedition idea; the Austrians pioneered this development, as well as the Poles; also later, the Japanese. Small groups of friends with limited personal means were able to achieve during the course of a four to five weeks' holiday several first ascents, exploring much new country into the bargain. Each summer more than a dozen parties ranged over these mountains. By the late 1960s every peak above 7,000 metres and a very large number of those above 6,000 metres had been climbed. Modern maps had become available, supplementing the old Survey sheets which lacked detail of the glaciers and showed only the largest peaks. While scanning the area for an objective to justify our venture to Chitral we discovered to our surprise that the Lunkho group in the north-east had not been fully explored. A Japanese expedition in 1967 had reached the east summit (6,872 m) but the west summit (6,868 m) was still unclimbed. We decided to work out plans for a visit to the area in 1968.

During British rule in India, Chitral, like other states situated on the remote frontiers, was semi-autonomous with relative freedom from outside pressures and influences. The British generally kept aloof from its internal politics, and the administration was headed by a hereditary ruler with the title of Mehtar whose balance of power usually varied in accordance with the force of his personality. British protection was provided in matters of defence and a levy force was maintained known as the Chitral Scouts, commanded by British officers. With Afghan territory on Chitral's northern and western borders it suited the British to have a friendly state lying between the north-west frontier of India and a neighbour whose actions often seemed unpredictable. Afghanistan itself, living then in fear of Russian ambitions, followed a policy intended to strengthen by whatever means her own independence. In 1894 Curzon was told by the Amir of Afghanistan, Abdur Rahman Khan, that his country was as a poor goat threatened from one side by a bear from the other by a lion and it was the bear he feared most. The Amir Abdur Rahman was an absolute ruler, courageous and cruel. He was also a practitioner of many crafts, including medicine. Internal disorders, he was confident, were caused by a worm. His treatment for which was starvation for one day after which he sat in front of a huge and delicious meal until the parasite was driven to crawl up his throat in search of food. When it appeared he would seize its head and draw it forth.[1]

When the influential Mehtar of Chitral Aman-ul-Mulk died in 1892 and the British nominated his son Nizam-ul-Mulk as his successor, powerful intrigues began to take place supported by the Amir of Afghanistan in favour of Sher Afzal, a brother of the late Mehtar, who was known to be disposed towards Afghan suzerainty. In 1894 a serious crisis developed following Nizam-ul-Mulk's murder; this had been brought about internally by an uprising of the discontented upper classes, and externally through the Amir of Afghanistan, under whose protection Sher Afzal lived as a refugee in Badakshan. In the valleys between Chitral town and Drosh a battle was fought in which about a third of a British force of 150 was destroyed. The remainder, six British officers and detachments of the 14th Sikh Regiment and Kashmir Imperial Service Infantry, were held to siege in Chitral Fort for forty-six days during March/April 1895. They were relieved by Colonel Kelly's force who had marched from Gilgit over the Shandur pass (3,124 m) and by Sir Robert Low's column marching from Peshawar through Swat and Dir.[2] After peace was restored in the state and Shuja-ul-Mulk was installed as Mehtar, Chitral came under the Political Agency which included Dir and Swat, the headquarters of which was at Malakand. Chitral later became loyally attached to the Government of India and the status of its frontiers, which had been defined under an agreement signed at Kabul in November 1893 between Sir Mortimer Durand and the Amir of Afghanistan, was no longer questioned. The tribal belt facing Afghanistan on the north-west frontier of India, which stretches south-west from Chitral to Quetta had provided the British with a number of notorious trouble-spots. The frontier tribesmen who lived in British-protected territory were turbulent and undisciplined; some of them, like the Mahsuds and Waziris, remained to the end untameable. Their loyalties, always delicately balanced, shifted as it suited them from the Amir in the west to the British in the east.[3]

Chitralis are of mixed descent. In the upper valleys there is almost certainly an amalgam of the races which are spread over northern Gilgit and Turkestan. It is believed that the *adamzadas*, or land-owning upper classes, originate from Khorasan, a north-eastern province of Iran. But there are also descendants, especially among the middle and lower classes, from the aboriginal race of Kalash Kafirs. These Kafirs, i.e. non-believers, with their predominantly Aryan features probably spring from an ancient Indian population of Afghanistan who in their refusal to embrace Islam during the powerful Moslem rule of the tenth century fled to the hills for refuge. Even in the present day they have not assimilated with the population of Chitral and they are still confined to a few narrow valleys in the northern and eastern parts of the state such as Birir, Bimboret, Rumbur. The language of Chitral is Khowar, distinct from Pushtu spoken by Pathans and Burushaski spoken in Hunza and Nagar. It resembles some mid-European language; and to my ears when a Chitrali speaks English he does so with a mid-European accent and intonation. The country which is mountainous and rocky has extremely hot summers; but the winters are severe and the upper valleys remain snowbound for nearly six months. The people are superstitious and have formerly had a reputation for cruelty and treachery. In my experience the villagers appear simple and unimaginative; and, arising probably from fecklessness or indolence, they seem to lack loyalty to a cause or to an individual.

Alexander Gardner was probably the first European to traverse the Gilgit valley crossing over to Chitral and thence to Kafiristan. He made two journeys between 1826 and 1828.[4] W. W. McNair of the Indian Survey Department, disguised as a Pathan chieftain and accompanied by two tribal elders from Nowshera visited Kafiristan in 1883 and managed to accomplish some survey work with a plane-table. George Cockerill was probably the first of the British surveyors sent out to explore the western Karakoram and eastern Hindu Kush. In 1892, after having helped, together with Younghusband, to raise and train the Hunza levies, later known as the Gilgit Scouts, he set out on the first of his two journeys, which covered an area from Shimshal to Chitral.[5] Between 1889 and 1891 Sir George Robertson carried out extensive travels in Kafiristan bringing back detailed information about the country and the people.[6]

Between 1927 and 1930, during the course of a more extended survey, all the main peaks of the Hindu Kush were triangulated, although many of the upper glaciers were only roughly filled in. The Shandur pass provides the most direct link from Gilgit through Punial, Gupis and the Ghizar valley to Chitral. An alternative route is via Swat and through the Panjkora valley in Dir over the 3,048 m Lowari pass; although this pass, like the Shandur, is snowbound for most of the winter, it is used by heavy vehicles in summer. In 1923 during the heyday of the British raj, Lord Rawlinson, Commander-in-Chief, India carried out a round trip to Chitral crossing both passes with a large retinue in befitting style with cases of port in their baggage. Nowadays an air service operates between Peshawar and Chitral, reducing the journey time to about one hour. By a lake near the foot of the Shandur pass in August 1968 a contest of their national sport was held between two opposing polo teams from Chitral and Gilgit; an event that was enthusiastically attended by large numbers of supporters from both sides.

Although British officers in the early years of the century had ranged widely over the hills, mostly in search of game, very little mountaineering had been done in Chitral. *Markhor* are still fairly well distributed in the upper valleys; snow leopard, once plentiful, are now sadly diminishing. Immigrant wildfowl settle on the river banks for several weeks in the winter, and various cruel methods employed for trapping them have recently been banned. The higher regions were the subject of much folklore and superstition, and practically no attempts had been made to travel up the glaciers and to approach the peaks. Prior to 1950, when the Norwegians climbed Tirich Mir, no major mountain in the Hindu Kush had been ascended.

In the summer of 1968 other eyes apart from ours had fallen upon the Lunkho group. Parties from Yugoslavia, Austria and Scotland, all having as their objective the highest Lunkho peak, had entered Afghanistan to launch attempts from two adjacent valleys in the Wakhan, though we were not aware of this at the time. In order to minimise transport and other problems which rob heavyweight expeditions of so much enjoyment, we had agreed that we would travel light. Hugh Thomlinson, a doctor engaged on cancer research at a London hospital, was invited to complete our party of four. Food, based upon lists which I had built up during previous journeys, was as simple as possible; and most of it was purchased in Pakistan. Only a limited number of items such as pre-cooked meat and concentrated high-altitude packs were brought out from England; and since the weight involved was small we could afford the luxury of flying these items out. The glaciers south of the Lunkho group, where we planned to set up a base, were about ten days' journey from Chitral town and this seemed to be within reasonable range of our time limit of six weeks.

We met in Peshawar on 21 July. Sally Westmacott and Hugh Thomlinson had not visited Pakistan before, but Michael had done a spell of Army service on the sub-continent several years before. He could not only follow my negotiations conducted in Urdu, but before long his knowledge came back sufficiently to enable him to conduct his own. Urdu is the *lingua franca* which I have been able to use throughout my travels in the Himalaya, Karakoram and Hindu Kush. An ability to establish direct communication with the people has often paved the way towards easier local relations; at the least, it has made possible the avoidance of any major misunderstanding. Of the many Japanese groups in Chitral that summer I met one which was obliged to engage an English-speaking interpreter and another which was unable to communicate even in English. Of course, in certain circumstances, complete ignorance of the language can be turned into a positive advantage.

The day after our arrival in Peshawar we flew to Chitral. This flight, though not as spectacular as that from Rawalpindi to Gilgit, is interesting because it is possible to pick out theMalakand pass and the Swat valley, the peaks of Mankial and Falak Ser, and the Lowari pass. Within an hour we touched down on the airfield at Chitral, raising a storm of dust as the aircraft taxied to a halt on a brown plain encircled by rocky hills. One of the first persons to greet us, apart from members of the police force who scrutinised our entry passes, was Prince Burhan-ud-din. As a descendant of a former ruler he is one of the diminishing aristocracy, in a country where the *adamzadas* still command some respect and influence. A wide range of interests had helped to fill his fifty-odd years with, among other activities, soldiering, mining for precious stones and wine-making. We found the main street of the town decorated with archways and flags, as this was the week of the *Jashn* or Annual Festival. The State Rest-House was full, and we were given rooms in a semi-completed hotel. Among others residing there was a large Japanese expedition from Kosei University with a Pakistan army liaison officer; there were five other Japanese expeditions in Chitral that summer in addition to eight small Japanese groups of 'tourist' climbers.

Before departing from Chitral town, we attended two functions. The first was a lunch-party hosted by Prince Burhan at his country estate for a large gathering of visitors, including some Japanese climbers. While we sat under the shade of plane trees with a wide view of the hills beyond a foreground of wheat fields, home-made wine, some of it very good, flowed from the proud hands of our host. Around his hunting lodge, situated a few miles up the valley, *markhor* used to be plentiful in the winter, and he showed us several heads which he had acquired. Shooting has recently been restricted, and he was good enough to allow me to have a beautiful head from his large collection. In the evening we attended the concluding match of the polo festival. The polo ground, a lush meadow surrounded by hills, provided a picturesque setting. The huge gathering included the young Mehtar, who had just completed his schooling in Lahore. He presented trophies to the winning team; the losers had to perform a dance. Polo, as played in these parts, looks wildly dangerous, and a band provides musical accompaniment matching the excitement of the game.

Early on the morning of our departure we heard parade-ground noises outside, and discovered that the Japanese expedition were doing their pre-breakfast P.T.; our degenerate party were still in bed. We got away at eight o'clock in two jeeps. Twice on the bumpy track winding between rice and wheat fields the vehicles were bogged down by floodwater escaping from irrigation channels; ahead was a spectacular view of Tirich Mir. By noon we had covered twenty-two miles to Maroi; the jeep-road beyond this point was damaged. Whilst we ate lunch on the shady village green, eight donkeys were arranged to carry our baggage to Uhznu, sixty-three miles away. Since we adopted the more satisfactory system of fixing their rate per mile rather than per day, it was as much in their own interest that the donkeymen should complete the journey early. Leaving Maroi late that afternoon we did a short first stage, camping at dusk on a private meadow near Barenis.

The next three days in the lower Mastuj valley provided the hottest marches I have ever experienced. Temperatures exceeded 105°F, and along miles of shadeless paths there was no escape from the sun's blinding rays. We were following a broad valley enclosed by cliffs of red and brown rock under deep blue skies that were absolutely cloudless. In a state of semi-stupor I once plunged fully-clothed into a shallow pool beside the river; the water was warm and in an atmosphere practically devoid of humidity my wet clothes were soon quite dry. We were never really able to satisfy our thirst, especially as it was necessary to filter every drop that we drank in the lower valley. We adopted a routine of 5 a.m. starts on mugfuls of cold lime-juice, stopping for breakfast three or four hours later.

One of the most agreeable features of the Chitral landscape is the rich green belt surrounding each village. These oases, which are fed by irrigation streams, seem by their contrast a veritable paradise of meadows, trees and fields. Seated in the cool shade of fruit orchards with the sound of water rippling through innumerable channels we were content during our breakfast halts to gorge on freshly picked apricots, apples and mulberries. On the third day we left the Mastuj valley and crossed the Kagh Lasht plateau, a deserted waterless stretch ten miles long; then we continued up the Mulikho, a western tributary. The Buni Zom group rose directly to our right; and suddenly close to the left was Tirich Mir. This contrast of desert and dazzling white peaks without any intervening forest belt and upper alpine zone is a feature of the landscape of Chitral, as it is of much of the Central Asian plateau. The nights were mild and it was pleasant to sleep out in the open below a canopy of trees, listening to the leaves rustling in the breeze and tracing an ever-changing pattern under clear skies.

Presently we entered a greener landscape, the air was filled with the scent of plane trees, and stately avenues of poplars lined the track. The plane trees which were then in full summer foliage were amongst the finest that I have seen. Ahead there was a view of Sararich Zom (6,216 m) a sharp-featured peak situated south of the Chutidum glacier. We reached Burzum, four miles short of Uzhnu, on 27 July. The don-keymen had done extremely well; but since the short stretch beyond was unfit for their animals we released them. Here we spread ourselves out in an apricot orchard whose owner, Maqsood Murad Khan, was most hospitable and offered to assist us over recruitment of porters.

Little did we realise how fiercely the villagers in these higher valleys guard their rights. From Wasisch, a village across the river, we hired two men, Abdul Akak and Abzar Khan; two years before they had both been high with an Austrian party who had climbed Akher Chioh (7,020 m) from the Kotgaz glacier. We asked them to arrange porters to carry for us up the Uzhnu valley to our Base Camp on the Chutidum glacier. But after fifteen selected men had lifted our loads the next morning and started to move out, they were apprehended by villagers from Uzhnu and threatened with dire consequences if they advanced any further. There was nothing for it but to release the Wasisch men; then Michael Westmacott and I walked over to Uzhnu. Squatting on a shady patch of grass beside the headman's house we found ourselves encircled by the male population of the village, and negotiations were opened. Through the help of Syed Aman, a retired *havildar* of the Chitral State forces, arrangements were concluded in the friend-liest atmosphere and we were able to resume our journey the following day.

Below Uzhnu we crossed a suspension bridge spanning the main river, here called the Rich Gol; this valley leads north to the Phur Nisini and Ochhili passes into Wakhan; and eastwards over the Shah Jinali pass to the Hindu Raj mountains. I believe that the Phur Nisini, Shah Jinali and Ochhili glaciers have not yet been fully explored. There are three peaks in the area above 6,000 metres one of which may still be unclimbed, plus a wealth of other interesting mountains. The ascent of the Uzhnu Gol began steeply; we started on its left bank, then crossed over by a snow bridge to the other side. After traversing a meadow of tall grass filled with partridge who seemed surprisingly tame, we camped in a tangle of birchwood scrub about six miles up the valley.

20. Lakhpa and Karma Bahadur, my porters from Kaigaon (10 October 1964)

21. Chitral landscape near the junction of the Mulikho and Mastuj rivers (25 July 1968)

22. Buni Zom group seen from the Kagh Lasht plateau (25 July 1968)

Hugh Thomlinson went down with a temperature here; Michael decided to stay behind with him whilst Sally and I moved on with the main caravan.

There were no further tracks beyond this point and at two places we had to traverse steep alluvial slopes above the river after a narrow path had been fashioned in order to make things easier for the laden men. The dreaded Shahgologh tributary which entered from the right was our main obstacle that day. It is fed by a glacier flowing from the north-west face of Sararich Zom, and when we reached it at noon it was in high flood, a mass of white foam falling between steep walls of rock. Mohamad Rahim Gul, known as Hercules, excelled himself here. First a logging party was organised who cut three birch trunks which they had to transport about half a mile to the bridging point. The logs were then thrown across the torrent from an embankment on our side to a projecting boulder on the other side. After the logs had been crudely bound Hercules ventured across, protected by a waist rope; on reaching the opposite bank he was able to reinforce the embankment there. It was a remarkable performance. Within an hour and a half the whole party had crossed over by a bridge that was serviceable and surprisingly sound. That evening we camped at about 3,300 m near the last of the birch scrub. The unexploited wood supply around that camp was a source of wealth to the porters, many of whom spent the evening fashioning ploughshares. They built three large fires, and the sound of their singing echoed through the valley late into the night.

The next day, 31 July, a two-hour ascent of the moraine brought us to the junction of the Chutidum and Kotgaz glaciers. On a level patch of boulders below the snout of the former we selected a site at about 3,200 metres for our Base Camp. The north face of Noghor Zom (5,935 m) towered above the Kotgaz glacier opposite; while a wide moraine slope about 220 m. high obscured our view of the Chutidum glacier to the north. Between boulders and streams surrounding the camp there were patches of grass scattered with pink willowherb, (*epilobium fleischeri*), and polygonum. We paid off the porters and they descended at once, a few of them having complained of headaches. When Cockerill was engaged on his early surveys in Chitral in 1894 he saw a headman of Turikho apply a remedy for mountain-sickness by piercing a vein on the victim's forehead until blood spurted out; this treatment was described as infallible. We did not try anything so drastic, distributing instead a few pills as we sent the men home. Hugh and Michael joined us that evening; Hugh had recovered fully, as he must have done to have accomplished the journey in one stage from their camp.

Michael Westmacott and I set out the following morning moving up Chutidum glacier, which was one and a half km. wide, in order to get our first glimpse of the Lunkho peaks. The moraine was quite steep and troublesome at first; but by crossing over to the right we were able to make rapid progress up an ablation valley and along a moraine ridge. The distance to a snow basin at the head of the glacier was about eight km., and the snowline appeared to be at 4,500 metres. When we reached the edge of the basin we were struck by the steepness of the two Lunkho peaks from this side, and it was clear at once that any route, especially on the higher peak, would involve technical difficulties of a high standard. Looking back we could see the larger Kotgaz glacier sweeping out of sight to the north-west. We spent a day ferrying loads from Base to a camp-site at about 4,500 metres below the snow basin. Hugh Thomlinson and I occupied that camp on 4 August, which was situated below a névé slope steepening up towards the foot of the Lunkho peaks. In the south-west there was a view of Noghor Zom, impressive from Base Camp, but now dwarfed by Akher Chioh looming up behind. It was a peaceful evening at our camp with changing colours playing upon the peaks against a background of deep blue sky.

We made a careful study of both the Lunkho peaks which now faced us barely one kilometre away. We were not aware that on the same day an Austrian and Yugoslav team had reached the West summit; and that nine days later they were to reach the East summit, approaching the peaks from the Khandud valley in Wakhan. Although the route from that side was probably longer, it was much less steep and relatively free from objective dangers. Avalanches fell regularly from the face above us, scattering the head of the basin with ice debris. On Lunkho East there were two routes which appeared feasible. One, by the south-west spur, was fairly lengthy and would require about two camps, with plenty of quite serious climbing. The other was by a rib further to the east which had been used by the Japanese. On Lunkho West the eye of faith scanned the face in vain for a line of weakness. A German party in 1967 had, however, thought otherwise; they had tackled an ice-wall forming its lower section in an attempt to reach a col situated on the long ridge connecting the East and the West summits. They called off their climb following a crevasse accident; to us this route looked dangerous. The same col, reached from the Wakhan side, was used by the Yugoslavs for the ascent of both the peaks.

In the morning Hugh Thomlinson and I went up to explore the head of the basin. An early start permitted a quick ascent of the névé slopes, but in the ice beyond we struck a crevassed area where great care was necessary. There seemed to be no major problems on the Japanese route on which we judged that only one additional camp would be required, provided snow and ice conditions were satisfactory. But a more appealing prospect was the peak marked 6,442 metres situated on the southern rim of the basin. Both of us, and later Michael and Sally Westmacott, felt that we could probably find a route up it from the west. After Thomlinson and I descended to Base the Westmacotts went up to occupy the camp which we had vacated, and were in agreement with our impressions about the Lunkho peaks.

Meanwhile a new and unfortunate development took place. Probably as a result of the unusually hot marches in the lower Mastuj valley, I had developed a blister on my right foot. This in itself was not exceptional for me, and I gave it my usual treatment which was to ignore it until it would harden sufficiently to be of no further trouble. But now it had grown steadily worse, until walking had become a conscious effort. On returning to Base Camp Hugh looked at it and said that my toe had turned septic. After three days and nights of intense pain, pus flowed out of the swollen toe while Hugh dosed me with antibiotics. It was eleven days before I was able to wear my climbing boots again.

We were now having a spell of what Sally called 'Welsh' weather; somewhat unusual for Chitral, though indicating the exceptionally heavy monsoon that was active further south. We had a visit from Hans Gassner and Fritz Iglar of the three-man Austrian party, whose Base Camp was situated quite near by on the Kotgaz glacier. A few days earlier we had watched them climb to the summit of Noghor Zom; they were now leaving, having climbed two 6,000 metre peaks from the upper Kotgaz glacier. They had travelled out by road from Austria and had climbed five mountains after spending a little over one month in the area. Two days after they left a party of three Japanese students occupied their campsite. For a while our camp seemed to attract a flow of visitors from Uzhnu. They meant well, nearly always bringing gifts of fresh food such as eggs, apricots and potatoes; but I think that we would have preferred the freedom from intrusion which we had intended when releasing all our porters.

It became necessary to modify our plans, and a suitable alternative appeared to be the examination of a northern bay of the Chutidum glacier. It was our impression that this was unexplored, but we came across traces of a former visit. We learned later that in 1967 the Germans had visited the area making an unsuccessful attempt to climb Wakhikan Rah (5,681 m), and that they had ascended a peak to the north-east, marked 6,405 metres, which they called Chutidum Zom. Heights shown on modern maps often vary with each other, and disagree with those shown in the old Survey sheets upon which they are mostly based. It seems unlikely that a modern survey will be carried out officially; and official maps of these areas are in any case not made available for general use.[7]

I spent a few nights alone in Base Camp. My foot was healing slowly but I could do no more than hobble about with a tennis shoe on one foot and a bandage on the other. In all my previous journeys to the mountains I had never before been laid low for longer than twenty-four hours, and this enforced inactivity was a new and distressing experience. My only companion was a solitary pied wagtail (*motacilla alba*) who hopped about outside my tent accepting eagerly the crumbs which I offered. Despite periods of frustration and deep dejection, there were sometimes moments of illumination brought about by an increasing sense of harmony with the mountains. Through the long daylight hours my mood seemed to alternate with the infinite changes in their colour and appearance; with the harsh noonday light which they reflected and with the deep shadows that transformed their shapes at dawn and sunset. The summits seemed remotely distant from the glaciers, dominating them and providing them with life and movement. It was an environment both wild and solemn, whose chief elements were a profound isolation, loneliness and silence—a silence broken occasionally by the sound of rushing waters wafted up by some breeze from the glacier below.

Whilst I was confined to my tent the others set up a camp at 4,500 metres with the intention of climbing Wakhikan Rah. After nearly two weeks of clouded skies and occasional drizzle the weather cleared on 16 August. There was a sharpness and clarity in the air that hinted of a change of season; the days were shorter and the nights cooler. Michael and Sally Westmacott occupied a camp at 5,200 metres below Wakhikan Rah on 17 August, with Hugh Thomlinson in support at the lower camp. The next day they reached the top and were treated to a wonderful view of Akher Chioh and other Kotgaz mountains, of the Lunkho peaks and, beyond Wakhan, of the distant Pamirs.[8] The day following this climb I arrived at the 4,500 metre camp; after two weeks of inactivity I had a great struggle to get there, and I retired into the tent with a temperature and a severe attack of urticaria, probably caused by a delayed reaction to the antibiotic treatment.

In the morning I decided to accompany Hugh to the upper camp, whilst Michael and Sally descended to Base. Within two hours we reached the basin of the upper glacier, below Wakhikan Rah and a peak to its right marked 6,185 metres. There seemed to be no difficulty in finding a way to the latter, and we would have much liked to climb it from the high camp, which was little more than an hour's walk away. But I realised now that I was too feeble to continue. It had become an effort to move, even in the almost level snow basin; and reluctantly I had to face the reality that I must go down. Hugh Thomlinson was very forbearing especially as I did not feel able to descend to Base, and another night had to be spent at the 4,500 metre camp, where once again a temperature and an attack of urticaria kept me awake. Although Hugh intended to accompany me back to Chitral, Michael and Sally Westmacott rightly decided to seek out further climbs from the upper camp. The two Wasisch men, Abdul Akak and Abzar Khan, were re-called to assist them. But they were very unlucky with the weather, and after sitting out three days of continuous snowfall at the 4,500 metre camp they descended finally to Base on 30 August in order to begin their return journey.

Hugh Thomlinson and I started back on 23 August. The *havildar* with Hercules and another porter had come up from Uzhnu, and we made the journey down to their village in twelve hours. Our bridge over the Shahgologh torrent, which at first had barely cleared the water, now stood several feet above it. Below our first camp we saw some cattle, but most of the herds had been moved down, as the grazing season was almost over. At dusk we reached the green in front of the *havildar*'s house and found ourselves surrounded by a dozen willing hands offering sweet tea, apples and baked potatoes. We slept out under a sky filled with an astonishing display of stars, and before their glow had faded we were on our way accompanied by two porters.

The march back was in complete contrast to the outward journey. The summer heat had receded, and there were autumn harvest scenes in the villages. In cooler weather our stages exceeded twenty miles each day, starting early and finishing late.

Crossing the Kagh Lasht plateau there were views of Saraghrar, Istoro Nal and Tirich Mir, etched with striking clarity against a background of the most intense blue. Landslides, following heavy rainfall, had destroyed houses in some of the lower villages and washed away a portion of the jeep-road below Maroi. We walked into Chitral town on the fifth day where we learnt that owing to unusually bad weather there had only been two flights from Peshawar during the past fortnight. Since the arrival of the next flight seemed uncertain, we hired a jeep for the seventy-two-mile journey to Dir.

On the outskirts of Chitral town we crossed the suspension bridge beyond which stands the Fort, scene of the siege in 1895. We halted briefly at Drosh, thirty miles beyond, headquarters of the Chitral Scouts. Below this, the road enters a narrow valley, winding at first through forest then above the treeline to the bleak crest of the Lowari pass. At dusk, we were deposited in a vast barrack-like inn at Dir. Two hours ahead of dawn the next morning we made a surreptitious departure in a jeep, whose ownership we considered it wiser not to investigate too closely. In the gathering morning light, the rich timber country for which the Panjkora valley is famous rushed past us, and we were thankful to reach Peshawar safely a few hours later.

If one must judge success or failure by purely material considerations then our visit to Chitral had been a failure. But none of us who made the journey look upon it as anything but an enjoyable experience. For me it was filled with a number of new impressions; and it was different in essence from other ventures in areas seeming to possess superficial similarities of scale and environment. From a narrow climbing viewpoint most of the plums have fallen in Chitral; and I think it is true that there are practically no genuinely unexplored corners left. But these mountains still contain a wealth of enjoyment. There is a high summer snowline; and, generally, absence of prolonged bad weather; also a relatively short approach to the peaks. Chitral will always appeal to those who are chiefly attracted by isolated and unspoilt regions where it is possible to achieve ascents of a standard quite as hard as any in Europe on peaks that are much bigger, and without any of the physiological barriers and logistical problems that are essential to ascents of the highest mountains.

X

Kaghan

*Happiness is most often met by those who have learned to live in
every moment of the present; none has such prodigal opportunities
of attaining that art as the traveller.*

T. G. Longstaff

Like the Kashmir mountains, which lie further to the east forming part
of the same geographical trend-line, the mountains of Kaghan rise
south of the Great Himalayan range. In scale and character they are
Alpine rather than Himalayan, the highest peak Mali-ka-Parbat rising
to only 17,356 feet. Though there are few glaciers, and these are small
in size, the region possesses in abundance all the features which are
attractive to lovers of mountain country. The valley is easily accessible
from Rawalpindi and Abbottabad, but with road communications restricted its upper reaches have remained backward. The area is still
relatively unspoilt, having kept surprisingly aloof from any political
influences or pressures. The main valley, which is almost a hundred
miles long, is drained by the Kunhar river whose source lies near the
Babusar pass (13,684 ft); this is situated on the crest zone to the north
which divides the valley from the tribal area of Chilas and the Gilgit
Agency. South of the valley lies Abbottabad and the Hazara district.
To the west lies the Indus gorge and the little-known area of Indus
Kohistan; Kashmir runs along its eastern boundary*. The district was,
indeed, part of the former Kashmir dominion, though the inhabitants
possess characteristics differing in many ways from those of their eastern
neighbours. Unless I have been particularly fortunate in the Kaghanis
I have met, it could not be said of them as it could be said of the boatman
of Kashmir who, according to his wont, encouraged his neighbour to
row harder so that he might row less hard himself. Maharaja Gulab

* See Map 9 on page 137.

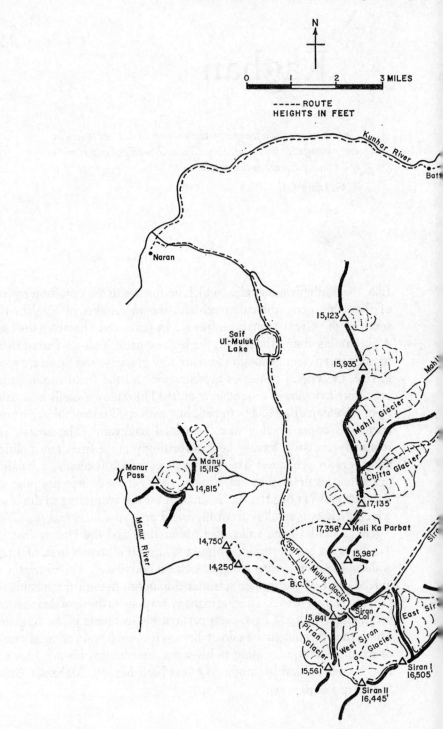

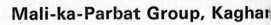

N

0   1   2   3 MILES

----- ROUTE
HEIGHTS IN FEET

Kunhar River

Batt

Naran

15,123'

Saif
Ul-Muluk
Lake

15,935'

Mahli Glacier

Mahl

Chitta Glacier

Manur
15,115'

Manur
Pass

14,815'

17,135'

Manur River

17,356' Mali Ka Parbat

14,750'

15,987'

Saif Ul-Muluk Glacier

14,250'

B.C.

Siran
Col

15,841'

Piran
Glacier

West Siran   Glacier

East Sira

15,561'

Siran I
16,505'

Siran II
16,445'

MAP 14

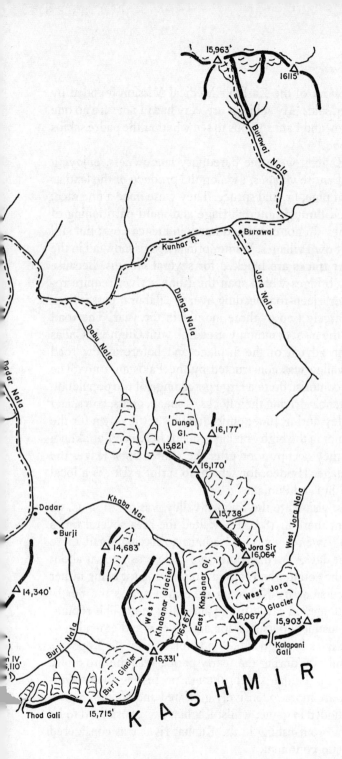

15,963'

16115

Burawai Nala

Burawai

Kunhar R.

Jora Nala

Dunga Nala

Dabu Nala

Dadar Nala

Dunga Gl.

16,177'

15,821'

16,170'

15,738'

West Jora Nala

Khaba Nar

Dadar

Burji

14,683'

Jora Sir
16,064

West Jora Glacier

14,340'

West Khabanar Glacier

16467'

East Khabanar Gl.

16,067'

15,903'

Kalapani Gali

Burji Nala

IV
110'

Burji Glacier

16,331'

Thod Gali

15,715'

KASHMIR

Singh, viewing the work of the Kashmir Medical Mission founded by Robert Clark in 1854, said: 'My subjects are very bad; I am sure no one can do them any harm, and I am anxious to see whether the padre sahibs can do them any good.'

The *Sayyids* of Kaghan were the hereditary landowners, enjoying feudalistic control of entire villages, owning the produce of the land as well as rich forests of pine, fir, and spruce. They were once a fine race, but have degenerated through intermarriage and multi-partitioning of hereditary lands. They do not command much influence now; but still enjoy respect in their own villages. Winter brings heavy snowfall in the valley and the upper tracks are blocked for several months. Because the crude cantilever bridges which span the Kunhar river require re-building each summer a jeep-road leading over the Babusar pass is fit to take vehicles for scarcely two or three months in the year. The road however used to be the most commonly used link with Gilgit via Chilas and Bunji before the advent of the airplane and before a new road through the Indus valley was constructed by the Pakistan army. The herdsmen who still comprise quite a large percentage of the population lead a nomadic existence driving their flocks of sheep, goats, cows, and buffaloes up the valley during June; entire families settle down for the duration of the summer in the high grazing grounds between Battakundi and Gittidas which they occupy soon after the winter snow leaves the ground. Their language, Hindco, for which no script exists, is a local dialect related to Pushtu and Punjabi.

One of the earliest visitors to the Kaghan valley was the Hon. C. G. Bruce who first went there in 1890. He visited the area several times during the following twenty years and admits to having spent there some of his happiest days.[1] At that time very little was known about the mountains; and the country had earned a reputation for being rather wild because of incursions by Kohistani tribesmen across the north-west border who indulged in cattle-lifting and petty theft. This reputation, not entirely unjustified, persisted for many years and extended to the tribal areas of Chilas in the north. A possible reason for Kaghan's relative lack of popularity during that early period was the proximity of Kashmir and the Pir Panjal which, though possessing many simi-larities in character, are more extensively glaciated and contain higher peaks. Kashmir abounded in game, whilst Kaghan was considered to be gameless, though the trout-fishing in the Kunhar river was considered to be the best in the sub-continent.

Very little mountaineering had been done in Kaghan until Captain

B. W. Battye of a Gurkha regiment climbed Mali-ka-Parbat in the late 1920s. No record exists of his climb, which is believed to have been made from the north. In 1940 the peak was climbed from the west by two British army officers, Lieutenants Willoughby and Price. Although the mountain has been tried several times before and since, no further ascents have been recorded.[2] In 1926 J. B. P. Angwin of the Survey of India spent five months in the valley, in the course of which he established about fifteen triangulation stations on mountains ranging from 13,500 to 15,500 feet. His work provided the basis for a subsequent topographical survey and the publication of the first map-sheets. These are substantially the same as the maps in existence today since, so far as I know, no further survey has been carried out.[3] In the border area near Chilas, Angwin had an encounter with Kohistani tribesmen who attempted to loot his camp, wrecking one of his survey signals. He describes a meeting held with Kohistani village elders who when offered some tobacco made a pile of mud on the ground, bored a hole through it horizontally, filled one end with tobacco, and lay on their bellies one after the other sucking smoke through the other end. I have seen this curious *chilam*, or tobacco bowl, used in a similar way by Garhwali porters from Mana village above Badrinath; it was their favourite method of smoking.

I have found the people of Kaghan unspoilt and honest, and, like most hillfolk, they are cheerful and friendly. Their method of carrying loads looks awkward and uncomfortable, with the weight supported between the shoulder and the head, and held in position with both hands. Although I have seen them carry up to seventy pounds in this fashion it is obviously an unsuitable method for traversing routes where a delicate balance is required. For the mountaineer the Kaghan valley is still only partly explored; but it is gradually becoming a popular area for tourists. Visitors go there for a limited period of the year, mostly during July and August when the jeep-road has been re-opened to traffic. Generally they do not move far beyond the central village of Naran where the Tourist Department have provided rest-houses and camping facilities. While trout-fishing is one of the main attractions, short treks are often undertaken through the forests to the upper alps and lakes. Saif-ul-Muluk lake, fed by a glacier of that name is situated at about 10,000 feet, below the north-west face of Mali-ka-Parbat; it is easily reached from Naran, and during the summer it is possible to travel there by jeep. There is a legend that Saif-ul-Muluk is the home of a fairy princess who was banished to its depths by her father as punishment for marrying a mortal with whom she had fallen in love. She lies in a cold grave, for the lake is frozen for more than half the year.

In 1965 I had two weeks' leave, and because of its easy access the Kaghan valley seemed to be an ideal place to visit. I was not aware then of any previous ascents of Mali-ka-Parbat, or of climbs on any other mountains in the valley. I was joined by John Austin, a young civil engineer working on an Indus Basin project near Lahore, whose experience was limited to rock-climbing on British hills. We had not expected to be able to do more than explore the upper valleys and examine alternative routes on Mali-ka-Parbat.

We left Lahore by car on 16 June, carrying the minimum of food and equipment and arrived the same afternoon at Balakot. There the Kunhar river, near the end of its journey, flows through a broad cultivated plain on its way south where it meets the Jhelum river twenty-five miles lower down. Balakot is approached from Mansehra over the Patrasi ridge which is covered with pine forest; it commands fine views, especially of the broad snow-covered mountain called Musa-ka-Musalla. The road beyond Balakot has since been improved, but in 1965 it was suitable only for one-way traffic and it had been re-opened after its winter closure only two days before our arrival. The 53-mile journey to Naran took six hours, and it was a bumpy ride for most of the way. In the lower valley the slopes are covered by terraced fields of rice and maize irrigated by hillside torrents; higher up, the hills have an abundant forest cover. At Kaghan village there is a broad background of snow-covered ridges; from there the thirteen miles to Naran are the roughest of the whole journey, with the road in many places hardly wide enough to accommodate a jeep. Travelling along this section seven years later, I did not observe any improvement in the state of the road, a disadvantage that will inevitably delay the development of Naran as a tourist resort. Winter snow lies late on this north-facing road, and at three places our vehicle skidded across an icy surface over which twigs and boulders had been placed. The margin of safety is narrow and a minor driving miscalculation can, and often does, end in disaster.

When I first saw Naran it was a quiet village not yet awakened from its winter slumber; and the government rest-house where we stayed was almost empty. With gentle snowslopes situated 1,500 feet above, this village if situated in Europe would probably have become a thriving ski-centre. On 19 June we left Naran with five porters to set up a camp near Saif-ul-Muluk lake. Above the village we entered a branch valley to the east, and this provided a beautiful forest track for the first two miles. We had our first glimpse of Mali-ka-Parbat when the valley took a southerly bend; and after crossing a bank of hard snow we climbed 1,000 feet up a hillside which bore remnants of what must have been a rich pine forest. At the top a winding track brought us within sight of the lake. We placed our camp half-a-mile north of it, at about 10,750 feet. Mali-ka-Parbat, with its steep north-west face in full view, looked quite formidable. With snow lying thickly everywhere and the lake completely frozen over, the valley gave us a rather chilly reception.

We retained two porters, Abdul Rashid, a bright youth keen to prove himself, and Mar Wali Jan who was slow but reliable. John Austin felt unwell, and after two nights in camp he was obliged to descend to Naran. Accompanied by a porter I made excursions to about 13,000 feet on both sides of the valley. Then I climbed 1,000 feet up the north-west spur of Mali-ka-Parbat from where I was able to study the route which R. L. Holdsworth had pioneered in the late 1930s. It seemed too early for a serious attempt from this side; and in view of the heavy snow cover I felt that it might be worth examining the mountain from the north. Three of the six nights spent at this windy camp were stormy. The forest rest-hut beside the lake was closed, and the log bridge approaching it was unserviceable. Small groups of dwellings beyond the lake, used by shepherds in summer, were almost completely buried by snow. We came across colonies of marmots, announcing their presence with shrill cries; and now and then the call of a cuckoo would echo through the valley. On patches of hillside recently cleared of snow there were clumps of purple iris and mauve primula. One day near the foot of a gully choked with old avalanche snow we dug out the remains of an ibex, his legs and spine shattered by a fall; his horns, which I was glad to acquire as a trophy, measured forty inches.

We descended to Naran on 25 June and moved up the valley. Our first halt was at Battakundi which is overlooked by alpine meadows and faces a northern cirque of snow-covered *aiguilles*. In this secluded spot Sir Aurel Stein, the noted archaeologist and Central Asian traveller, camped while writing his memoirs. There are a number of small glaciers to the south-east containing groups of peaks rising to about 16,500 feet. Practically all of these are still unexplored, and some of them would give quite hard climbing. The summer migration had begun and we met large numbers of people moving up the valley with their livestock. They had begun their journey in Balakot several days before, and their destination was the wide rolling plains below the approaches to the Babusar Pass. These nomads were an unattractive-looking people, appearing unkempt and dirty; while some of them begged for alms others asked for medicine. Practically all the bridges were down, and it would be several weeks before the jeep-track to the Babusar pass would re-open. At Burawai where we arrived on 26 June a two-mile detour was necessary up the Jora *nala* in order to cross the stream by a snowbridge. The rest-house situated at 9,596 feet was small but very adequate and it served us as a convenient base. We were now above the treeline; flowing through the brown plateau which surrounded us were numerous streams which were joined by smaller torrents from the snow-covered slopes on either side racing down towards the Kunhar river.

On our first day we climbed the slopes to the south-east, traversing a snow dome and moving on to a col at 14,000 feet situated at the foot of a rocky spire 500 feet above; the latter looked quite hard and we did not attempt to tackle it. A mile away to the right was a small glacier containing a cirque of rock peaks. We looked in vain for Mali-ka-Parbat which was concealed behind an intervening group of mountains, some of which exceeded 16,000 feet. There are several small glaciers approachable from the Jora *nala*, and at the head of the valley is the west Jora glacier situated on the Kashmir border. Above this glacier rise two peaks of 16,000 feet. From the Jora valley a pass can almost certainly be found to the Khabanar glacier system further west, which contains three peaks above 16,000 feet. None of these mountains has ever been approached; indeed, I doubt whether any of the glaciers have been fully ascended. When we turned to descend we were attracted by a row of three peaks situated north of Burawai, one of which we decided to attempt.

Taking Mar Wali Jan, we started at seven the next day and crossed a footbridge over the Kunhar river. On the opposite side we entered the Burawai *nala* to the north; near its entrance we noticed a handful of deserted huts. Where the snow had left the slopes there were clusters of mauve iris, primula denticulata and forget-me-not. We ascended steep snow-covered moraine, beyond which lay a small basin enclosed by a rocky ridge. We had chosen the left of three peaks situated on the ridge, the highest of which was Burawai peak (16,115 ft) to the right. Branching left we climbed out of the moraine heading for a col (14,250 ft), situated on the west rim of the basin. We reached this at about noon; the porter who was feeling unwell waited here. Ahead was a long snow ridge which provided a straightforward ascent to the top of our peak (15,963 ft).

Standing on the summit we appeared to be at the north-west end of the Kaghan crest-zone with the ridge declining in the west towards the Indus gorge. Beyond were higher ranges in Swat and Indus Kohistan, a line of familiar mountains from which I was able to pick out Falak Ser, Mankial and the Siri Dara group. To the north were bigger peaks: Haramosh and the great mass of Nanga Parbat. It was the view to the south-west that intrigued me. Mali-ka-Parbat dominated all the other Kaghan mountains, and its north-east face seemed to provide the clue to an attractive route. While we rested on the summit an aircraft on the daily flight between Rawalpindi and Gilgit passed not more than 600 feet above us. We waved a greeting. If the pilot noticed our axes glinting in the sun we must have been an unexpected sight, for climbers on Kaghan peaks are exceedingly rare. We returned to the rest-house shortly after 6 p.m. and were back in Naran the next day. There, two very green rods with spinners and flies caught twelve rainbow trout within two hours; a pleasant end to a light-hearted holiday.

Two years later interest was re-awakened in Mali-ka-Parbat; or rather in trying out the route I had spied from the peak above Burawai. Friends living in Pakistan were keen to join in the attempt, and we thought that with luck we could do it in twelve or fourteen days including judicious use of weekends, which was all the time that two of us could spare. Gene White, an American civil engineer, had climbed in North and South America and also in Chitral. He had lived in Pakistan for almost seven years and spoke Pushtu fluently, his early years in the country having been spent in the areas around Peshawar. Norman Norris had climbed in Britain, Switzerland, Chitral, Swat and Kaghan. He and I had enjoyed many climbing weekends in Pakistan. He possessed qualities which made him an ideal companion in the mountains. Completely sincere, not talkative by nature, but communicative when in a small group. He was quite oblivious to the normal frustrations encountered on mountain journeys, and one seemed to draw strength from his calm, relaxed manner in the face of cold or physical discomfort. I have never seen him emotionally upset, nor have I known him ever to press a personal demand that might conflict with another's interest. Yet his amazing toughness and reliability in difficult places always qualified him to stay out in the front. I do not think that there is any other person with whom I would rather share a mountaineering expedition.

We had been approached by the Karakoram Club in Lahore to allow one of their members to join us. At first I refused, because I was anxious to avoid publicity. We had not sought permission for an attempt on Mali-ka-Parbat, although it had been hinted during my first visit that permission was necessary. The Club's candidate was Abdul Rauf, a final year geography student at Punjab University. He had visited Swat and Kaghan, and as he seemed genuinely keen, we agreed that he should come.

At Lahore, where we had arranged to meet on 30 June, the summer heat was so intense that the air was oppressive even at 4 a.m. when we drove out through the dark streets of the city and over the Ravi bridge on the road to Rawalpindi. We ran into belts of heavy rain on the way. Norman Norris, who met us at Rawalpindi looked very fit after his return from Swat, where he and the Austrian climber Wolfgang Stefan[4] had climbed Miangul Sar (19,500 ft). We reached Balakot the same evening and noticed that the Kunhar river looked brown and turgid, confirming reports that we had heard about heavy rainfall in the valley.

We set out from Naran on 3 July with three pack-animals and two porters; we also hired a pony for Gene's wife and two-year-old-son who accompanied us to our Base Camp. Since motor traffic had not been fully resumed we saw few tourists in Naran although the snowline seemed higher than it had been two years before. Beyond Naran villagers were busy in their fields hoeing crops of young wheat and maize and digging water channels. At Battakundi on 4 July we left the main valley and branched south into the Dadar valley. It appeared to us that the best way to approach Mali-ka-Parbat from the north-east would be via the Chitta glacier. Once we entered the Dadar valley there was no further rainfall and from then on we had an unbroken spell of fine weather. This minor valley contained few settlements and there was practically no cultivation. A handful of people occupying the one village which we passed looked almost as primitive as the small Kafir communities whose dwellings I had seen in the valleys south-west of Chitral. There were several patches of old snow lying across the track and one of our pack-animals slipped and lost its load, although this was fortunately recovered.

We placed our Base Camp on a lush meadow about one mile long and half a mile wide which was situated above the meeting-point of two streams. The Siran, which we hoped to follow to the Chitta glacier, entered from the south-west; the Burji, in the south-east, gave access to the unexplored Khabanar group. About five miles away to the south was Thod Gali a pass leading into Kashmir. It was a beautiful spot for a camp. Numerous fresh water streams ran through the meadow, and

23. Camp at 4,600 metres near the head of the Chutidum glacier; Noghor Zom (5,935 m) centre, Akher Chioh (7,020 m) right (4 August 1968)

24. Mali-ka-Parbat, 17,356 feet, seen from Burawai peak. The Siran basin and its peaks are in shadow to the left (28 June 1965)

there was a view of a peak of the Siran group which we mistook at first for Mali-ka-Parbat. Three dwellings stood in a corner of the meadow, occupied by a priest and his family. A fourth structure, no more than a stone shelter with an earthen floor, served as a mosque. We were permitted to take this over as a cook-house and mess provided we agreed to enter without shoes. This settlement, as well as the neighbouring settlement of Burji one mile above, was inhabited only during the summer; we found the people hospitable and unintrusive, despite the stir which the sight of our orange, yellow and green tents must have caused. The pass into Kashmir appeared to be in regular summer use and occasional groups of travellers passed our camp on their way to the Kishanganga valley. Some of them looked quite prosperous, employing porters or pack-animals. From the head of the Siran valley it seemed quite possible to reach the upper Siran basin, which contains two peaks of about 16,500 feet.

Since our time was limited I had worked out a plan for a rapid advance, based upon moving with loads to a higher camp on every alternate day and sleeping at a lower one. Accordingly, on the day following our arrival in Dadar, four of us accompanied by two porters moved up the Siran valley to search for the Chitta tributary. For over one mile we followed boulders and scree, puzzled by the non-appearance of our branch valley. To the right was a hanging valley, 1,500 feet of steep grass and scree ending in a patch of snow, beyond which we could not see. Could this be our Chitta (white) valley? Despite some doubt, we thought that we had better take a closer look. Ascending beyond the snow patch we came upon a meadow covered with pale blue and deep purple gentians. We rested in the sunshine intrigued by the enclosed glen which we had entered and which at this point appeared to alter course, making a 90° bend to the south-west. As soon as we rounded the corner the mystery was over. We saw a glacier ahead and a steep ascent of moraine took us over the snout. Then suddenly in front of us was Mali-ka-Parbat, a perfectly shaped pyramid of snow filling the head of the glacier. My first reaction was how utterly different the peak looked from the other side; and my next was that we should almost certainly find a route up it. The photograph I had taken two years before from the Burawai peak had come to life.

During the next three days we built up and occupied two camps. The first was on the lower glacier at 12,500 feet and the next in an upper snow basin at 15,700 feet. On 8 July we occupied the high camp and in the afternoon Norman Norris, Gene White and I reconnoitred the route above. We reached a col at 16,000 feet on the north ridge of Mali-ka-Parbat, and found ourselves looking down almost sheer into the Saif-ul-Muluk valley 5,000 feet below. From the col the ridge began with a 400-foot rock-cliff that could not be avoided, and as a route it did not appeal to us. The north-east face seemed preferable, though I judged that it was somewhat exposed to objective dangers. It was justi-fiable as a route provided the threatened area could be traversed quickly while it was frozen. The atmosphere was amazingly clear, with hun-dreds of miles of mountains visible in the blue and gold afternoon light. Nearby were the familiar Swat mountains and beyond them the distant line of the Hindu Kush. Of the Karakoram peaks I could pick out Hara-mosh, Rakaposhi, and the Batura. Nanga Parbat filled the middle dis-tance, dwarfing the Chongra peaks and other satellites. That evening we ate supper outside the tents. The air was calm and I watched the light on the peaks fading through an infinite variety of shades until the cold drove me inside.

It was decided that Norman and Gene should comprise a rope of two for the summit climb. It froze hard during the night, and they set out soon after 5.30 a.m. Crossing the *bergschrund* at the foot of the north-east face, they climbed diagonally to the right, cramponing quickly up the steep snow face towards the north ridge. On reaching it they moved round to the north-west face. After three rope-lengths of moderate ice and rock, they stood on the North summit of Mali-ka-Parbat (17,135 ft). The South summit, about 200 feet higher, was nearly three-quarters of a mile away, separated by a narrow and rather broken ridge, very exposed on both sides. Although Norman was inclined to give it a try, proposing to traverse below the ridge on the steep right-hand face, Gene estimated about six hours for the climb to the South summit and back, and decided that it was not justified. This climb can probably be claimed as a second ascent of the North summit, assuming that Captain Battye climbed the mountain from this side. We considered it doubtful that he had traversed the technically difficult ridge leading to the higher summit, especially as his only companions were four Gurkha soldiers from his regiment. At Camp II, I was able to follow much of the climb. Perhaps it was a pity that Abdul Rauf was not able to take part in it, but I am sure that our decision to provide a fast rope of two was the right one. Rauf had done very well, and had contributed his full share of load-carrying to the high camp. I think that he gained something from this trip; and later on he led several parties of students on hiking and scramb-ling trips in the hills.

By the time Norman Norris and Gene White began to descend, the snow on the north-east face had turned soft revealing ice underneath, and they had to move very cautiously. Later all of us descended to Camp I, where we found two porters who had come up that morning; with their help we packed up and carried everything down to Base, arriving there the same evening. The ascent had been achieved within a week exceeding our most optimistic estimates, but we had been very lucky with the weather. We spent a rest-day ascending a ridge south of Dadar to about 13,000 feet. From there the North and South summits of Mali-ka-Parbat appeared as two distinct peaks. West of the Siran basin, which contains two attractive peaks, it was intriguing to see a possible pass leading into the Saif-ul-Muluk valley. Looking towards the east there was the unexplored Khabanar group containing three peaks above 16,000 feet. There was quite enough in this area to keep an active climber busy for two or three weeks, provided the main attraction was exploratory mountaineering and not the ascent of high mountains.

On leaving Dadar we could not persuade the caretakers of the mosque to accept money. They had been scrupulously honest, and had occasionally brought us gifts of food. I can recall the *muezzin*, huddled in his shawl, patiently watching for the appointed hour after dusk to enable him to make the day's fifth and last call to prayer.

In Naran, learning that the jeep-track to Saif-ul-Muluk lake had been re-opened, we hired a vehicle and drove there on 12 July. Spring had arrived in the valley and I found it altered beyond recognition. Above the lake, now a striking blue-green colour, there were rich pastures and the valley walls on either side were almost free of snow. Looking across at Mali-ka-Parbat from the upper slopes, the North summit of the mountain appears merely as a high point situated on the long north ridge. Seeing the 5,000-foot west face below it, one was tempted to use the word vertical; and we upheld Gene and Norman's decision to forego the traverse of the ridge to the South summit. But it would be interesting to come back one day and climb to the South summit from this valley; a prominent snow face seemed to be the crux and it looked quite steep, though under the right conditions it should provide an excellent climb. We lunched in the warm sunshine by the lake with a group of tourists gathered outside the rest-hut. One of them had heard that we had climbed Mali. As he was a senior police officer from Abbottabad, we feared a mild reproof. Instead we received effusive tributes and a threat to release the news to the press, which happily we were able to avoid.

It was not until 1972 that another opportunity occurred for a visit to the Saif-ul-Muluk valley. Increasing responsibilities and the passage of time (I was married now and had entered my fiftieth year) had inevitably diminished my fervour for long expeditions, though heightened sensibilities provided deeper impressions during each fresh visit to the mountains. I had not lost what Eric Shipton has called a 'sense of wonder'.

Mid-June once again and less than a fortnight to spare. Curiosity aroused by that peep into the Siran basin from Dadar hinting at a pass into Saif-ul-Muluk, and excellent companions with whom to share a new venture. Norman Norris and his wife Jean, Wolfgang Stefan and his wife Helga, now living in Karachi, Frederick Höflin, my wife's 28-year-old brother who travelled out overland from Switzerland on the eve of his final medical examinations in order to join us.

I had been in the hills earlier. From Murree, which is thirty miles north east of Rawalpindi, a long ridge or gali leading north contains a group of village settlements and summer resorts situated at heights above 7,000 feet. Nathia Gali (8,800 ft) is the most westerly and the highest of these. From it the forests gradually recede, and the spurs of a diminishing range begin to level out westwards to the valleys surrounding Abbottabad. Situated at 8,500 feet about three miles below Nathia Gali is Dunga Gali. There, in a cottage surrounded by forests of pine, cedar and oak, I had spent days of deep contentment accompanied by my wife and small son in an atmosphere that was filled with a peacefulness I had not known since my boyhood.

Rising 1,000 feet above the cottage is the hill Mukshpuri, the top of which I used to visit frequently. I would go there at dawn or sunset, when I would be sure to find the solitude I wanted. I used to climb to the top of this mountain from four different directions, sometimes scrambling on rock or traversing the exposed northern slopes or struggling through the undergrowth in forests inhabited by fox and wild monkey. My favourite route, which followed the south-west spur, started from a meadow formed by a prominent col in the ridge that divides Dunga Gali from Nathia Gali. Narrow tracks ascend through a forest filled with the scent of pine. Before the upper alps are reached the pines, seemingly more stately in their isolation, provide a vivid foreground against the sky; through them there are glimpses of distant foothills and a first peep of the snows. In May, when the first primula and irises are beginning to appear, the upper meadows are strewn with edelweiss in a profusion that would seem unbelievable in Europe. In

June when these are all gone I have stridden through the same meadows calf-deep with daisies.

From the summit of Mukshpuri I have watched the changing scene in all weathers. Some of the variations of cloud and sunshine, lighting up a peak or silhouetting a ridge, have been quite unforgettable. Perhaps my sharpest memories will be of clear skies at dawn and a line of peaks across the northern horizon, the eye sweeping across nearly 400 miles of high ranges. On days of exceptional clarity I have seen in the distant west the Hindu Kush, seeming to merge into the mountains of Swat and Indus Kohistan; then the Kaghan hills, close enough to enable me to pick out familiar peaks and ridges on which I have climbed. Dominating all, the bulk of Nanga Parbat—not a single mountain but a dazzling white structure standing above a purple plinth, containing several peaks and isolated from lesser ranges. To the east the soft outline of lower summits comprising over a hundred miles of the Kashmir and Pir Panjal mountains.

About two miles north-west of Nathia Gali is the hill Miranjani, almost 10,000 feet high, which was used as a triangulation station when the early surveys were carried out more than 60 years ago. Rising in isolation above its neighbours it commands views of all the ranges to the north, of the Jhelum river 6,000 feet below to the east, of Rawalpindi and Abbottabad and the plains to the south. Three times I have slept on its summit. Once in mid-winter, inside a tent pitched amid deep snow banks, twice in summer under the open sky, waking in the morning to see Nanga Parbat and other peaks on the northern horizon lit with orange and gold. Then racing down the steep and bouldery forest-tracks to a car waiting below, and back to the cottage for breakfast.

At the forest cottage in Dunga Gali our 'expedition' met; and from there on 17 June we set out, motoring in one day to Naran. The valley seemed to be filled with summer tourists. Five years had brought about some changes; the people looked more prosperous and they seemed to place a much higher value upon their services. One could not really blame them, for the tourist season is a short one of less than three months. Abdul Rashid, one of my 1965 porters, was a tourist guide now, and much too elevated in status to carry a load. With his assistance we engaged three porters, who together with two pack-animals moved all our baggage to the rest-hut at Saif-ul-Muluk lake the next day. Winter had not yet left the valley; the lake was partially frozen and snow still lay thickly everywhere. Since the caretaker of the hut had been one of our porters he permitted us to use the hut that night. It had not been occupied since the autumn and was in disarray but we were glad to be able to light a wood fire in the hearth and to spread out our sleeping bags on the floor.

Wolfgang Stefan and I moved up the valley with light loads at 5.30 a.m. the next day. Although the sky had been clouded at sunset the morning dawned beautifully clear and we were cold for the first two hours as we plodded up the snow-filled valley under the shadow of Mali-ka-Parbat. For nearly five miles we advanced south gaining height steadily. Then, passing the snout of the Saif-ul-Muluk glacier, we turned south-east and the slopes began to steepen. We were now moving round to the south side of Mali; the valley had narrowed and our view was confined to steep rock cliffs on the left and receding snow slopes on the right. Reaching the top of a steep spur on the medial moraine we struck a small patch of grass, only recently clear of snow. Here, about three and a half hours from the lake, we sat down to eat our second breakfast. At 12,000 feet this seemed an ideal site for a camp. Leaving our sacks and a coloured flag as a signal for the others, we moved up the glacier to search for the Siran col. We made quick progress up moderately steep névé, arriving before noon on a saddle at about 14,000 feet. There were no signs that it had been visited before and it was exciting to look into the upper basin of the West Siran glacier from which rose the two highest Siran peaks. The descent to the basin, though steep, looked straightforward and we thought that we could see a route on Siran II. From this peak the ridge dropped to a high col leading south-east then rose steeply to Siran I whose north ridge divides the two Siran basins. We built a cairn and descended to our breakfast site. Here, finding that the rest of the party had arrived, we began to dig ourselves in.

Three tents were pitched and food and equipment were made up into individual loads. Only one porter-ferry from the lake was required in order to fetch all our stores, then the two Naran men were released. This camp was our base for the next few days. It was ideal in many ways, although it was windy and the morning sun arrived late. On one side rose the southern cliffs of Mali-ka-Parbat, too steep to hold any snow; on the other was a high ridge enclosing the valley; almost directly ahead lay the Siran col, obscured behind a steep rise in the glacier. Wolfgang Stefan, with his accumulated experience of big Alpine climbs, went through each stage meticulously. The essential and the necessary comprised two distinct categories when the weight of a rucksack really counted. Routes were worked out in Alpine fashion on a strict time-schedule, with provision for vagaries of weather and conditions. Stefan, relatively small and light of build, appeared to move slowly though this may have been the effect produced by the economy of his style. If he was a slow starter, he seemed to be fresh at the end of a climb. Every plan, like every move, was carefully considered with a view to ensuring success; a wild scheme or a slender chance was out. I found him very likeable as a companion. What appeared to be almost his only fault was an inability to relax, even when at the end of the day to relax seemed to be the only thing left to do.

On 21 June a camp in the Siran basin was occupied and the following day Helga and Wolfgang Stefan with Frederick Höflin reached the summit of Siran II (16,445 ft). A cairn was found on the top left by two British climbers John Winning and Keith Stott who had made the first ascent in 1969 from the south side. The next day all of us ascended a snow point of 14,750 feet north-west of our camp from which we were able to make a fresh study of Mali-ka-Parbat. On an off-day I climbed a neighbouring summit of about 14,250 feet, a fine viewpoint which bore a cairn and had probably been used as a survey station. There was an extensive view of the Manur valley to the south, with massive banks of monsoon cloud building up beyond. On 24 June Wolfgang Stefan and Frederick Höflin bivouacked on a small platform at 14,000 feet at the foot of the steep north-west face of Mali. The next day, after a climb of six and a half hours, they reached the South summit (17,356 ft). The last part of their route was similar to that followed in 1940 by Willoughby and Price, whose cairn they found. The average angle of the face is about 50° and they were lucky to have had good conditions for the ascent, although with the upper layer of snow turning soft during the descent extreme care was necessary owing to the presence of ice. Stefan and Höflin followed this climb by shifting to the Siran basin from where they made the first ascent of Siran I (16,505 ft). Then they descended the Siran valley to Dadar and Battakundi.

The trip had been a complete success. The whole journey was done in under two weeks and the cost was much below that of my first two journeys. This was partly because there were six to share the expenses but chiefly, I think, because we travelled really light, and some familiarity with the area had enabled us to work out a plan which made maximum use of the limited time available. Thus no day was lost in unnecessary load-shifting, and very little use was made of porters.

I have had many enjoyable days in the Kaghan valley. The mountains are modest in size; and although they might have a limited appeal they provide that most delightful of contrasts, an evening descent to a camp among flowers after a day spent on snow peaks. With its easy accessibility the area provides a wonderful opportunity for a short holiday. Many such opportunities have I seized; sometimes no more than a long weekend in winter; sometimes a quick reconnaissance with an eye for some future project. From the eight visits I have made altogether, I have never come back disappointed.

XI
The Freedom of the Hills

'Tis not too late to seek a newer world.
Push off, and sitting well in order smite
The sounding furrows; for my purpose holds
To sail beyond the sunset, and the baths
Of all the western stars, until I die.
It may be that the gulfs will wash us down:
It may be we shall touch the Happy Isles,
To see the great Achilles, whom we knew.
Though much is taken, much abides; and though
We are not now that strength which in old days
Moved earth and heaven; that which we are, we are.

Tennyson

For over a decade I lived in Pakistan. When I first went to the Punjab in 1961 Khanewal was a quiet country town, which the description of a former day, 'a small upcountry station', would have fitted perfectly. The five rivers of the Punjab enclose large tracts of country which were not long ago desert with a water level eighty feet below the surface, peopled by nomad tribes who grazed their goats and camels on scanty scrub. But the British rulers had observed that the slight north-east to south-west decline in the land-level combined with a watershed pattern existing between every pair of rivers seemed to provide an ideal situation for the construction of canals whilst also dictating their main alignment. By 1890 work had begun on building the first canals in the Punjab; around them grew colonies and villages, with sites selected every twenty or thirty miles for country towns. Before colonists were brought to settle, model towns had been designed, connected with roads and railways, whilst extensive tree-planting was carried out. The desert suddenly blossomed; the colonies grew into rich agricultural belts and became a major source of supply for the country's requirements of wheat and cotton. Seventy years later, when a new link-canal system was under construction in the Punjab with the use of modern earth-moving equipment, one could begin to appreciate the staggering task that the pioneer canal-builders must have faced working under the most primitive conditions. It has been said that if the English were to choose one monument by which their years in India were to be remembered it might be the canals.

Khanewal, situated in the central canal zone of the Punjab, was in 1961 a mixture of fertility and desert, with green fields and sandy belts existing side by side. Like all deserts, it experiences extremes of temperature. The winters are cold and clear with ground frost common during January; but the summers are extremely hot. During my first summer it seemed hardly possible to believe the midday thermometer which stood at 118°F day after day during June. The annual rainfall is about four inches; it is the absence of humidity that makes such high temperatures easier to bear. I was fortunate to have inherited a large garden which had matured over a period of forty years into an oasis of trees, shrubs, hedges, lawns and flower-beds. In summer passing out of the garden gate into the sandy atmosphere outside it was possible to feel a distinct rise in the air temperature. At sunset on summer evenings I would walk across the empty sandhills, which had not quite shed their daytime heat; or by the canal banks on a narrow verge of grass lined with trees, providing an undisturbed landscape for endless miles. Sometimes I was a source of puzzlement when declining the offer of a passing cyclist; an actual preference for walking seemed incomprehensible.

In this country town one heard in the quiet of the night the whistle of a steam engine from the nearby railway station, the bells of a camel caravan carrying freshly-picked cotton to a ginning factory, or the clatter of a horse and *tonga** on the metalled road. There were few other sounds, except the occasional call of a nightwatchman on patrol. Life seemed reminiscent of a former era, and one lived almost as the planter on his estate, insulated from the world. But there were many frustrations; and without patience, forbearance and a readiness to improvise, there was a real danger of early disenchantment. There were, of course, compensations. One of the chief of these was the devotion and loyalty of household servants. In this unique relationship the model

* Two-wheeled passenger carriage.

mentor and provider received their protection and affection, and accepted the headship of a family. Only those who have spent earlier decades in the Indian sub-continent will understand the depth of the attachment. It was not unknown during those years for the old retainer, introducing his grown son with pride, to say: 'This is my son, now he is your son'. Of equal value was the steadfastness of one's office staff. To give way to a fit of impatience would fill one with remorse because you knew that they trusted your integrity and judgement, and it was wrong to display any symptom of weakness.

Unlimited opportunities existed for me to get away to the mountains. By putting to the best possible use a fairly generous quota of public holidays, and by reducing my needs to the barest essentials, I have managed in long weekends to visit areas as far distant as the limestone ranges of Quetta, sandstone mountains of lower Baluchistan; forbidden tribal hills in Waziristan, isolated escarpments in the Salt Range, and wintry Kaghan summits. With these and many other mountain groups have I dallied; unencumbered by local difficulties and going just as far as my strength allowed, entering uninhabited valleys and building cairns on lonely mountain tops. Sometimes achieving a grateful success and never troubled by the despondency that follows defeat on bigger objectives.

Some of my happiest journeys have been undertaken, often alone, during stolen weekends in winter and spring. From them I have always returned greatly refreshed. Knowing myself a little better; and, while the after-glow lasted, shedding the pettiness and meanness that often enter into our daily lives. In one year I made seven such visits to various ranges, hardly believing the good fortune that had enabled me to do so.

On my first journey to Quetta* in 1964 I travelled by car across the plateau west of the Suleiman range, a journey of about 200 miles through rocky desert. The road consists of rough gravel, sometimes winding through ravines and sometimes stretching in a straight line for miles with curiously contorted limestone ridges on either side. Geographically this is the commencement of a wide belt of arid and mountainous terrain that extends westwards in an almost uniform pattern for over 1,500 miles from Pakistan through Afghanistan and Iran. Often a single road serves large tracts of country where the

* The areas described in this chapter can be found in the front end-papers.

population is scanty and the way of life has changed little over the centuries. The inhabitants live mostly by subsistence farming or as nomadic herdsmen. Brigandage, a traditional occupation, is even today not entirely unknown. From Dera Ghazi Khan, situated on the west bank of the Indus, I had my first view of the hills which form part of the Suleiman range. Since it was spring I crossed the Indus by a boat-bridge which spanned shrunken channels along the eight-mile-wide bed of this mighty river; in the flood season I would have had to use a ferry.

Dera Ghazi Khan is the divisional headquarters of an administrative district, and in 1866 Robert Sandeman was posted there as Deputy Commissioner. It was regarded in those days as a frontier district; across the border were independent Baluchi tribes who accepted the Khan of Kalat as their titular head. There were the fierce Marris and Bugtis in the south, also the tribes of Zhob and Pishin. In the north were the Sheranis and other Pathan tribes of Kurram and south Waziristan. Often under opposition from his superiors, Sandeman introduced new methods of dealing with the tribes, risking his life to enter tribal territory under tribal escort and visiting the headquarters of every clan in order to keep in friendly touch with them. As an alternative to their habitual looting raids he adopted a system of employing the tribes as messengers and patrols, thereby keeping the caravan routes open, and creating a force of men who were available when required. For nearly twenty years he exercised great influence in these areas, gaining the respect and affection of the tribal leaders. When he died some of them nearly came to war for the privilege of burying his remains.

The country contains great charm of a primitive sort; yet no man wanders about these hills without a rifle. My first night was spent in a two-roomed mud hut, one of about a dozen in a village called Kingri situated fifteen miles from its neighbour. I had received a personal welcome from the headman, and I slept unarmed and with doors unlocked. Earlier an armed policeman had requested a ride in my car. As we drove through the dusk I noticed two figures beckoning us to halt; I had begun to slow down when my policeman urged me to drive on, fast. Only then was the danger brought home to me. The next day, on which there was a religious festival, I approached the picturesque village of Mekhtar which is built around green fields and circled by low hills. I could see the road ahead filled with a procession consisting of the whole male population dressed in their finery and led by the village chief and elders. I halted the car and walked a hundred yards towards the crowd, feeling very lonely and exposed and eyeing cautiously the movements of the headman in front. As we drew close I pondered nervously about an opening gesture. Then I walked towards the chief with my right hand outstretched; a moment later he had clasped it firmly in a handshake and the tension was over. The gesture was repeated by a score of his followers and a passage was given to my vehicle.

Loralai, centrally situated between the Zhob and Sibi districts, used to be a British army station and there are now derelict acres of sand behind the village containing the skeleton structures of a former cantonment. Fifty-nine miles beyond is Ziarat, 8,030 feet high, where juniper forests bring about a sudden change in the character of the country. Situated between miles of barren hills it is refreshing to see sheep grazing on green pastureland. The air is fragrant with the scent of artemisia, and there are slopes strewn with the bright yellow spikes of Foxtail lily, *eremurus*. Ziarat is a summer resort for dwellers in Sibi and Quetta; but under its winter cover of snow it is deserted. When I saw it in April, the trees were filled with apple, apricot and peach blossoms.

I visited Ziarat again in March 1966 with Betsy and Gene White and Richard Blandy. The weather was still wintry and the night temperature was 20°F. Among a handful of local inhabitants we found an old *shikari*, Mohamed Noor, who was willing to guide us to our objective the peak of Khalifat (11,434 ft). British officers formerly stationed at the Army Staff college in Quetta[1] explored most of these hills, discovering some good climbs on the sound limestone rock.[2] A narrow track winding for eight miles south of Ziarat was just wide enough to accomodate our jeep wagoneer. At the end of the track lies Zezri meadow, surrounded by forests of dwarf juniper. We camped beside a woodcutter's hut with the snow-covered north face of Khalifat rising above. Mohamed Noor tried to discourage us from making the ascent in winter, but after he had been out with us on an afternoon reconnaissance of the rock face he agreed to accompany us. We traversed the mountain the next day, going up by the north-east face and down by the west ridge; a very satisfying climb of seven hours. In the late autumn of 1972 Wolfgang Stefan and I repeated this climb taking just over six hours, the route having been made easier by the absence of snow on the rock face.

On another occasion Gene White and I spent a night at a small village nestling under the face of Tukatu, a peak of 11,390 feet situated twelve miles outside Quetta. The mountain is a striking sight from the centre of Quetta town, and when it is snow-covered in winter it has quite an impressive appearance. With its twin summits it probably contains the best rock climbing in the region. In August the weather was terribly dry and hot. Gene and I slept out in the open but we were glad to have brought blankets. The climb was done by the south face and the south-west ridge. The upper part, though never more than a scramble, reminded me of Crib Goch and provided plenty of interest. On the return we raced down the bouldery track across dry ravine beds to an apple orchard fed by spring water. Seated on thick turf under the luxurious shade of the trees we gorged on unripe though marvellously juicy fruit.

Twice more, during Christmas weekends, I visited this region. On the first occasion in December 1968 my companion was Mick Briggs, school-teaching in the Punjab during a year of voluntary service overseas. We drove through Sukkur to Jacobabad which is reputed to be the hottest town on the subcontinent. It is named after John Jacob who colonised the region in the middle of the nineteenth century. Starting with a few huts in the desert he built a town of 7,000 inhabitants with a laboratory, a workshop and a large library. The Commissioner of Sind, Sir Bartle Frere, visiting him in 1855 wrote: 'I went with Jacob nine miles into what four years ago was real desert without a tree, a drop of water or a blade of grass; all is now stubble as far as the eye could reach.' This 'real desert' stretches for ninety-eight miles from Jacobabad to Sibi. There is a narrow strip of road along which the impression is not so much of motoring as of sailing, with heat-haze creating the illusion of a shimmering ocean on either side. A single railway track runs through it, and from Sibi the railway climbs, with the road, through the hills to the Bolan pass, dropping down from there to the Quetta plateau. Like the railway through the Khyber pass this was constructed in the early 1920s; and with its numerous tunnels it is a tribute to the engineers who designed it.

Our objective was Koh-i-Maran (10,751 ft) situated forty miles northeast of Kalat. We approached the mountain late one afternoon, climbing over an intervening ridge and crossing two miles of flinty sand. The night was spent at a settlement comprising half-a-dozen huts surrounding a pool of brackish water. The pool and the settlement bore the owner's name, Haji Baber Khan; the next settlement was twelve miles away across the desert at the next well. The primitive nomads with their camels and goats treated us kindly. Next day the ascent turned out to be no more than a steep walk, but from the summit, where there was a sharp wind, we had an extensive view across the Quetta and Kalat hills. Near the top we saw tracks of *markhor*, which looked very fresh. On the way down we filled our two billy-cans with snow, having politely declined the murky liquid which our hosts had produced from their well.

My next climb in those hills was on Christmas day in 1971. About fourteen miles south of Quetta stands the Chiltan range (10,500 ft), which is one of the few refuges for diminishing herds of *markhor*. The morning was cold and clear when I entered one of the *nalas* at the foot of the mountain, hoping to climb to the snow-covered summit which rose about 5,000 feet above. I was alone, and except for two wood-cutters busy at the entrance to the *nala*, I saw nobody for the remainder of the day. Climbing steadily for four hours I arrived at a point about 500 feet below the summit ridge, having long since realised that I had entered the wrong branch valley and I would not make the main summit. The sun had disappeared and clouds drifted across the skyline adding an air of mystery to the untrodden ground ahead. I had decided that at one o'clock I would have to turn back. When I did so the peak was no longer visible and a black mushroom cloud stood poised over Quetta. I returned to the car in the afternoon and the next day, driving 500 miles in twelve hours, I reached Khanewal just after dark.

A trip to Takht-i-Suleiman in the winter of 1967 was one of my most enjoyable weekend ventures. Norman Norris and I travelled to Dera Ismail Khan by car, driving across the twelve-mile wide Indus bed, which was almost dry during January that year. Dera Ismail Khan remains an important frontier headquarters. It is situated at the southern end of the political agencies of Kohat, Bannu and Waziristan, populated by tribal communities some of whom, like the Mahsuds of South Waziristan, are still thought to be unpredictable. Beyond, a wide road-way, submerged under several inches of dust, leads to the Suleiman hills. The dust turns to gravel and the level track begins to wind and climb through the range. There is a fort at Daraban situated at the entrance to the Sherani tribal area. From there fifteen miles of rocky and undulating road leads to Darazinda, district headquarters of the Frontier Constabulary. The officer commanding the fort generously permitted us to use his guest-house and provided us with a *havildar-major* and a *lance-naik* as escorts. Ahead of us stood Takht-i-Suleiman (11,325 ft), rising nearly 7,000 feet above the plain. We drove eight miles along the Fort Sandeman road, on which there was a thrice weekly bus service to Quetta through the isolated Zhob district. Branching west, we reached the village of Ragasar situated at the foot of our mountain. There we were able to engage two tribesmen as porters, and they took on a third man for good measure.

In the evening, after a climb of about 4,000 feet we camped on a high summer pasture situated below the final rock face of Takht-i-Suleiman. Water was obtained from a nearby pool after breaking the icy surface. The following morning we entered a rock gully which provided a steep scramble for about 1,500 feet. The next stretch of about 300 feet was ascended by means of crude wooden scaffolding attached to a smooth 75° rock face. The men took a delight in this cat-walk which they called Sherani *sarak*, i.e. road. Beyond, we gained the north ridge of the mountain, and descended to the easier north side which had a substantial snow cover. From the summit, which we reached after three hours, we could see in the extraordinarily clear atmosphere hundreds of miles of brown hills to the west and south, and an unexpected belt of pine forest, the home of *markhor*, lay below us to the north. Our escort, one of whom carried a rifle, were in high spirits. I think that a rather trigger-happy attitude prevails amongst these tribesmen, which has resulted in a serious diminution of the wildlife population. If shooting could be controlled within supervised limits this would keep the inhabitants reasonably happy, at the same time preserving a desirable balance in the natural environment. We left the summit at noon and returned to Ragasar the same evening, stumbling over steep moraine for the final hour in total darkness.

Situated on the watershed between the Siran and Kunhar rivers in Kaghan, and about fifteen miles north-west of Balakot is Musa-ka-Musalla* (13,374 ft), a prominent whaleback hill whose summit is snow-covered throughout the year. In summer its ascent involves a steep though fairly lengthy ridge-walk. It had never been climbed in winter; and with others I made various attempts to climb it from the east, south and west via each of its three main ridges. The winter snowline in the Kaghan valley is usually about 9,500 feet; but there are occasions when I have seen snow lying thickly at 7,500 feet. In February 1970 I made another attempt to climb Musa-ka-Musalla from the west. Seen from Mansehra, sixteen miles beyond Abbottabad, the mountain dominates a line of peaks comprising the lower Kaghan range. A narrow track branches north from Mansehra following the Siran river for about thirty miles to Domel,† where a stream from the north enters the

* The prayer-mat of Moses see Map 9 on page 136.
† Literally, where two points meet.

25. Chitta glacier and North peak of Mali-ka-Parbat, 17,135 feet (5 July 1967)

26. Norman Norris standing on the North peak of Mali-ka-Parbat. The South peak is behind, showing the upper part of the north-west face (*photo G. White*) (9 July 1967)

27. Siran II, 16,445 feet, seen from the col Siran (21 June 1972)

28. Approaching the summit of Siran II. Siran Col centre left. Mali-ka-Parbat behind (*photo W. Stefan*) (22 June 1972)

29. Frontier Constabulary at Darazinda Fort; Takht-i-Suleiman, 11,325 feet, behind (15 January 1967)

kept the fire going all night partly, I suspect, because of their fear of leopard, and they claimed to have stayed awake throughout. I caught fragments of their conversation. Young Muskeen spoke nostalgically of summer pastures below this hut where a drink of warm sheep's milk was always at hand.

We started before dawn the next morning; it was cold and the sky was cloudless. We ascended the ridge, kicking steps in firm snow. The pale summit above us turned orange, then gold as we climbed up to meet the sun's warming glow. After two and a half hours we stepped onto an immaculate white dome and the slopes fell away on all sides. The *ziarat* was buried under eight feet of snow and only its upper flags were visible. There was a thrilling view of the entire Kaghan range, standing out sharply in the blue-tinged wintry atmosphere; and I was able to pick out many familiar peaks dominated by Mali-ka-Parbat. Neither the sharp wind nor the freezing temperature could contain the enthusiasm of the two porters; their friends in Jhacha would never believe that they had reached the *ziarat* in winter. On the way down we came across fresh tracks in the snow criss-crossing ours at the entrance to the forest; the men were certain that these had been made by a snow-leopard during the night. The greetings received on our return to the village were spontaneous and sincere; as was the farewell of Ghazi Khan, 'Will you not come back again?' He had refused to accept payment on behalf of the men. But I was able to compensate them when they continued with me down to Domel that evening.

In July 1970 Mick Briggs, who had accompanied me on a weekend venture to Baluchistan in 1968, came out from England with two companions, C. Meredith from Manchester and E. Thurrell from Stockport, to join me on a short trip to the Karakoram. Hunza and Nagar were closed that year, so we went to the Naltar valley, which joins the Hunza river twenty miles north of Gilgit*. The village of Nomal is situated at the junction of the two valleys and we were able to travel by jeep to this point and eight miles beyond to the forest rest-house above Naltar village. There we engaged five pack-animals, setting out on 10 July for a two-day walk to the head of the valley. Beyond the Shani glacier we placed a camp at 12,500 feet situated below the Naltar pass leading into Ishkuman. The Karambar river flows through the Ishkuman region; a pass at its head provides a route into Wakhan, and its headwaters lie north of the Hindu Raj mountains.

* See map 7 on page 120.

Several large glaciers which drain into the Karambar valley from the east and the north are a fitting reminder of the great range which borders this valley; for the Karambar forms a natural dividing-line between the Karakoram and the Hindu Kush. Before the glacial recession which commenced around the turn of the present century the Karambar valley above Imit was often rendered impassable by ice-dams formed by these great glaciers, the bursting of which would cause the river at Gilgit, 150 miles away, to rise to flood level. Many of the glaciers draining into the Karambar have not been fully explored because entry to this region has always been restricted. The largest settlement in the valley is at Imit which used to be the seat of the Raja of Ishkuman; the first Raja, an exiled Mir from Wakhan, settled there in 1883.[3]

Our map, which was based upon surveys carried out sixty years earlier, showed a peak of 20,646 feet, situated about fourteen miles north-east of the Naltar pass. While the heights of some of the larger peaks had been accurately determined, the position and alignment of glaciers were largely conjectural, since in those days it was rare for surveyors to explore to the head of every valley. The map indicated a route over the Shani divide into Ishkuman, from where it seemed possible to follow an approach west of the peak, but the glaciers to the north were only roughly sketched in and I was fully prepared for some surprises. My three companions had indicated beforehand that their primary interest lay in the ascent of the 20,000-foot peak. I welcomed in addition an opportunity to try to clear up some of the confusion on the map and to fill in the blanks. It seemed possible thus to combine their purely climbing objectives with my own mainly exploratory interests; but after much searching we failed to find a passage over the watershed into the Baj Gaz valley above Imit, and the route to our peak appeared to be barred from that side.

To the east was the Daintar divide; whilst the others tried to climb a snow dome situated on the dividing ridge, I crossed the divide and dropped into the Daintar valley. From there I ascended to the upper basin of the Karengi glacier, discovering a feasible approach to the 20,646-foot peak, via an exit out of that basin to the west. The basin appeared to provide another exit to the north-east towards the wide stretch of glaciated country, only partly explored, south of the Batura group whose highest peaks are still unclimbed.[4] It was four days' journey from our Base and I was inside Nagar territory where I had no right to be. My presence had been accepted because my Shani porter was reduced to a camp-follower and I engaged a Nagari porter in his stead. I found here another instance of inhabitants of adjacent valleys speaking a different dialect, their homesteads differing in style and each side hardly aware of the other's existence. Dadu, my Nagari porter, was a lively and intelligent youth. He was aroused to considerable emotion when describing the uprising that had occurred six months before at the Mir of Nagar's winter home in Chalt. When Government forces arrived to establish their rights following the merging of the State with Pakistan (see Chapter VI, Note 2) loyal subjects of the Mir, Dadu amongst them, fought a pitched battle outside the Mir's residence which was quelled only after reinforcements had been called from Gilgit. Dadu visited our Base Camp at the end of the Karengi journey; during the night he crept rather shamefaced into my tent for shelter during a severe storm. In the half-light of dawn, with the storm only partly abated, he slipped outside into a dense fog to make his way back home over the Daintar pass.

On an off-day a rock feature above Base Camp was tackled by each member of the party in turn, as a challenge that had to be met. All three of my companions represented the younger generation of keen enthusiasts whose main interest in the mountains lies in the opportunity which they provide for overcoming difficult technical problems on rock faces. One of them was an exponent of artificial techniques, having done grade six rock climbs in Britain. By dint of continuous perseverance the modern climer is able to reach an astonishing degree of technical skill, tackling climbs that a previous generation would have labelled impossible. Theirs is essentially an acquired art, differing in essence and in quality from the skill of the natural climber, such as that of the native mountain dweller with his inborn mountain sense, fearlessness and sheer grace of movement. One member of the party, physically the most impressive, was unhappily unable to acclimatise, suffering great discomfort every time he went above 12,500 feet, which deprived him of any climbing. Perhaps the comment of one of my companions on the last day should not have surprised me. I had remarked upon a striking snow ridge leading to the highest summit of an unclimbed group of 19,000-foot mountains situated behind Naltar when he observed, 'I'm on holiday now; no interest.' To attempt to define modern attitudes to climbing or to compare them with those of the pioneers would be futile. After all, have we not witnessed revolutionary changes during the past hundred years in the material quality of the lives we lead, accompanied by an evolution

31. Shani peak, 19,310 feet (25 July 1970)

in social and moral values which would have seemed strange only two or three decades ago. Each new generation creates its own trends and introduces different standards of acceptability. As each passing generation recedes into the background it should wisely recall its own earlier attitudes and attempt to find a measure of compatibility towards its successors. What remains unalterable is man's striving after self-satisfaction and his ability as an individual to live with his conscience. The greatest satisfaction is a feeling of gratitude for having seized one's chance at the proper time, without recrimination or envy over the future.

Near our Shani base were Shani peak (19,310 ft) and the Twins (19,230 ft). The former appeared to be beyond our powers. Although we thought that we had found a route on one of the Twins, a freak storm lasting for four days put an end to our attempt. We left the valley at the end of July with only one ascent of a peak of 17,918 feet, situated on the Ishkuman watershed. For the others it was only the technical challenge of reaching a summit that seemed important, so that the possibility of discovering a pass into an unsuspected valley did not raise a glimmer of enthusiasm. I think that the absence of an alternative plan after our main objective was denied failed to give them the satisfaction of achievement which seemed lacking at the end. Adjustment to the scale and the conditions delayed a proper assessment of the problems involved. If there had been more time I am sure that other climbs would have been made.

I would have liked to return to that region. Of the many unexplored glaciers east of the Karambar river one of the largest is the Karambar glacier in the north which would provide access to the peak Kampire Dior (23,434 ft). No climbers have so far approached this mountain, and there does not seem to be a way to it from the south or the east. But much of that country is still unexplored, and a few geographical enigmas still await unravelling in odd corners of the Karakoram. Unfortunately, political upheaval in Pakistan has resulted in a veil being drawn across most of the region.

In 1971 I was able to introduce my wife to the Himalaya when we paid a short visit to Rama. We travelled by jeep from Gilgit to Astor, much impressed by the Pakistan army's bull-dozing operations on sections of the new road which were under extension. At Bunji, neatly laid out bungalows and messes occupied by the Gilgit Scouts recalled an earlier British era. Just beyond we had our first spectacular view of Nanga Parbat, a gleaming mass rising straight out of the heat-haze without any intervening forests or alps to soften the contrast between the brown desert. The commandant of the Scouts welcomed us hospitably in Astor and from there we walked to Rama, 3,000 feet above. Occupying a picturesque forest bungalow situated at 10,500 feet we spent the next week in a glorious setting of pinewoods and meadows below a glacier which flows from peaks situated on the north-east rim of Nanga Parbat. We ascended the ridges enclosing both sides of the valley. Situated at the farthest end of the northern ridge was a high point, c. 16,000 feet, which bore a survey cairn. From it we faced the highest Chongra peak, not more than four miles away. Extending from that peak in a great south-westerly curve I could see the incredible ridge almost nine miles long which supports the two lower Chongra peaks, Rakhiot peak, the Silver Saddle and the huge summit structure of Nanga Parbat. The intense clarity of the atmosphere made the spectacle seem almost unreal. I suppose that there are not many mountain groups that can be compared with this in structure and size throughout the length of the Himalaya and the Karakoram.

And so I have come to the end of my wanderings.

In the north-west are deserts, hundreds of miles of barren uplands streaked with low ranges of contorted limestone stretching across Baluchistan and Waziristan and forming a natural barrier to the rolling hills of Afghanistan which lie to the west. The people belong to fiercely independent tribes who are physically attractive and possess strange manners, being hospitable and docile in their homes but warlike and quick to anger against trespassers. North of this zone lie the valleys of Chitral, a land of legend and superstition where the harshness of the landscape is relieved by the lush fertility of small settlements which are surrounded by groves of poplars and plane trees; where the economy has remained backward because the inhabitants must hibernate for almost half the year during their snowbound winters. Mile upon mile of rugged mountains stretch into the distance beyond their habitations, forming the chain of the Hindu Kush whose glaciers recede unusually high into the folds of the peaks and whose peaks stand sentinel on a rim overlooking the sparsely-peopled valleys of Wakhan. Towards the south and the east there are the unexplored regions of Kohistan and the Hindu Raj where hundreds of mountains of diminishing size await the climber.

Eastwards the Karambar valley forms a geographical dividing line; in its upper reaches it provides access to little-frequented passes through the main chain. Here the scale begins increasingly to impress, for this is an area of massive glaciers dominated by giant mountains with valleys inhabited by a people whose history and traditions precede the Christian era. For over 300 miles the Karakoram extends in a great arc to the south-east. Practically all its highest peaks have been climbed, but mountaineers have done no more than touch the fringes of this range, some of whose upper valleys and glaciers have seldom been visited by man. There, from a high summit it is possible to look out on to chain upon chain of peaks, the procession of icy mountains in every direction seeming to be without end; only in the remote horizon to the north changing colours hint at the limitless plateaux of Central Asia. The great Indus river flows south of this range, its waters joined by rivers issuing from distant glaciers of enormous size. Curiously this river follows a northerly trend before pushing out into a spectacular curve above Nanga Parbat to meet the Gilgit valley. When it emerges at last, through a series of gorges, at the foot of the hills near Tarbela it continues its journey through the plains for over 900 miles before reaching the Arabian sea.

The softer landscapes of Swat and Kaghan are situated on both sides of the great gorge carved by the Indus river. Their rich soil yields abundant food and fruit crops; green meadows merge with scented forests of pine, fir, cedar and spruce; the snowpeaks are of modest size and easily approachable. Near this point the Great Himalayan Range curves sharply to the south-east with the Pir Panjal and Zaskar ranges dividing Kashmir from Ladakh, and the Deosai plains separating the Karakoram from Kashmir. For over a hundred years Kashmir with its lakes and forests, hills and glaciers has been a happy playground for travellers and sportsmen. But no less beautiful are the hills of Chamba and Kulu to the east. There are gentle hillsides of the deepest green ideally suited to the cultivation of cereal crops which grow on terraced fields of symmetrical beauty adorned with a wealth of chestnut, oak and elm trees and orchards filled with apples and pears. The people here look healthy and contented, as they have every reason to be. Across the passes to the north lie the bleaker landscapes of Lahul and Spiti, the watershed between these zones filled with ranges of enchanting mountains. Beyond the borderlands to the north and north-east lies Tibet, land of enigma and mystery, whose former self-imposed isolation has given way to a remoteness more complete. Fabled mountains exist there, Kailas, Gurla Mandhata, Gosainthan and many others mostly unnamed.

Spread across the tops of the foothills which rise from the plains of India are the small towns built by man eager to savour the climate of Europe in an atmosphere of contrast and luxuriance found only in tropical lands. The presence of large mountains, never very far away to the north, adds a touch of magic to the changing though changeless landscapes of Simla, Ranikhet, Almorah, Mussooree, and a dozen other small settlements. The hills beyond these, comprising folds and ridges of blue and purple, contain joys and rewards that in a lifetime of travel would never grow dull or stale. There is a variety of country to stimulate and to challenge; forests, alpine meadows strewn with flowers; a stark barrier of torrents and gorges guarding large glaciers; and mountains that rise above 25,000 feet. There are the habitations of people whose simple hospitality and charm have remained unsullied in a world where these qualities seem to have lost much of their meaning.

Across the eastern borders of Kumaon and Garhwal lie the mountains of Nepal whose ranges extending in a great sweep from west to east occupy over 450 miles of the Great Himalaya. No longer a forbidden land, this has become the best known part of the whole range and it is considered by some to be the most impressive and the most beautiful. There is much variety in the landscape affording equal delight to the traveller, explorer, botanist, scientist, and climber. In this monsoon land the luxuriant foliage alters through a series of climatic belts, each possessing its own distinct character; the low-lying Terai, the tropical forest, the lower foothills, the temperate alpine zone and the heavily glaciated upper regions. The largest number of the world's highest peaks is situated within this part of the range, and it is perhaps the finest testing-ground for the high-altitude climber. To obtain a view of Everest and other great mountains from a spur above the foothills is to see in a single glance probably the most impressive assembly of mountains on the surface of this planet. The people are full of good humour and charm, an amalgam of races who are varied as the regions in which they dwell. In the rugged lands to the north which impinge on the borders their culture and centuries-old way of life are akin to that of their Tibetan neighbours. In the north-east corner is the home of the Sherpas, traditionally immigrants from Tibet, who more than any other of the mountain races have played a part in the extension of Himalayan exploration and mountaineering during this century.

Adjoining Nepal is the small Kingdom of Sikkim, an impressive chain of high mountains comprising the seventy-mile-long border between the two kingdoms, with Kangchenjunga the crowning jewel of the chain. On all sides Sikkim faces large and powerful neighbours. The rim of mountains to the east and north forming a geographical borderland is broken here and there by a series of passes into Tibet. To the south lie the plains of India, easily accessible yet easily isolated when the winding hill roads are washed away by rain. The monsoon rainfall is sometimes cataclysmic, and in this small country where the mountains are on a grand scale, the valleys are narrow and steep containing densely forested hills, and there is a sharpness in the form of the peaks which even their heavy mantle of ice and snow cannot conceal. In the damp primeval forest of the lower foothills and in the wildness of the upper regions the country seems to have remained untouched, untrammelled by man from the beginning of time. During spring on the lower slopes there are wide banks filled with hydrangeas in every combination of white, pink and blue. Higher up the rhododendrons appear, first in small patches then in thickets until there are complete forests of rhododendron of innumerable colours and varieties. There are giant magnolia of the purest white filling the air with their scent; and orchids climbing wild over tree-trunks, bushes and ferns. In the north there is a complete contrast of wide open spaces, an expanse of windswept plateaux dotted with snow mountains.

From a high point on the Singalila ridge which divides Sikkim from Nepal it is possible to see all this on a clear day; the deep valleys, the dense forests, the brown northern desert and the great range of peaks, Makalu, Everest, Lhotse, Jannu, Rathong, Kabru, Talung, Kangchenjunga, Pandim, Simvu, Narsing, Siniolchu, Lhonak, Chomiomo, Kangchenjau, Pauhunri, Chomolhari and scores of others. The majesty and beauty of Kangchenjunga seems to pass beyond the realm of earthly reality. The eye that has seen this gigantic spectacle of mountains in Nepal, Sikkim and Tibet filling the horizon has had an opportunity to comprehend the greatness of the Himalaya. Darjeeling possesses something of this magic for it is a part of this enchanted land and each season it renews and fulfils its freshness and beauty—in the crisp air of spring, and in the crowded summer, in winter when deserted roads and cottages lie under cover of fog and rain; in the monsoon when mists obscure the pine-trees, drawing apart for an instant to reveal some unidentified ice ridge; in the autumn sun, when skies of unbelievable clarity seem to spread an atmosphere of serenity across the great ranges.

Happiness is a combination of the physical ability to act and the objective capacity for contentment. The intensity of enjoyment that we derive from our pursuits depends upon the depth of our susceptibility to the influences that attract us. I have been very fortunate. For thirty years I have wandered about the Himalaya amidst a variety of landscapes and peoples, enthralled by the mountain environment whether I have found myself in the icy world of the giants or in the mellow atmosphere of the foothills. I have seized many opportunities; from some has sprung a sense of fulfilment; from others a greater degree of self-knowledge. Failure and success equally have been my teachers; each in its own way has deepened my involvement. Those are nearest to having won the freedom of the hills for whom each fresh encounter is a source of enrichment.

NOTES

Chapter I: Historical Background

1. For a more detailed account of the founding of the Himalayan Club see G. L. Corbett's Introduction to Volume I of the *Himalayan Journal*, published in April 1929. See also Kenneth Mason's *Abode of Snow*, pp. 189–92 (Hart–Davis, London, 1955). Professor Mason's book is an authoritative source of reference on the historical and geographical background to the entire Himalayan range. I know of no other single volume that contains such a concise and comprehensive history of Himalayan exploration covering the period up to 1955. Innumerable are the occasions on which I have turned to its pages for information and guidance.

2. Volumes I to XII of the *Himalayan Journal*, which appeared regularly every year from 1929 to 1940, constitute the most complete record available of all Himalayan activity during that period. The first four volumes were printed by Thacker's Press in Calcutta and the remaining eight in Oxford at the Clarendon Press. Copies of these volumes are exceedingly scarce. In order to meet a growing demand from all over the world the Himalayan Club had a scheme under consideration for their re-printing.

3. The 1929 attempt is described in Bauer's book *Im Kampf um den Himalaya* (Knorr & Hirth, Munich, 1931). Also *Himalayan Journal*, Vol. II, pp. 13–20. An account of the 1931 expedition is contained in *Um den Kantsch* by Paul Bauer (Knorr & Hirth, Munich, 1933); also *Himalayan Journal*, Vol. IV, pp. 116–22. *Himalayan Campaign* by Paul Bauer, translated by Sumner Austin (Blackwell, Oxford, 1937) contains the story of both expeditions. See also *Kangchenjunga Challenge* by Paul Bauer (William Kimber, London, 1955).

4. This expedition is described by F. S. Smythe in his book *Kangchenjunga Adventure* (Gollancz, London, 1931).

5. Under the Expeditions Section of the *Himalayan Journal*, a brief summary of this expedition's achievements is given in Vol. I (1929), pp. 88–90, and Vol. II (1930), pp. 107–9.

6. See *Himalayan Journal*, Vol. IV (1932), p. 46: 'My Expedition in the Eastern Karakoram' by Professor Giotto Dainelli.

7. A full account is given in *Himalayan Journal*, Vol. IV (1932), pp. 27–45. See also *Kamet Conquered* by F. S. Smythe (Gollancz, London, 1932).

8. See *Himalayan Journal*, Vol. V (1933), pp. 65–74. 'The Attack on Nanga Parbat, 1932,' by Willy Merkl.

9. Fritz Bechtold, who had been a member of Merkl's 1932 party describes this tragic expedition of 1934 in the book *Deutsche am Nanga Parbat* (Bruckmann, Munich, 1935). An English edition, translated by H. E. G. Tyndale, entitled *Nanga Parbat Adventure* was published by John Murray, London, 1935. Bechtold is also the author of the account which appears in the *Himalayan Journal*, Vol. VII (1935), pp. 27–30, 'The German Himalayan Expedition to Nanga Parbat', 1934.

10. Paul Bauer who left Germany, heading a rescue team, as soon as news of the disaster was received reached the expedition's Base Camp about three weeks after the avalanche had occurred. His account, which contains extracts from the diaries of Karl Wien and other members of the party, appears in the *Himalayan Journal*, Vol. X (1938), pp. 145–57. 'Nanga Parbat 1937.'

11. See *Himalayan Journal*, Vol. XI (1939), pp. 89–106. 'Nanga Parbat, 1938' by Paul Bauer.

12. The official account of the expedition appears in the beautifully produced volume *Everest 1933* by Hugh Ruttledge (Hodder & Stoughton, London, 1934). A personal account is given in Frank Smythe's book *Camp Six* (Hodder & Stoughton, London, 1937). See also 'The Mount Everest Expedition of 1933' by Hugh Ruttledge in the *Himalayan Journal*, Vol. VI (1934), pp. 31–46.

13. The expedition is described in 'The Mount Everest Reconnaissance, 1935' by Eric Shipton in the *Himalayan Journal*, Vol. VIII (1936), pp. 1–13. See also *Himalayan Journal*, Vol. IX (1937), pp. 16–20. 'Survey on the Mount Everest Reconnaissance', by Michael Spender.

14. It was this expedition, which came back with so little achieved despite the relatively large outlay in terms of money and effort, that set about a reassessment of the problems facing successive attempts to climb Mount Everest. The expedition is described in *Everest, the Unfinished Adventure* by Hugh Ruttledge (Hodder & Stoughton, London, 1937). Also 'The Mount Everest Expedition, 1936' by Hugh Ruttledge, in the *Himalayan Journal*, Vol. IX (1937), pp. 1–15.

15. 'Mount Everest 1938' by H. W. Tilman, *Himalayan Journal*, Vol. XI (1939), pp. 1–14. *Mount Everest 1938* by H. W. Tilman (Cambridge University Press, 1948).

16. The 1938 expedition is described in the *Himalayan Journal*, Vol. XI (1939), pp. 114–27: 'A Reconnaissance of K2, 1938' by Charles Houston. An account of the 1939 expedition is given in the Expedition Section of *Himalayan Journal*, Vol. XII (1940), pp. 123–27.

17. See *Blank on the Map* by Eric Shipton (Hodder & Stoughton, London 1938). Also *Himalayan Journal*, Vol. X (1938), pp. 22–39, 'The Shaksgam Expedition, 1937' by Michael Spender, and 'Résumé of Geological Results, Shaksgam Expedition 1937' by J. B. Auden, ibid., pp. 40–8.

18. *Nanda Devi* by Eric Shipton (Hodder & Stoughton, London, 1936). Also 'Nanda Devi and the Sources of the Ganges' by H. W. Tilman, *Himalayan Journal*, Vol. VII pp. 1–26.

19. *The Ascent of Nanda Devi* by H. W. Tilman (Cambridge University Press, 1937). Also *Himalayan Journal*, Vol. IX (1937), pp. 21–37.

20. 'The Polish Ascent of Nanda Devi East, 1939' by S. B. Blake and Dr Jakob Bujak, *Himalayan Journal*, Vol. XIII (1940), pp. 65–80.

21. 'The Ascent of Nanda Kot, 1936' by Y. Hotta, *Himalayan Journal*, Vol. X (1938), pp. 71–8.

22. An account of the Gangotri section of these surveys is described by G. H. Osmaston in 'Gangotri Triangulation', *Himalayan Journal*, Vol. XI (1939), pp. 128–39. Eric Shipton describes survey work further to the east in 'Survey Work in the Nanda Devi Region', *Himalayan Journal*, Vol. IX (1937), pp. 74–87. See also *Himalayan Journal*, Vol. X (1938), pp. 177–8.

23. 'The Ascent of Kabru' by C. R. Cooke, *Himalayan Journal*, Vol. VIII (1936), pp. 107–17.

24. 'A Winter Visit to the Zemu Glacier' by John Hunt and C. R. Cooke, *Himalayan Journal*, Vol. X (1938), pp. 49–70.

25. An attractive volume with beautiful illustrations describes this expedition: *Himalayan Quest* by Paul Bauer translated by E. G. Hall (Nicholson & Watson. London, 1938.) Also 'The ascent of Siniolchu and Simvu north peak' by Dr Karl Wien, *Himalayan Journal*, Vol. IX (1937), pp. 58–73.

Chapter II: Sikkim

1. Sir Joseph Hooker, K.C.S.I., M.D., F.R.S., was born in 1817; his father was Sir W. J. Hooker, a Director of Kew Gardens.

His pioneer travels in Nepal and Sikkim during the years 1848–50 were undertaken mainly with a view to extending scientific knowledge; his observations covered geology, meteorology and human geography. His main interest, however, was in botany, and his seven-volume work, *The Flora of British India*, was long regarded as the standard work on Indian botany His *Himalayan Journals* or *Notes of a Naturalist* contain detailed accounts of his travels and of the scientific work which he accomplished. A reprint of this work has recently been issued by Today and Tomorrow's Printers and Publishers, 11/7 Milestone Mathura Road, Faridabad, India. Price 60 rupees.

2. For a proper appreciation of the background to Sikkim's relations with Tibet and the historical affiliation that existed between the two countries, a useful source is Sir Charles Bell who was closely associated with Tibet between the years 1900 to 1920, spending over a decade during that period as Political Officer in Sikkim, commencing in 1904. Bell lived in Tibet for nearly a year between 1920 and 1921 as head of a diplomatic mission invited to Lhasa; and since he spoke Tibetan fluently he was the only European at the time to have established intimate contact with the Dalai Lama. His book *Tibet Past and Present* was first published in 1924 and was reissued in 1968 by the Oxford University Press.

3. For accounts of this expedition see *India and Tibet* by Sir Francis Younghusband, (John Murray, London, 1910). *Britain and Chinese Central Asia* by Dr A. Lamb (Routledge & Kegan Paul, London, 1960). *Bayonets to Lhasa* by Peter Fleming, (R. Hart-Davis, London, 1961). *The Younghusband Expedition* by P. Mehra, (Asia Publishing House, London, 1968).

4. The origins of this once highly important trade lay in the Tibet Treaty of 1893, which was established as an appendage to the original Treaty of 1890 (see p. 34),

and a subsequent agreement reached at Simla in 1914. The trade route from Kalimpong passed through Sikkim into Tibet over the Jelep La following the Chumbi valley, a wedge of semi-fertile country that cuts between Bhutan and Sikkim to within twenty-five miles of the Bengal plains, to Yatung where a customs post was maintained. Through this route there used to pass more than one half of the entire trade between India and Tibet, the Tibetans exchanging wool, musk, rock salt, jade and borax for miscellaneous Indian manufactures and consumer goods.

5. Four decades of travellers and trekkers in Sikkim turned for help and guidance to the book *Tours in Sikhim and the Darjeeling District* by Percy Brown, which contains a mine of information about the country, as well as a good deal of practical advice of the 'hints to travellers' variety. The author was once Curator of the Victoria Memorial in Calcutta and the book was first published in 1917 by W. Newman & Co. Ltd., Calcutta. Its fourth edition appeared in 1944 and I believe that it has since then been out of print. I treasured my copy for many years as a valuable source of reference, and I treasure it today as a symbol of the manners and customs of a more spacious and leisurely age.

6. Dr A. M. Kellas was probably the first to enter Sikkim wholly for the purpose of climbing and exploration. His Himalayan record, which spans the period from 1907 to 1920, is probably unique. With only one exception, when he took European guides, he travelled alone accompanied by local porters. To them he imparted a basic alpine training, from which stemmed the creation of a nucleus of high-altitude porters who were to fulfil the demand from climbing expeditions during the next decade. In 1907 he was in the Zemu area making attempts to climb Simvu (22,346 feet), and to reach the Nepal Cap. In 1909 he visited Lhonak, climbing Langpo Peak (22,815 feet), and reaching 22,000 feet on Jonsong Peak. In the same year he made two attempts to climb Pauhunri (23,385 feet). He climbed this mountain in June 1910, and a month later he climbed Chomiomo (22,403 feet). In May of that year he had climbed Sentinel Peak (21,290 feet), situated on the Tibetan Divide near the Chorten Nyima Pass. He was probably the first European to cross the Sebu La (17,560 feet); and in August 1912 he climbed Kangchenjau (22,603 feet). In 1920, after reaching over 23,000 feet on Kamet in Garhwal, he returned to Sikkim and climbed Narsingh (19,111 feet), a southern outlier of the Talung glacier; also Lama Anden (19,233 feet), situated above Lachen. He joined the first Everest Expedition, but fell ill and died on the way through Tibet on 5 June 1921, aged 53. His grave is at Khamba Dzong. Accounts of some of his Himalayan climbs can be found in the *Alpine Journal*, Vol. XXVI, pp. 52–113; Vol. XXVII, p. 125; Vol. XXXIV, p. 408.

7. Wilfrid Noyce, whose father was Sir Frank Noyce of the Indian Civil Service, was probably the leading British climber of his generation; he was born in 1917. After war-time climbs in Sikkim, Garhwal and Kashmir, he returned to the Himalaya in 1953 as a member of Hunt's Everest team; in 1957 to Nepal for the climb on Machapuchare (22,958 feet); and in 1960 to the Karakoram, when he climbed Trivor (25,370 feet). He was killed with the young Scottish climber Robin Smith in 1962 in an accident following their ascent of Garmo Peak in the Pamir. Writing and mountaineering, in both of which he excelled, were the two absorbing

interests of his life. His personal qualities gained him the regard and affection of a wide range of mountaineers and climbers, equally among the older as well as the younger generation. He was the author of several books including climbing guides, poetry and a novel. His expedition books, especially *South Col*, are among the best of their kind.

8. Jim Thornley was himself involved in a tragedy three and a half years later. With W. H. Crace and Richard Marsh he had planned a twelve-months' expedition to the Shaksgam in 1950, hoping to continue some of the work that Shipton had planned to do ten years earlier. While travelling to their area they were informed that the permit granted to them by the Pakistan Government had been withdrawn. Returning south from Gilgit they entered the Rakhiot Valley in order to make a winter reconnaissance of Nanga Parbat. Tenzing, who was with them, remained at a lower camp with Marsh, while Thornley and Crace advanced up the glacier in the appalling mid-December conditions of storms and deep snow. They were never seen again.

9. The quotation is taken from a discussion by George Mallory of the chances of climbing Mount Everest and the means that should be adopted for achieving success. He had just returned from the 1921 Reconnaissance of Everest. The official account of this expedition is given by Col. Howard Bury, *Mount Everest: The Reconnaissance, 1921* (Arnold, London, 1922). Mallory's comments can be found on page 278 in that volume.

10. The best available map of Sikkim is the official Survey of India Sheet No. 78 A/NE and 77 D/SE on the half-inch scale. The copy which I used on all my journeys was the 1941 edition, which had been revised up to 1939–40.

11. In an article published in the *Himalayan Journal*, Vol. XXIII (1961), pp. 169–70, a Sikkimese climber, Sonam Gyatso, is reported to have climbed Kangchenjau; the account given is very sketchy and contains no details about the route followed. In the same account, an ascent of Chombu is said to have been made.

Chapter III: Kangchenjunga

1. Mrs Jill Henderson was then Honorary Local Secretary of the Himalayan Club in Darjeeling and I have referred earlier to the great regard in which she was held by the Sherpa community there.

2. Reference has been made in Chapter I to their expedition to the Zemu glacier in 1937, a full account of which appears in the *Himalayan Journal*, Vol. X (1938), pp. 49–70.

3. In an article entitled 'The Problem of Kangchenjunga', which appears in the *Himalayan Journal*, Vol. VII (1935), pp. 67–75, F. S. Smythe, after examining several possibilities, concluded that the route followed by the Germans in 1929 and 1931 was the only possible one by which Kangchenjunga could be climbed. It seems a pity that an Austrian Expedition scheduled to try out Paul Bauer's route on the Northeast spur in 1972 was not able to do so. It would have been interesting to see whether

a combination of advanced climbing techniques and considerably improved equipment over a period of forty years would have overcome the problems of this very lengthy route.

4. Aleister Crowley (1875–1947) referred to variously as the Great Beast or 'the wickedest man in the world' acquired notoriety for his debauchery, his ventures into the occult, and his various publications in poetry and prose. His brief mountaineering career included expeditions to K2 in 1902 and to Kangchenjunga in 1905. He wrote his own *Confessions*, published originally in 1930 by the Mandrake Press, and re-published in 1969 by Jonathan Cape, London, *The Confessions of Aleister Crowley* edited by John Symonds and Kenneth Grant.

5. This unique organisation was set up in the year 1953 with the surplus funds and accruing revenue that flowed from lectures, publications and royalties occurring as a result of the ascent of Mount Everest on 29 May 1953. Its board, which includes representatives from the Alpine Club and the Royal Geographical Society, receives applications every year from climbing and exploratory expeditions, providing sponsorship and financial assistance to deserving groups. It has been a powerful source of encouragement to young climbers, who otherwise might have found it impossible to raise all the finance necessary to launch expeditions to the Himalaya and other distant mountain ranges of the world.

6. Donald Stafford Matthews was a colourful character and his book *Medicine my Passport* (Harrap, London, 1957) contains an entertaining account of his varied life. He died in 1956, aged thirty-nine, when returning from an expedition to the Peruvian Andes which was led by John Kempe and included J. W. Tucker.

7. An account of our reconnaissance in 1954 was published in the book *Kanchenjunga* by John Tucker (Elek Books, London, 1955).

8. The official account of the ascent of Kangchenjunga in 1955 appears in Charles Evans' book *Kangchenjunga, the Untrodden Peak* (Hodder & Stoughton, London, 1956). Before the departure of the expedition Charles Evans had given a personal undertaking to the Maharaja of Sikkim, in deference to the religious significance in which the mountain is held, that the highest point would remain untrodden. Both the summit teams honoured that promise.

Chapter IV: Kumron and Garhwal

1. An English edition, edited by Malcolm Barnes, entitled *The Mountain World*, was started in 1953 by George Allen & Unwin Ltd., London. This publication, which was probably the most lavishly produced of all mountaineering journals, ceased in 1969. Though its coverage was worldwide the mountains of Asia and South America were prominently featured. The Swiss Foundation for Alpine Research were, of course, the sponsors of the two Swiss Expeditions to Everest in 1952, and of the Swiss Expedition in 1956 which climbed both Everest and Lhotse.

2. This journey is described by H. W. Tilman's article entitled 'Nanda Devi and the

Sources of the Ganges' in the *Himalayan Journal*, Vol. VII (1935), pp. 14–20. See also *Nanda Devi* by Eric Shipton (Hodder & Stoughton, London, 1936).

3. For references see 'Gangotri and Leo Pargial, 1933' by Marco Pallis, *Himalayan Journal*, Vol. VI (1934), pp. 106–26; also 'The German Expedition to the Gangotri Glacier, 1938' by Prof. R. Schwarzgruber, *Himalayan Journal*, Vol. XI (1939), pp. 140–6.

4. The first Europeans to cross the Mana Pass were the Portuguese Jesuits Father Antonio de Andrade and Brother Manuel Marques in July 1624. They had set out from Agra on 30 March on a journey to Tsaparang, a small and prosperous kingdom in Tibet situated on the Sutlej River. Their first attempt to cross the pass in June had failed due to a blizzard. After they had founded the first Christian Church at Tsaparang in 1626 the route was followed by several Jesuit missionaries during succeeding years. When the King of Tsaparang was baptised in 1630 a revolution followed, the church was sacked, 400 converts were reduced to slavery, and the King and two Jesuits were removed to Leh in Ladakh as captives. In 1912 a British traveller, G. Mackworth Young, was able to make a study of the remains of the church at Tsaparang. Full records of these and other travels by early Jesuits can be found in *Early Jesuit Travellers in Central Asia, 1603–1721* by C. J. Wessels S. J. (Martinus Nijhoff, The Hague, 1924). For this information I am indebted to Professor Kenneth Mason's book, *Abode of Snow* (see Chapter I, Note 1).

5. During the next six weeks the Swiss party made two more ascents. The first was of Balbala (20,760 feet), a mountain situated six miles south-east of the Mana Pass. Three weeks later they climbed Nanda Ghunti (20,700 feet), situated west of Trisul. By modern standards, the expedition's achievements might seem slight. But Ernst Feuz of the Swiss Foundation had, in advance, kept the venture on a low key; and it would be only fair to judge the results in that context and in its period. The time had not yet come for the international race to capture 8,000-metre summits.

6. R. A. Gardiner, in the course of his survey during 1936, is responsible for the discovery of the Bankund plateau, which is situated over 3,000 feet above the main glacier. This snow basin six miles in length and almost a mile wide, contains several peaks between 19,000 and 22,000 feet. In 1937 F. S. Smythe and P. R. Oliver camped on the plateau and climbed three of its peaks. The area is covered by the Survey of India half-inch sheet No. 53 N/NE. This sheet, like all officially published maps of the mountain regions throughout the Himalaya, Karakoram and Hindu Kush, is banned for sale to the general public for strategic reasons. An anachronism in these days of high-altitude survey, and a source of deep frustration to mountain climbers and travellers.

7. Dunagiri (23,184 feet), after resisting several early attempts was ascended in 1939 by an expedition sponsored by the Swiss Foundation for Alpine Research led by André Roch.

Chapter V: Kulu and Spiti

1. For a summary of the origin and composition of the Himalaya, two papers by a former Director of the Geological Survey of India, D. N. Wadia, are of great

interest. These can be found in the *Himalayan Journal*, Vol. XXVI (1965), pp. 20–37 and Vol. VIII (1936), pp. 63–9. Much of what has been stated in the past, conflicts with certain other theories about the origin of the Himalaya. Based upon oceanographic evidence it is suggested that the Himalaya were formed 45 million years ago when a plate of the earth's crust, travelling 5,000 km due north across what is now the Indian ocean carrying the landmass of India, collided with the plate carrying Asia. The concept of Continental Drift accepts that all the continents were part once of Gondwanaland, and that splits were caused by rifts in the ocean floor arising from volcanic activity below the earth's crust. In some cases it has been possible to reconstruct the theoretical lines of cleavage, but this so-called reconstruction is as yet by no means complete. Resulting from oceanographic surveys carried out in the Indian ocean by scientific teams from the USA in 1968, it has been suggested that the landmass of India broke away from Antarctica 75 million years ago and travelled north towards the landmass of Asia at a rate varying from 7 to 16 cms per year. If these theories are to be supported it will be necessary eventually to relate the composition and movement of Himalayan rocks to the remnants left on the ocean floor. (An article in *Scientific American*, Vol. 228, May 1973, p. 62 *et seq.*, discusses the latest research in this direction).

2. In September 1953 A. E. Gunther, together with John Kempe, travelled up the Chandra valley and camped on the Bara Shigri glacier, climbing a peak of 20,000 feet. They were the first to reveal the size of this glacier and the scope that it offered for exploration and climbing. It had been visited only once before by J. O. M. Roberts in 1940, when he climbed a peak of 21,148 feet. Within the next eight years seven expeditions visited the Bara Shigri glacier and many of its peaks have now been climbed. A description of the Gunther expedition can be found in the *Alpine Journal*, Vol. LIX (May 1954), p. 288. The Snelson expedition is described in *Himalayan Journal*, Vol. XVIII (1954), pp. 110–17.

3. At that time, approximately 13⅓ Indian rupees were equivalent to £1.

4. When travelling in Buddhist country, i.e. Tibet and Nepal, as well as Sikkim, Bhutan and Ladakh, prayer walls are a common sight. Built of stones they are usually no more than three or four feet high and are often decorated with prayer flags. The traveller always passes them to his right. Carved in bold Sanskrit letters on the stones is the symbolic Buddhist inscription *Om Mani Padme Hum* (Hail, O Jewel, in the Lotus flower). Also a familiar sight in these regions is the *chorten*. The Tibetan word means, literally, receptacle for offerings. Originally the *chorten* was a tomb erected over the body of a venerated Buddhist. But later it became less of a tomb and more of a cenotaph, 'built to recall some special fact, or for the salvation of him who erected it or of his relatives, or as a votive offering or expression of gratitude' (Prof. G. Tucci).

5. In 1958 a British party led by J. G. Stephenson and including J. P. O'F. Lynam as surveyor visited the Bara Shigri glacier. They discovered that a row of peaks enclosing a basin on the northern branch of this glacier connected with the Gyundi system; and in the east and south respectively they overlooked the Ratang and the Parahio. Crossing a pass over the northern rim they were able to descend into the upper Gyundi glacier. Lynam returned to the Bara Shigri in 1961. Extending his

earlier exploration, he made some corrections to his 1958 map and climbed the highest peak in the region, to which he gave a height of 21,800 feet. His map of the Bara Shigri glacier appears in the *Himalayan Journal*, Vol. XXIII, p. 60. For an account of Lynam's 1958 expedition see *Himalayan Journal*, Vol. XXI, p. 97.

6. He did so in 1956 with his wife and G. Walker, taking Rinzing and Sonam with him again. Since they made an earlier start the Ratang gorge provided fewer problems and the party reached the headwaters of the Ratang, two stages beyond our meadow camp, which enabled Holmes to establish its connection with the Bara Shigri system. Holmes climbed a few peaks on the Gyundi divide, then moved to the Parahio glacier and from there crossed over a difficult pass into Kulu. The party descended the Dibibokri glacier into the Parbati valley, connecting with Snelson and Graaff's journey in 1952. Holmes' second journey to the Ratang is described in his book *Mountains and a Monastery* (Geoffrey Bles, London, 1958). An Italian Expedition to Kulu in 1961 visited the glaciers south of the Bara Shigri; on their sketch map Holmes' exit route in 1956 from the Parahio can be traced. See *Himalayan Journal*, Vol. XXIV (1962–3), p. 86.

Chapter VI: Karakoram

1. Accounts of the campaign can be found in two books which make fascinating reading, describing adventures on the north-west frontier of India before the turn of the century: *The Making of a Frontier* by A. G. Durand (London, 1900), and *Where Three Empires Meet* by A. F. Knight (Longmans Green & Co, London, 1895).

2. After the establishment of the Gilgit Agency a number of territories and tribal districts were brought together under the administration of the Political Agent in Gilgit. In addition to Hunza and Nagar these included Chilas, Darel and Tangir in the south; Punial, Ghizr, Ishkuman and Yasin in the west and north. The hereditary rulers of these small kingdoms or tribal states were allowed to retain their privileges, and their customs were not interfered with. The Commandant of the Gilgit Scouts acted as military adviser to the Political Agent. The Scouts exercised the strong arm of the law, being called upon to act when incidents arose involving armed rivalry or petty warfare. When the British left the subcontinent in 1947, the mantle of protection was taken over by Pakistan. In February 1970 all State territories were merged with the Republic of Pakistan.

3. The Pakistan and Chinese armies combined to build an all-weather road, which was opened in 1970, forming an important strategic link connecting Pakistan and Chinese Turkestan. Construction took over four years, with the Chinese engaged on the northern section and Pakistan in the south. The road runs through Swat, and after crossing the Changla ridge twenty miles north-east of Saidu Sharif it enters the Indus gorge, passing through much difficult terrain in Indus Kohistan. The road follows the Indus river to Chilas, Bunji and Gilgit. There it meets the Chinese-built section which crosses from Turkestan into Hunza over the Mintaka pass.

4. In 1939 the Minapin glacier was surveyed by members of Eric Shipton's Karakoram expedition. Fazal Ellahi and Inayat Khan of the Survey of India carried out a plane-

table survey based upon a triangulation by P. G. Mott. This resulted in the publication by the Royal Geographical Society of a map on the scale of one inch to four miles, covering the Hispar and Biafo glacier regions, which includes Minapin. An account of the 1954 German Expedition appears in *The Mountain World*, 1955.

5. His reminiscences, which are full of amusing anecdotes and experiences, are entitled *Life Among the Pathans*. The book was privately published in 1969 and was printed by The Owl Printing Company, Tollesbury, Essex.

6. In 1972 the Pakistan Government deprived the Rajas of Gupis, Punial, Ishkuman and Yasin of their hereditary territories and feudal privileges. In exchange, they were accorded small annual grants and were permitted to retain their titles. A new system for the collection of land revenue has been introduced in these four political districts, designed ostensibly to ease the burden of small landholders.

Chapter VII: Swat and Indus Kohistan

1. Jimmy Mills, who was a member of the British Army Expedition to Rakaposhi in 1958, came out to Pakistan in 1960 to join the Army Staff College at Quetta. He climbed a peak of 18,000 feet in northern Swat during the winter of 1961. His enthusiasm spread among many of his young Pakistani colleagues whom he introduced to the mountains in Quetta and elsewhere. In 1962 he was leader of the Joint Pakistan–British Forces Expedition to Kunyang Chish (25,762 feet), situated north of the Hispar glacier. He and Captain M. R. F. Jones were killed on 18 July while climbing on the south ridge of that mountain. See *Alpine Journal*, 1962(1), for his account of Swat Kohistan; and *Alpine Journal*, 1963(1), for an account of the Kunyang Chish expedition. Kunyang Chish remained unclimbed until 1971, when a Polish expedition led by Andrzej Zawada made the ascent by the east face and the upper part of the south ridge.

2. In 1961 three British travellers were attacked by tribesmen while camping in a lonely forest eighty miles north of the State capital Saidu Sharif. Within twenty-four hours the Wali was present at the scene of the incident. He obtained a confession from two of the offenders, meting out punishment on the spot, and the travellers were accorded full compensation for the theft of their property. Evidently this incident was fresh in the mind of the Waliahad when he suggested that an armed escort should accompany me. The incident was described to me a few years later by the travellers themselves.

3. In February 1970 Swat, like all other semi-independent states was merged with the Republic of Pakistan. The Wali was deprived of all his powers and of most of his property. Political rivalry has reappeared, threatening internal stability and retarding progress. The introduction of a formal legal system, with its cumbersome bureaucratic processes, has caused an increase in the incidence of crime.

4. The ascent was made by two New Zealanders, C. H. Tyndale Biscoe and W. K. A. Berry, when the former was a master at Edwardes College, Peshawar. Tyndale Biscoe also climbed one of the Batin peaks to its south. The only other mountain known to have been ascended in Swat up to that time was Mankial (18,750 feet),

which was climbed in 1940 by R. L. Holdsworth, J. T. M. Gibson and J. A. K. Martyn, who visited the state at the invitation of the Waliahad, their former pupil at the Doon School Dehra Dun.

5. A new bridge has since been constructed, and the motor road up the Ushu valley has been extended northwards, leading in few miles beyond Paloga to the junction of the Falak Ser valley. This has made the area more accessible to tourists. In 1962, visitors to this isolated valley were practically unknown.

6. The higher of the two peaks (18,700 feet) was climbed in 1957 by Tyndale Biscoe, and the lower (18,000 feet) in 1968 by an Austrian party led by Wolfgang Stefan.

7. A German expedition, led by Steff Rausch, made an ascent by this route in 1965; the same route was used by Wolfgang Stefan for his ascent in 1968. It is believed that one other ascent may have been made after Tyndale Biscoe's first ascent in 1957, but no details have been recorded.

8. My initial exploration of the Siri Dara group was followed up by a young team from Cambridge comprising Lieut. Henry Day (leader), John Peck, Lieut. Hugh Samuel, Richard Isherwood, who went there two years later. This modestly organised expedition was a model of good planning. During a three-month period, and at a total cost of £600, the party travelled out from Cambridge to Pakistan and back by Land Rover, spending six weeks in the mountains. They climbed seven peaks and prepared a rough sketch-map of the plateau and its surroundings. Their ascents included the 'Breithorn' and Central Peak, also the peak enclosing the western corner of the plateau which turned out to be Mankial. The latter, the third ascent of Mankial up to that time, and the first from the north, helped to orientate the position of the plateau and to relate it to the few peaks such as Mankial and Falak Ser which had been plotted and measured on the old maps. But there are still many gaps in adjacent areas, and I believe that a good deal of interesting survey remains to be done in the mountains of Swat and Indus Kohistan. For details see 'Cambridge Chitral Expedition 1964', a booklet privately published by the expedition; also *Himalayan Journal*, Vol. XXVI (1965), p. 38.

Chapter VIII: Nepal

1. One of the most comprehensive works on the Kingdom of Nepal, which covers much of its early history, sociology, etc., is *Nepal* (2 vols) by Percival Landon, which was published in London in 1928. The work was commissioned by the ruling Rana Prime Minister, and of necessity it avoids controversial political comments.

2. With the approval of the Nepalese Government, the Survey of India as well as certain other private bodies have carried out fairly extensive surveys in recent years. The new maps, some of which have been published on the scale of 1:50,000, have not been made available, however, for general use.

3. I suppose that all travel brochures, while serving to lure the tourist, sometimes tend to mislead. The route-map to which I have referred appears in a brochure entitled 'Everest-trek', printed at Sree Saraswati Press Ltd., Calcutta, in March

1971 on behalf of His Majesty's Government of Nepal, Ministry of Industry & Commerce, Department of Tourism, Katmandu. The brochure also contains information about the Everest View Hotel, Songboche, situated at 13,000 feet between Namche and Khumjung, with an airstrip attached.

4. Following once again the Langu gorge, a way was found to the glaciers below the northern side of the Kanjiroba peaks, and attempts were made to climb them from the north-west and the north-east. From both directions the routes appeared to be lengthy and difficult. An account of those attempts along with a sketch-map appears in the *Alpine Journal*, 1970, p. 114–23. A sketch-map based upon survey work carried out during the 1964 expedition appears in the *Geographical Journal*, September 1967, facing p. 337.

5. I have not seen details of the recent Japanese ascent of one of the Kanjiroba peaks, but it is gathered that the mountain was climbed from the south, after the party had gained access from the west to the upper Jagdula valley.

Chapter IX: Chitral

1. For this story, and for some interesting sidelights on the political forces existing on the north-west frontier of India at that time, I am indebted to Kenneth Rose's portrait of Lord Curzon, *Superior Person* (Weidenfeld & Nicolson, London, 1969). In 1894 Curzon travelled through Hunza over the Kilik pass into Wakhan, discovering the source of the Oxus river, a journey which earned him the Gold Medal of the Royal Geographical Society in May 1895. Capt. F. E. Younghusband, who was appointed Political Officer in Hunza in 1892, was transferred a year later to Mastuj in Chitral, where he and Curzon first met. Later there grew between them a strong mutual regard and respect.

2. The *Himalayan Journal*, Vol. V (1933) and Vol. VI (1934) contain accounts of events leading up to the seige of Chitral Fort in 1895 including a detailed description of the seige itself, written by Lieut.-Col. B. E. M. Gurdon, who was Political Officer in Chitral. Gurdon had succeeded Younghusband in late 1894, and was one of the six officers who held Chitral Fort during the seige. The two accounts make extremely interesting reading, conveying the atmosphere of the political intrigue and rivalry that prevailed at the time. Perhaps one does not fully appreciate today that officers serving on the frontier during that period had to possess not only a command of the language but also the perspicacity to deal with the workings of a mind and a way of life wholly different from their own.

3. The problem was inherited by Pakistan after the division of the Indian subcontinent on the departure of the British in August 1947. In 1970 the State of Chitral was merged with the Republic of Pakistan.

4. Alexander Gardner, who was once described as 'one of the finest specimens ever known of the soldier of fortune', was of Scottish descent born in North America, a world traveller, a colonel in the British artillery; he later entered the service of Maharaja Ranjit Singh of Lahore. He died in Jammu in 1887, aged ninety-one, as a

pensioner of Maharaja Gulab Singh. *Memoirs of Alexander Gardner* was published in London in 1898 by Blackwood.

5. For more detailed accounts of the earliest travellers and surveyors in Chitral, commencing with the period around 1890, I would recommend the paper written for the *Himalayan Journal*, Vol. XI (1939), by Brig.-Gen. Sir George Cockerill. This also describes his own journeys between 1892 and 1894 with a winter spent in Gupis. Another paper dealing with this general area and with Kafiristan in particular is of great interest: 'Early Explorers of Kafiristan' by Lieut.-Col. B. E. M. Gurdon in the *Himalayan Journal*, Vol. VIII (1936), p. 25–43.

6. It was as Surgeon-Major Robertson of the Indian Medical Service that he had headed a military mission to Chitral in 1893, and he commanded the small force who were held to seige there in 1895, for which he was awarded a knighthood. He later joined the Indian Political Service. His book, published in London by Laurence and Bullen in 1896, entitled *The Kafirs of the Hindu Kush*, is still probably the most detailed and authoritative account of the region ever written.

7. Official maps, which were based upon field-work carried out about forty years before, had not been updated. One of the maps in more general use at the time was that prepared by J. Wala and published by the Polish Mountaineering Club, which had sponsored three expeditions to the Hindu Kush between 1960 and 1963. Basing the heights of the biggest peaks on the early triangulations, it was possible with the knowledge gained from later exploratory journeys to sketch all the glaciers and fill in practically all the blanks. It was the Wala map which was available to us. But sketch-maps prepared by other expedition groups tend to show minor height variations.

8. Wakhikan Rah stands on the watershed which divides Chitral from Wakhan. Its height is shown on the old maps as 18,639 feet, and Wala gives it as 5,681 metres; although Noghor Zom (5,935 m) could apparently be overlooked from its summit. Below Wakhikan Rah is Wakhikan An, or the Afghan Pass, said to have been in use once by Afghanis who carried out armed raids on upper Chitral villages. Above the Shahgologh torrent is Wakhikan Gumbat, or Afghan Grave, containing human bones pointed out to us by our Uzhnu men as the remains of Afghan raiders who had been killed in combat by their forefathers.

Chapter X: Kaghan

1. Descriptions of some of his journeys to the Kaghan valley can be found in his books *Twenty Years in the Himalaya* (Edward Arnold, London, 1910) and *Himalayan Wanderer* (Alexander Maclehose & Co, London, 1934). Bruce was much impressed by what he called the 'giant' of the Kaghan, Mali-ka-Parbat, which appeared to be a much more serious mountain than its height (17,356 feet) indicates. In 1907, accompanied by Swiss guides, he climbed a peak of 16,000 feet which he called Shikara, and he did a good deal of wandering in the valleys to the east, near the Kashmir borders.

2. In 1936 and 1939 R. L. Holdsworth, a master at the Doon School, Dehra Dun, made attempts to climb Mali-ka-Parbat. His second attempt very nearly succeeded

when, accompanied by two local men, he started from the lake Saif-ul-Muluk and climbed about 6,000 feet to within 750 feet of the summit in one day. The first ascent in 1940 was made by his route. I am indebted to him for most of my information about previous attempts on the mountain. His article in *Himalayan Journal*, Vol. XXV (1964), p. 85: 'Moderate Mountains for Middle-Aged Mountaineers' makes mention of his Kaghan climbs.

3. Angwin gives an account of his work in the *Himalayan Journal*, Vol. II (1930), pp. 48–60: 'The Kaghan Valley' by Lieut. J. B. P. Angwin. Official Survey maps which cover the area comprise Sheets Nos. 43F/9–10–13–14, all on the scale of 1 inch to 1 mile; they are filled with detail and are very accurate. Unfortunately these maps are not available for general use.

4. Wolfgang Stefan made the thirteenth ascent of the Eiger Nordwand in August 1958 with Kurt Diemberger, the Diemberger–Stefan partnership being one of the best known among the leading young groups from Austria at that time. Stefan had first come to Pakistan in 1960 as leader of the four-man Austrian expedition which climbed Disteghil Sar (25,868 feet). A month after that climb, he visited Swat and made the second ascent of Mankial peak. He took up a post in Pakistan in 1967 and has since made ascents in Swat, Chitral and Kaghan.

Chapter XI: The Freedom of the Hills

1. The Quetta Staff College was established in 1906 by General Kitchener as Commander-in-Chief, India. It operated on the lines of, and worked in association with, its counterpart in Camberley: a tradition which was retained by Pakistan after the departure of the British.

2. Detailed descriptions of climbs in the Quetta region, including various routes pioneered on the peaks of Tukatu and Khalifat can be found in the *Himalayan Journal*, Vol. IX (1937): 'Quetta Rock Climbing' by J. R. G. Finch, Vol. XII (1940): 'Some Quetta Rock Climbs' by W. K. Marples and R. O. C. Thomson.

3. Mention is made of Ishkuman in Notes 2 and 6 to Chapter VI, which give a general background to the former feudal enclaves that originally formed part of the Gilgit Agency.

4. The Karengi glacier and the larger basins to its north-east have been visited in recent years, but very few of its peaks have been climbed and a detailed map of this region has not yet been prepared. For references see *Two Mountains and a River* by H. W. Tilman (Cambridge University Press, 1949), pp. 95–111; *Road to Rakaposhi* by George Band (Hodder & Stoughton, London, 1955), pp. 81–99; 'Two Valleys in Nagir' by C. H. Tyndale Biscoe, *Himalayan Journal*, Vol. XX (1957), pp. 94 *et seq.*; 'German Karakoram Expedition 1959' by Hans-Jöchen Schneider, *The Mountain World*, 1960/61, pp. 108 *et seq.*

GLOSSARY

Ablation Valley Found on the side of a glacier below lateral moraine, usually comprising a level meadow formed by the removal of glacier waste following melting or water action

Bergschrund Large crevasse separating upper slopes of glacier from steeper slopes of ice or rock above

Barhal Blue sheep, *Pseudois nayaur*, in habits and structure a mixture of goat and sheep. Weighing up to 150 lbs with horns averaging twenty-four inches

Chapatti Flat cake of bread roasted over an open fire and prepared from coarse unleavened flour of wheat, maize or barley

Chit A common Indian term derived from the word *chitti* meaning letter; thus note, certificate

Chowkidar Literally, keeper of the seat: caretaker

Col A depression or saddle between peaks

Crampons A metal frame comprising up to twelve spikes which is strapped on to a climbing boot

Crevasse Deep split or crack in glacier-ice

Cwm A small partly-enclosed basin.

Divide Watershed

Havildar Non-commissioned rank equivalent to sergeant

Ibex Wild sheep, *Capra ibex linnaeus*, inhabiting both sides of the main Himalayan range from Afghanistan to Kumaon. The greatest recorded horn length in Gilgit is fifty-five inches

Icefall Steep part of glacier usually broken into cliffs

Khalasi Surveyor's assistant, usually entrusted with carrying survey instruments

Lumbardar Village Headman

Markhor Himalayan wild goat, *Capra falconeri*, whose horns assume a spiral twist. Record horn measurements are sixty-five inches (Astor)

Moraine Rock debris covering the ice bed of a glacier

Muezzin Mohammedan reader, not necessarily a priest

Naik Non-commissioned rank equivalent to corporal

Nala Side-valley, ravine, stream

Névé Snow-ice found usually in upper level of glaciers

Patwari Village record-keeper charged with maintaining details of land revenue

Scree Small loose stones

Seracs Pinnacles of ice shifting and breaking with movement of glacier

Shikari A hunter

Sirdar Leader, chief, head

Snout Terminal point of glacier, usually of bare ice from which issues a stream

Subedar Non-commissioned officer holding charge of a small detachment of men

Tehsildar Revenue official holding charge of civil administration in a small district

Tsampa Roasted barley flour, the standard diet of Sherpas and Tibetans, usually eaten as a raw dough or a gruel

Ziarat Moslem shrine; often found on the summit of a prominent hill

INDEX